Africans in Harlem

AFRICANS IN HARLEM

An Untold New York Story

Boukary Sawadogo

EMPIRE STATE EDITIONS

AN IMPRINT OF FORDHAM UNIVERSITY PRESS

NEW YORK 2022

Fordham University Press has no responsibility for the persistence or accuracy of URLs for external or third-party Internet websites referred to in this publication and does not guarantee that any content on such websites is, or will remain, accurate or appropriate.

Fordham University Press also publishes its books in a variety of electronic formats. Some content that appears in print may not be available in electronic books.

Visit us online at www.fordhampress.com/empire-state-editions.

Library of Congress Cataloging-in-Publication Data available online at https://catalog.loc.gov.

Printed in the United States of America

24 23 22   5 4 3 2 1

First edition

CONTENTS

PREFACE

Africans in Harlem: An Untold New York Story is a narrative of the African presence and influence in Harlem from my own perspective as an African-born immigrant scholar at the City College of New York, writer, filmmaker, and founding director of the Harlem African Animation Festival who lives and works in the neighborhood. My intention is to document lesser-known facets of the history of Harlem, New York City, with special attention to the story of Africans who have migrated there since the 1980s, a migration that has resulted in a considerable economic and cultural presence. I am originally from Burkina Faso, West Africa. Before landing in Harlem, my life trajectory in the United States started with graduate studies in Cedar Falls, Iowa, then Lafayette, Louisiana, followed by teaching positions in Marlboro, Vermont, and Boston, Massachusetts. This personal perspective partly informs the structure and style of the book, infusing a dimension of self-examination as a member of an ethnic minority who addresses contemporary African mass migration within diasporic community building in twentieth- and twenty-first-century American history. I have made the decision not to write myself out of the text, given that I am a member of the African community in Harlem, writing from this place. I would not have written this book if I did not happen to reside in Harlem at this specific time in history.

Harlem is the New York City neighborhood located between the Harlem River and the Hudson River, east to west, and between 110th and 155th Streets, north to south (though it used to begin on 96th Street, encompassing what is now known as Carnegie Hill); it is subdivided into East or Spanish Harlem, West Harlem, and Central Harlem. Famously, from the 1920s to the early 1960s, Harlem was the intellectual and cultural center of the Black world; the Harlem Renaissance movement, with its wealth of literary and cultural expressions, was a hallmark of that vitality. It brought together Black writers, artists, and musicians from different backgrounds who helped rethink the place of Black people in American society at a time of segregation and lack of recognition of their civil rights. This questioning of systemic oppression had reverberations beyond the US; it inspired the works of the Negritude literary movement to denounce French colonialism and to extol Blackness, which in turn laid the intellectual foundations for the quest for independence of French-speaking Africa.

The inspiration to write this book was birthed in Harlem on a Saturday afternoon in fall 2015, a few months after I moved into the neighborhood from Boston. I was sitting in a café working on materials for courses I teach at the City College of New York when a double-decker tour bus—of the type ubiquitous in New York City—pulled up on the other side of the street. The tourists streamed in to get beverages before proceeding on their tour of Harlem. As one of the tourists stood by my table speaking on her phone, I overheard her saying that she was on a tour of the Jewish history of Harlem. I had never heard of a Jewish tour of Harlem and wondered which landmarks and places they would be visiting. Many more questions entered my head that day: I wondered whether there are African history tours of Harlem. If not, should I consider creating one—to put Africa in Harlem, on the map of New York City sightseeing tours? What places would such a tour cover? Where is the history of Africa in Harlem?

With these questions planted in my mind, others began to crop up: In what ways should I document and communicate the strong presence of African-born migrants in the neighborhood, particularly francophone West African communities? What did I personally know about the different community networks and vibrant cultural venues that exist in the neighborhood? How can African immigrants' relationship to Harlem and with African Americans be characterized? When and how have Africans and African Americans intersected? What does Africa mean to African Americans in Harlem, as well as to African émigrés? What is the future of the various African communities in today's fast-gentrifying Harlem? To find answers to my questions, I realized, would take extensive and sustained research. So I set out to do just that.

Over the next few years I immersed myself in the history and culture of Harlem, perhaps the most storied neighborhood in America. In doing so, I understood what an emotional experience it is for Harlemites and visitors alike to walk the same streets as famous former residents such as Philip Payton, Madam C. J. Walker, Madam St. Clair, W. E. B. Du Bois, Marcus Garvey, Langston Hughes, Claude McKay, Alain Locke, Malcolm X, James Baldwin, Duke Ellington, Adam Clayton Powell Jr., Amiri Baraka (Leroi Jones), and Ossie Davis. Strolling around Harlem makes it possible to re-visit in memory and lore the cultural vibrancy and political activism that are closely connected to the neighborhood. Physical markers of its cultural history fill the place: the Apollo Theater, the Cotton Club, Studio Museum in Harlem, Schomburg Center for Research in Black Culture, City College of New York; the corner of Lenox Avenue and 138th Street, where Marcus Garvey held his first public meeting in 1916; 409 Edgecombe Avenue, which has landmark-preservation status thanks to its former occupants, including Duke Ellington, Countee Cullen, Thurgood Marshall, and W. E. B. Du Bois; the YMCA, which has seen generations of Harlemites pass through its doors for at least a century, including Nnamdi Azikiwe, in 1925, who would later become the first president of Nigeria; and the historic district of Strivers' Row.

Today's Harlem is a place where old and new coexist: the classic brown-stones with their unique stoops standing side-by-side new retail development, restaurants, bars and lounges, and high-rise business and residential buildings. In some areas the erasure of the old is unfolding at an alarmingly accelerated rate, causing great concern for longtime residents who feel anxious at seeing Harlem lose its identity. Indeed, the paucity of physical memorials denoting African present made researching and documenting this history challenging. Whereas usually monuments and street names help derive the history of a space and the people who inhabit it, the only prominent historical landmark in Harlem with "African" in its name is African Square at the intersection of 125th Street and Seventh Avenue. Named African Square in the 1980s, this is the gathering place where Malcolm X regularly addressed crowds during the height of his influence in the 1960s. Although African storefront signs and places of worship exist, they do not provide the full scope of the African presence in Harlem, as they date back only as far as the late 1980s.

But Harlem is more about its people than its landmarks, important though they are. Harlem is about the diverse population we see on the streets today, particularly the ever-growing African immigrant communities that have sprung up since the 1980s when the first Senegalese started arriving in Harlem. From Little Senegal, along 116th Street between Lenox Avenue and Frederick Douglass Boulevard, to the African street vendors on

125th Street, to African stores, restaurants, and businesses throughout the neighborhood, the African presence in Harlem has never been more active and visible than it is today. As a member of the Mossi ethnic group from Burkina Faso, I was first surprised to overhear conversations in Mooré when I moved to Harlem a few years ago from Boston, whereas today I frequently hear Mooré and other West African languages being spoken in the streets, restaurants, taxis, or places of worship. That feeling of surprise has gradually subsided as I have come to understand that diversity is part of the local ecosystem. One might say that New York City is such a cosmopolitan city that one is bound to hear all languages of the world spoken here. What makes the linguistic diversity in Harlem so unique, however, is the seamless interaction of residents from various backgrounds who share a strong connection to their neighborhood and its people. Harlem has become a microcosm of the traditional idea of the United States melting pot, from its founding in 1658 as a Dutch farming community under the name of Nieuw Haarlem (named after the city of Haarlem in the Netherlands) to its historical place as the mecca of Black culture and politics. The influx of different populations from elsewhere in Manhattan over the centuries also has contributed to the area's diversity, as can be seen in Italian Harlem, Spanish Harlem, the Jewish history of Harlem, in Irish immigrants moving to the neighborhood in late nineteenth century, and West Indians in the early twentieth century.

This is to say, although the book is focused on Harlem, this is also a story about New York City, particularly its self-renewal brought about by the contributions of new human capital, creative energies, dreams nurtured and fulfilled, and good neighbors. In this respect, certain parallels can be established between the history and stories of the African presence in Harlem with those of other ethnic immigrants to New York City. By the early 1900s the population of Harlem was a mix of Italians, Jews, Irish, Germans, and African Americans. Italian immigrants formed a large, thriving community in East Harlem between 96th and 125th Streets until the Great Depression. Tens of thousands of Italian immigrants lived and owned businesses in what could be referred to as the Uptown Little Italy, which was larger in size than the current Little Italy in Lower Manhattan; its legacy and material history today is mostly located on Pleasant Avenue and at Our Lady of Mt. Carmel Church on 116th Street, where the remaining Italian families attend Sunday mass.

Several decades later, waves of African immigrants would make their impact on the city and its neighborhoods, especially in Harlem. The story of African immigrants should be understood in the larger context of building commonalities in immigrant experience across generations of New Yorkers—Italians, Jews, Irish, Germans, Chinese, and others—who changed New York City as each ethnic group moved there in the nineteenth and twentieth centuries to create new lives for themselves. Considered in a framework larger than New York City, moreover, this book can also serve to demonstrate how global diversity derives from local diversities, especially in cities. African immigrants have transformed Harlem economically and culturally as they are themselves transformed. The embodied experience of the city, segregation in the city, and the materiality of the city offer alternative epistemologies to think about global cities and the lived experience of their racial and ethnic minorities.

My own first encounter with Harlem goes back to high school in Burkina Faso, in literature and world history classes, where I learned about US history, particularly the transatlantic slave trade and the civil rights movement of the 1960s. In my literature classes I learned how the Harlem Renaissance inspired poets of the Negritude literature movement, such as Léopold Sédar Senghor and Aimé Césaire. For both older and younger generations than myself, music (particularly jazz), hip-hop, blaxploitation and Hollywood movies served as entry points to Harlem and the African American experience. The year 2019 marked the one-hundredth anniversary of the Harlem Renaissance. This book has personal significance for me not only as a Burkinabe living in Harlem but also as a faculty member at the City College of New York. Historically, City College has had connections with some of Africa's notable writers and intellectuals such as Chinua Achebe, who taught there in 1989 for two years and was the 1993 recipient of the Langston Hughes Festival Medal. The Langston Hughes Festival, held annually at City College, honors highly distinguished Black writers, of which Wole Soyinka, James Baldwin, Toni Morrison, Amiri Baraka, Maya Angelou, Octavia Butler, and Walter Mosley are but a few.

As a faculty member of the City College of New York, I am honored to follow in the giant footsteps of my illustrious predecessors and to celebrate them. For instance, I had the privilege of chairing on December 5, 2018, a panel on the sixtieth anniversary of the African classic *Things Fall Apart* by Chinua Achebe; there, the former South African President Kgalema Motlanthe was one of the panelists. The panel showcased continued physical and intellectual encounters of Africa and the diaspora in Harlem, which follows a long-standing tradition. I am working in a space that is known for its progressive history of providing minority and immigrant groups access to higher education as a means of social mobility. The date of April 22, 2019, marked the fiftieth anniversary of the protest and takeover of the City College of New York by minority students. This protest led to the creation of the Black and Puerto Rican Studies departments and programs throughout the City University of New York system. The recent racial justice movement of Black Lives Matter, featuring people from diverse backgrounds, highlights the continued fight for racial justice and the activist engagement of young people to bring about systemic changes in society. Prior to that historical event, City College was the site of some contributions to what would later pave the way for the civil rights movement. In the broader context of the fight against segregationist practices, as Michelle Young noted in her article,[1] the Lewisohn Stadium, a Roman amphitheater-like stadium, on the campus of City College of New York hosted in 1946 an NAACP fundraiser for Sgt. Isaac Woodward, known as "The Blind GI." Some 20,000 people attended performances by musicians such as Billie Holiday and Duke Ellington. In 1964, Martin Luther King Jr. was the commencement speaker in the Lewisohn Stadium.

Writing is a solitary endeavor, but the research and information gathering stages preceding the writing are very often collaborative. Generosity and cooperation of third parties determined progress of the book project. I owe a great debt to the poet and educator Rashidah Ismaili AbuBakr for hosting conversations at her Harlem-based Salon d'Afrique, the literary salon where I presented chapters of this book to a very diverse audience of African immigrants and African Americans; their generous feedback has been incorporated. Thank you so much, Rashidah, for the many insightful conversations over dinners, and for putting me in contact with community members whom I would not have otherwise encountered. Auntie, or Mama Rashidah—a couple of the many affectionate names by which she is known—moved to New York City in 1957 from her native Dahomey (the present-day country Benin in West Africa) and is regarded within the community as a living repository of the collective memory of the African presence in Harlem.

Oral histories of community and religious leaders and long-standing residents of Harlem constituted a major beneficial resource. In these interviews it was particularly important to address the African presence in Harlem from the perspective of both Africans and African Americans. Dior Dieng, a graduate of City College of New York, opened the doors to the Little Senegal community for me, enabling me to interview Senegalese community members, store owners, and workers. Dieng's family moved to Harlem in the 1980s from Senegal, where some family members still live. I am grateful to you, Dior. My gratitude goes to the many other community members who shared their stories and experiences of Harlem:

Clara Villarosa, the cofounder and co-owner of Hue-Man Bookstore, the only Black-owned and -operated bookstore in Harlem in the mid-2000s; Wodajo Mogues who settled in the neighborhood in 1968 from his native Ethiopia; Daoud AbuBakr and Maimouna Sow for documenting and sharing the history of Harlem through photography; Kader Ouedraogo, from Burkina Faso, who owns and runs several live-music venues and bars in Harlem. The generosity of author and journalist Ernest Harsch is greatly appreciated for sharing a personal account as an eyewitness to President Thomas Sankara's visit to Harlem, which took place at the auditorium of Harriet Tubman High School in 1984.

To uncover evidence documenting the strong African presence in Harlem, I am also indebted to several cultural, religious, and research institutions in Harlem that granted me access to their archives. The Schomburg Center for Research in Black Culture in Harlem is one of the largest repositories of source materials on Black people in the United States; it gave me access to their collection on the visits of Third World heads of state and governments to Harlem. The Apollo Theater and the Riverside Church also maintain valuable repositories of records of the African presence and influence in Harlem. Special thanks to the Apollo Theater's resident historian for information on African artists who performed at the iconic venue, and to the Riverside Church for generously opening its archives of the South Africa Task Force to my inquiry.

Learning and sharing this story has provided the opportunity to better situate myself in relation to the history and people of the place I now inhabit. This book was written around the time when two historical events were commemorated, each having some correlation to my own presence today in the United States. First, the four-hundredth year since the establishment of slavery in the United States was commemorated in 2019. Without the gains won by the civil rights movement in the 1960s, led by descendants of slaves, the conditions would not probably have been conducive for me to be here now. Second, the year 2020 marked the sixtieth anniversary of most French-speaking African countries gaining political independence from their former colonial power. As we shall see in some detail, the confluence of these historic trajectories contributed to the formation of the large community of French-speaking West Africans in Harlem.

The source materials for this study, then, consist of living pieces of today's Harlem: interviews, visits to archive and collection sites in New York City, group conversations with segments of the Harlem community, teaching a graduate course on Global Harlem, and my own experience as a West African immigrant living and working in the neighborhood. For all the help from various people and institutions, I am grateful, and I shall be responsible for the imperfections of the book. My aim was to write a book that will live on bookshelves and educational syllabi for years to come as the definitive book on Africa in Harlem and New York City. To date, the story of Harlem has been about the African American experience. It is indisputable that Harlem is a household name and enjoys a historical legacy in Black culture and politics thanks to the Harlem Renaissance movement, African American civil rights leaders, and cultural and literary icons who have contributed to the fame of Harlem in New York and among Black populations around the world. Now, with a new focus, with an eye to another diversity, I hope you'll take the journey with me to discover the important and untold story of African-born migrants and the vibrant African influence in Harlem.

Africans in Harlem

⠏⠇

Africa in Harlem

THE FIRST TWO DECADES of the twenty-first century have seen a series of historical, racial-justice, and media events which have spotlighted the rise of Africa and the African diaspora—both historical and contemporary—through the flows of immigration and their ties of interconnection. Let us consider a few:

In 2020, seventeen African countries celebrated the sixtieth anniversary of their political independence from their former colonial powers; of these, fourteen are French-speaking West and Central African territories. This sovereignty meant, among many other things, full-fledged citizenship with the possibility to travel on a passport, which enabled Africans to meet and exchange with the diaspora or settle relatively freely. Legacies of the past sixty years have been the focus of debates at commemorative events, though the necessary question concerning the future of Africa over the next sixty years often has not been sufficiently addressed.

The year 2020 also witnessed, in the context of the COVID-19 health and economic crisis, the global resonance of a racial-justice movement in the wake of the killing of African American George Floyd at the hands of Minneapolis police officers. The ensuing protests against racism and police brutality by multigenerational and multiracial crowds in the United States found echoes in minority communities across Western European cities as part of the Black Lives Matter movement. Thousands of French people, Blacks for the most part, protested in Paris in early June 2020 to demand justice for twenty-four-year-old Malian French Adama Traore, who died in police custody in July 2016. No justice had been rendered. In North America, Europe, and parts of Africa, the initial demands for systemic changes to policing practices evolved into a larger sociocultural moment centered on memory and justice as evidenced by protesters' removal of symbols, monuments, and statues tied to colonialism, slavery, and racism. The protest over racial injustice fueled debates on relational history and memory reconstruction that has found resonance beyond national borders, racial lines, and age groups.

The previous year, 2019, marked the four-hundredth anniversary of the start of slavery in the land that would become the United States. In the wake of this confluence, the General Assembly of the United Nations declared the years 2015 to 2025 the "Decade for People of African Descent" to promote and protect their human rights. The African Union now includes a fifth and virtual region covering the African diaspora from the initial four geographic regions encompassing the pan-African political and economic organization (discussed in Chapter 8). Public events and media coverage brought further attention to the commemoration, which might otherwise have passed by unacknowledged within the general public. Through its *1619 Project*, for instance, the *New York Times Magazine* special issue of August 18, 2019, brought focus to the subject with contributions from poets, academics, journalists, and artists. What was glaringly obvious about the various commemorative activities in the United States is the relative absence of prominent African voices, and the fact that the anniversary did not get as much attention and coverage on the continent as it did across the Atlantic. More work in bridge-building, healing, and sharing history remains to be done.

In the first two decades of the twenty-first century the media message concerning Africa has changed noticeably. This is exemplified by two issues on Africa published eleven years apart by the British news magazine *The Economist*, presenting diametric perspectives on the trajectory of the continent. The first issue, titled "Africa: The Hopeless Continent," appeared in May 2000, and the second, "The Hopeful Continent: Africa Rising," in December 2011. Both issues offered a prospective analysis of Africa from a Western perspective, assessing the African presence and trajectory in the world over the preceding two decades.[1] These controversial cover stories spawned debates and op-eds by journalists, development experts, and academics sparring over Afro-pessimism and Afro-optimism. The "hopeless continent" thesis appeared to reinforce the Western discourse of Africa's chronic failure to achieve substantive economic development despite numerous programs created to put the continent on the path of development. Economic progress was insufficient during what is often referred to as the "lost decades" of the 1970s through the late 1980s. These times were marked by military coups and authoritarian regimes, drought in the Sahel bioregion, currency devaluation of the CFA Franc in January 1994, and structural adjustment programs imposed by the World Bank and the International Monetary Fund.

Yet the lost decades need not determine the future standing of the continent in the world—because Africa is rising. There exists no inherent reason that prevents Africa from becoming an economic powerhouse in the world.[2] Africa has vast natural resources to drive the development of entire industries and businesses, and more significantly, the relative youth of the fast-growing African population stands as more of an asset than a liability, contrary to the population-control discourse and policy efforts of the West directed toward Africa. The current population of 1.2 billion is projected to double around 2050, which means that by then one person in four in the world will be African, and every other young person will be African around 2070. Africa has already tripled its middle class between 1980 and 2010,[3] which has in part sustained and will continue to foster demands for better practices of governance, democratic standards, human rights, and economic development. Africa will soon become a world hub of production, creativity, and consumption. And the contemporary African diaspora, its encounters and exchanges, is one of the lenses through which the continent's presence and trajectory in the world can be examined.

Indeed, the very concept of the African diaspora is changing as it showcases a new profile as an outgrowth of globalization and economic development driven by creative and uninhibited talents. African diaspora historically refers to communities around the world whose ancestors were forcefully removed from the continent. But the notion of "diaspora" describes not only a dispersal of human beings but also the permanent connections and ties to the homeland, such as those, for example, of Indian, Chinese, and Lebanese diasporas with their home countries. The new African diaspora—that is, the voluntary migration of Africans mostly to the economically developed countries in search of better life opportunities—should be considered an outgrowth of globalization and the consequence of inequalities in economic development. The relation between globalization and the new African diasporas may be understood, as Donald Carter observes, in the context of "the tumultuous patterns of social, cultural and economic dislocations of global capitalism and the complex interplay of power relations in and across nation-states [which] has often been associated with the creation of vast interconnected global systems of cultural, economic and social relations and the decentering of the people, objects and ideas that move across the 'hypermodernity' of late capitalism."[4] In addition, climate change and extremist violence are increasingly significant factors of dislocation in Africa. The movement of African immigrants to New York and other cities around the world, and the relatively recent settlement of African Americans on the continent, are realities that complexify the concept of the new African diaspora. As a result of global African migration in postcolonial contexts, major cities in the global North are now homes to large African communities, inscribing their cultural identity in spaces they inhabit while also contributing to the renewal of these cities. New York is a prime example of such a global city, where Africans have a strong cultural and economic presence in the Harlem neighborhood of Upper Manhattan. This is a presence that many New Yorkers are hardly aware of; and the newly arrived African immigrant is surprised to see such a community presence. This is an invisible presence and a story yet to be told.

According to data published in 2018 by the Pew Research Center, the number of foreign-born Blacks in the United States was 4.2 million in 2016 (an increase from 800,000 in 1980, 1.5 million in 1990, and 2.4 million in 2000).[5] The number of Black immigrants in the United States has almost doubled every ten years. Of this total, Africans make up 39 percent (1.6 million) of the foreign-born Black population, up from 24 percent in 2000.[6] The top five African countries of origin in 2015 were Nigeria, Ethiopia, Egypt, Ghana, and Kenya. The top five countries of origin for West African immigrants to the United States in 2015 were Nigeria, Ghana, Liberia, Cape Verde, and Sierra Leone.[7] Since 1990, immigration from Africa has increased rapidly, giving way to a new trend: More Blacks are coming to the United States from Africa now than during the slave trade.[8] This story needs exploring and to be told, given Africans' influence in shaping neighborhoods and communities. Every immigrant enclave imbues its bars, live-music venues, restaurants, and places of worship with a distinct regional personality.

Indeed, through their earnings and tax contributions, sub-Saharan immigrants in 2015 contributed significantly to the economies of California, Texas, Maryland, New York, Georgia, Virginia, and New Jersey. The New American Economy, a coalition of Republican, Democratic, and independent mayors and business leaders advocating for immigration reforms to help the American economy, published a twenty-two-page report in January 2018 titled "Power of the Purse: How Sub-Saharan Africans Contribute to the US Economy," which outlined the significant economic contributions of Africans to state economies. The report states that in 2015 African immigrants earned $55.1 billion, of which $4.7 billion went to state and local taxes, and $10.1 billion went to federal taxes, leaving them with $40.3 billion in spending power.

The US cities with the greatest number of sub-Saharan immigrants between 2011 and 2015 were the greater New York City area, Washington, DC, and the Atlanta metropolitan areas, which together accounted for about 27 percent of sub-Saharan Africans in the United States. During the same five-year period the metropolitan area of New York/Newark/Jersey City welcomed about 200,000 foreign-born immigrants from sub-Saharan Africa through such pathways as the diversification lottery, family ties, and resettlement programs for refugees and asylum seekers. The official statistics do not include undocumented immigrants or those already here with expired visitor visas, which together could account for as much as five times the number of immigrants. Though there are not yet official statistics on the distribution of African immigrants in New York City's five boroughs, Manhattan (where Harlem is located), the Bronx, and Brooklyn appear to be the top three destinations, as Africans tend to move into areas that already have the largest numbers of their countrymen. In terms of Black nationalities in Harlem, there are the Afro-Caribbeans, native-born Africans, born-and-bred Black New Yorkers, and Black Southerners. These groups exist alongside Afro-Latinos and Puerto Ricans. However, the complex realities of intermarriage, intermingling of communities, and how later generations of (im)migrants identify themselves sometimes defy any practical attempt to effectively categorize these groups.

Thus, the influence of Africans in Harlem has been not only cultural but economic as they have made major contributions to reviving the neighborhood in the 1980s and 1990s in the wake of violence, drugs, and disinvestment in the city's communities of color. Though Harlem has been gentrifying since the late 1990s, it was once made attractive by African immigrants moving there en masse and opening restaurants, taxi companies, and ethnic food stores. Thousands of Africans have moved to Harlem, the most famous Black neighborhood in the United States, because of its perceived affinity with Blackness and its historical standing as the mecca of Black culture and politics. In moving to a neighborhood, many of these African migrants may be encountering American notions of race and "Blackness" directly for the first time. They were born, raised, and have developed professionally in contexts where their Blackness was either normative or even not a significant factor in identity and public discourse. Then they migrate to the United States where race is historically present—subtle at times and overt at others—in interactions and perimeters of private and public spaces. Like African Americans, foreign-born Blacks in the United States are at risk of being caught in what the African American writer and sociologist Tressie McMillan Cottom refers to as "the anti-blackness dragnet that does not ask if you have an accent before it shoots you."[9] This is an essential dimension to consider in critically exploring how foreign-born Blacks make sense of themselves and relate to their African American neighbors in private and public spaces. In other words, the entry into spaces of racialized identities and politics shapes African immigrants' relations with African Americans, and even their own identities, beyond ethnicity as the basis of how they may have defined themselves or are defined in the homeland. The designations of Africans and African (im)migrants are used interchangeably throughout the book; I would like to emphasize from the outset that this should not be read as my intention to deny any group within the Black diasporas their Africanness or African heritage. This is simply how African-born migrants very often self-identify in relation to African/Black Americans. Also, African migrants are referred to as "Africans" by members of groups of the Black diasporas.

These Harlem-bound migrations of Africans since the 1960s can be divided into two major trends. The first trend comprises the mostly English-speaking African artists, writers, political activists, and liberation leaders who moved to Harlem in the 1960s and 1970s. This migration must be examined within the larger context of solidarity movements: the civil rights movements, anti-apartheid struggle, and anti-colonial struggles for independence in African countries. This generation built and occupied spaces in New York, especially in Harlem, for later *émigrés* to inhabit. The second migration trend consisted of predominantly French-speaking West African immigrants who arrived in Harlem from the late 1980s to the present. This economic migration may be explained by the untenable living conditions at home, as the more able-bodied and educated left in search of better prospects for themselves and their families. The decision of these immigrants to reside in Harlem was based on several factors: major shifts in international migration patterns of Africans to Europe from the late 1970s to early 1990s, Harlem's history as a center of Black culture and politics, and some shared identification of Blackness. But these two migratory patterns do not capture all the complexities of migration; refugee settlement programs and winners of the Diversity Immigrant Visa Program (the "green card lottery") are additional mechanisms by which nationals of African and other countries have moved to the United States.

The diverse makeup of the neighborhood has been reshaped as this second wave of francophone West African immigrants, primarily from Senegal, Mali, Guinea, and Burkina Faso, moved to Harlem beginning in the 1980s. The cultural diversity infused in the neighborhood by the arrival of West Africans has been particularly noticeable in the neighborhood's schools, mosques, churches, hairdressing salons and barbershops, grocery and convenience stores, restaurants, cultural and community organizations, and live music venues, and in immigrant enclaves such as Little Senegal. Walking the streets of Harlem, one notices that African immigrants are contributing to the sense of fashion for which Harlemites have long been known. These Black bodies in traditional African garments occupy spaces with dignity, grace, and pride, thus adding to and expanding the history and cultural practices of the neighborhood. Yet the African presence in Harlem remains relatively unexplored beyond a few existing publications on Little Senegal, the Murid Islamic community, and the consequences of gentrification for longtime Harlemites.

The history of the African presence in Harlem is a testament to New York's emergence as a center of exchanges and encounters between Africans, African Americans, and West Indians for the development of a Black consciousness and enabling the pursuit of individual and community dreams. Why is this story not told more widely? It is high time that New York's role in building bridges in the Black world be acknowledged— notwithstanding the fact that Paris has often been considered the global nexus of encounters between Africans, African Americans, and West Indians. Several books and movies have been produced about African American writers, musicians, entertainers, and soldiers in Paris; others, on the encounter of Africans, African Americans, and Caribbeans in Paris through literary and solidarity movements: the Harlem Renaissance, the struggle for liberation against colonialism, and the civil rights movement.[10] In addition to Paris, London is a global city where the African immigrant presence is the subject of scholarly investigations.[11] Perhaps precisely because New York has no colonial ties to African countries—as contrasted with Paris and London—the experience of African immigrants in New York City remains largely unexplored apart from three books on the subject: Paul Stoller, *Money Has No Smell: The Africanization of New York City* (2002), Kane Ousmane Oumar Kane, *Homeland Is the Arena: Religion, Transnationalism, and the Integration of Senegalese Immigrants in America* (2011), and Zain Abdullah, *Black Mecca: The African Muslims of Harlem* (2013). Although there is no straightforward, simple answer to the question why this story is not told more widely, the first step is to note major differences in articulating race, both historically and in terms of policies and politics.

France has long cultivated an image as a land of human rights, with Paris as a cosmopolitan place that welcomes and nurtures diversity in its various forms. But between the carefully constructed image and the reality of race relations, there could not be a larger gap—one that has yet to gain attention in academic scholarship and the media. In France, the official discourse does not cover race or ethnicity per se; one is simply "French." Duality in French identity is often brushed off as divisive, undermining national cohesion. For example, the feud between the South African comedian and *Daily Show* host Trevor Noah and Gérard Araud, the French ambassador to the United States, in the summer of 2018 reflects the unease that surrounds any talk of hyphenated French identities.[12] The feud was sparked by Noah's comments about the African roots of certain soccer players, noting how Black people around the world celebrate the Africanness of the players Paul Pogba and N'Golo Kanté. The French ambassador Araud wrote a letter to the comedian arguing that the focus on the players' African roots was denying their French identity. Noah responded that the two are not incompatible, that one can be both French and African.

This dichotomy further complicates the task of attempting to understand or compare Paris and New York as the nexuses of encounters between Africa and the Black Atlantic.[13] Paris has traditionally represented a place of liberation for Black writers, intellectuals, and artists. Yet as the example above demonstrates, France does not celebrate multiple identities. If anything, hyphenated identities—Afro-French or Afro-European— might be a burden to those who wish to claim them. In contrast, one is enabled to celebrate multiple heritages or hyphenated identities in New York and throughout the United States, as the various parades in New York celebrating different ethnicities and cultures illustrate. I am not suggesting that the United States treats racial and ethnic minorities better than France does, but I am pointing out a different level of acknowledgment of race issues and their deliberate inclusion in the public discourse.

In 1947, the Senegalese intellectual Alioune Diop created the journal *Présence Africaine* in Paris to circulate ideas among Blacks from Africa, the Caribbean, and the United States who were under various forms of oppression.[14] The name of the journal carries symbolic significance for its attempt to give voice and presence to Africans and West Indians in Paris as they address the condition of Black people. The historical circumstances of Black Paris in the 1940s may be different from that of New York City in the twenty-first century, but the parallel is about an African presence that needs (re)telling and discursive construction in its transnational dimensions, especially in global spaces of encounter. This book is a bid to render the visible more present and to open lines of inquiries on migration and diaspora.

Several factors have to be considered in mapping the networks of contemporary African mass migration, forming the patterns of diaspora. In this regard, it is important to underline Donald Carter's observation that "African diasporas emerge not only in sites where relationships have been established through colonies but in new contexts, often following the circuitous pathways of NGOs, religious organizations, political affiliations, transnational refugee networks and familial reunification."[15] Trade networks have historically been a factor in the immigration of African groups such as Senegalese, Malians, Guineans, and Nigeriens to New York City.[16] Today, other equally significant factors are shaping routes and destinations of African migrants. Effects of climate change—less rainfall or flooding in traditionally arid zones—are already a lived experience for the vast Saharan region stretching from Senegal to Ethiopia. For these populations, specifically in the West African Sahelian region, the drought of the 1970s left an indelible scar in the collective memory of the devastating impact of climate change on their livelihoods. The drought brought tremendous suffering to humans and animals across the Sahel region, causing migration within and outside the continent. Climate migration is an urgent issue of contemporary relevance. Today, internal displacement due to jihadist attacks has seen agro-pastoral villagers flee their homes for big cities and countries along the coast such as Côte d'Ivoire, Ghana, and Guinea. The resulting fast-moving urbanization will in turn either cause cities to implode because of the infrastructure's inability to accommodate these mass arrivals or generate a mass movement toward the global North.

The movement of African-born migrants since the 1970s and 1980s, which should be considered in globalized and postcolonial contexts, challenges the conventional definition of African diaspora or, at the very least, calls for a new concept to render a new migratory pattern and process. Historically, it is widely known that tragic processes of forced removal of Africans contributed to the formation of the African or the Black diaspora; the transatlantic slave trade, the trans-Saharan slave trade, and the Indian Ocean slave trade dispersed millions of Africans from their original homes to different parts of the world. Colonialism also led in certain contexts to the displacement of Africans outside of their homes. Up to the early 2020s, however, a significant portion of publications on African diaspora appears to be focused primarily on descendants of slaves, with Blacks in the United States getting much of the attention.[17] In this respect, the concept presented in the volume edited by Khalid Koser, *New African*

Diasporas (2003), provides the linking thread to examine the settlement of francophone West African immigrants in Harlem since the 1980s. These new African diasporas are the outcome of mass migrations throughout the twentieth century. As members of the new African diaspora, Koser writes, "the status of recent African migrants ranges from the highly skilled and professional (diplomats, academics, doctors) to the near-destitute (illegal migrants, asylum seekers)."[18] The volume also draws on research on new immigration to New York by the scholar Nancy Foner, who considers as new immigrants to New York City those who have arrived since 1965 from many countries and cultures.[19] The end of the quota system under the Hart-Celler Immigration Act of 1965 allowed in-migration of more diverse groups than was previously possible, including ordinary, nonelite Africans for whom international travel became an accessible reality when their countries gained independence in the 1960s (discussed in Chapter 3). In this regard, the trajectory and experience of Africans in New York fit in with the larger context of the city's newcomers.

On the topics of African immigrants in New York City and their migration to Harlem, some scholarly investigations include works by Paul Stoller, Zain Abdullah, Édouard Glissant, Irma Watkins-Owens, and Vivek Bald. The anthropologist Paul Stoller examines the Africanization of New York City through the economic, spatial, and communal presence of African street vendors in *Money Has No Smell*, already mentioned. The migrants he describes, mostly from francophone West African countries, have successfully navigated politics of space to establish a presence in Harlem; for example, in Malcolm Shabazz Market in Little Senegal and Lower Manhattan (stalls on sidewalks). This is particularly significant for migrants who often have a limited command of the English language and little access to decision-making circles. As is well known to New Yorkers, the city can be tough on newcomers or those lacking access; however, many of these migrants appear to have overcome these obstacles. Stoller depicts this as a community formed on the basis of informal and grassroots networking, which the present book seeks to build on, exploring the cultural negotiation techniques used by African migrants to thrive as a community. Stoller's study is the first of its kind and offers insights into the economic presence and contributions of African migrants in New York City, notions that he further develops in *The Power of the Between: An Anthropological Odyssey* (2009). This concept refers to the capacity to adapt and thrive in a space radically different from one's original milieu. In other words, not being from here or there is not regarded as an obstacle but rather an asset in thriving personally and professionally: The new or adopted space becomes a site of rebirth and creativity. The concept of the *power of the between* guides the present book's examination of the processes of African migrants' new identity-formation and the relationships between African immigrants and African Americans in Harlem. Closely connected with this is the question of whether and how their sense of identity and community is based on nationality, race, ethnicity, class, or religion.

Zain Abdullah addresses the presence of African Muslim communities in Harlem, particularly the Murid community from Senegal, in *Black Mecca: The African Muslims of Harlem* (2013). The book explores the visible African Muslim presence in Harlem as changes to the US immigration law of 1965 led to French-speaking Africans immigrating to New York and Harlem. This African Muslim presence is examined in the context of the "double minority" standing of immigrant Black Muslims in the United States after the 9/11 terrorist attacks and relations between West African Muslims and their African American neighbors. Among many other spaces, the *masjid* (mosques) are places where relations between African Americans and African migrants are established and nurtured. Faith becomes an element of identity and community formation beyond race and nationality.

What interconnects New York's African immigrant community? In his writings on creolization in the Caribbean, the Martinican philosopher and literary theorist Édouard Glissant offers a critical lens for understanding African migrants in the diaspora, particularly in New York. This is the case with Glissant's notion of the rhizomatic (multilayered) identity formation of the African diaspora in the Caribbean. Glissant's work draws on the *véçu*, the lived experience of the Caribbeans, where identity formation points to a passage of unicity to multiplicity. Glissant's creolization intersects with Stoller's power of the between to explain displacement, rootedness, and belonging in diasporic community-building. In *Poetics of Relation* (1997), Glissant defines relation as what connects us beyond filiation, as he distinguishes identité-relation from identité-filiation. One of the laws of relation is opacity, meaning to accept what we don't understand in ourselves and in others, which can lead to acceptance of difference. Diversity is created and maintained when one's own opacity encounters or enters into relation with that of others. The concept of opacity not only brings difference into relation but also advocates for acknowledging difference and accepting it. This is particularly important for immigrants today and the disenfranchised or historically oppressed racial and ethnic groups. In the end, it is all about our shared humanity, in which differences are only one facet of manifestation.

In terms of the wider scope of scholarship on immigration and the lives of immigrant communities in Harlem, this book can be contextualized and put in conversation with other works such as Irma Watkins-Owens's *Blood Relations: Caribbean Immigrants and the Harlem Community, 1900–1930* (1996) and Vivek Bald's *Bengali Harlem and the Lost Histories of South Asian America* (2015). Both books underline the migratory American experience through the history and journey of poor, working-class migrants from different parts of the world. They also show how migrant spaces have transformed cities across the United States and have consistently contributed to renewing American society and the economy. The present book adds to those critical interventions by bringing attention and focus to African immigration to Harlem, a subject matter that holds resonance for conversations on immigration, the rise of ethnonationalism, and the (dis)continuity of history and culture between Africa and the diaspora and global cities.

In short, I have written this book to rectify that absence of Africa from the Harlem narrative, while also addressing the intellectual, artistic, and creative exchanges between Africa and New York dating back to the 1910s, a story that has not been told in its full form. Writing from my area of expertise—cinema, literature, Black studies—the book takes an interdisciplinary approach to the topic of Africans in the history, culture, and diversity of Harlem, drawing on history, politics, art, literature, film and media studies, anthropology, and migration and diaspora studies. The chapters are conceptually framed from the intersection of these fields of scholarship, deploying the new African diaspora as a critical lens to appropriately render patterns, processes, and experiences of the global African migration since the 1960s, though the book does not lay claim to open a new paradigm or theoretical construct in migration and diaspora studies. Throughout the book, qualitative methods of research and analysis are preferred over quantitative methods.

While Harlem's ties to Africa are often examined in the context of Harlem Renaissance and Negritude movements—the struggle for independence and civil rights in Africa and the different global struggles against racism and systemic oppression—what is lacking in the existing narratives of Harlem are the economic and cultural transformations that francophone West African immigrants have brought to the neighborhood since the 1980s. This book seeks to challenge the hiddenness of the historical presence of Africans in Harlem and in turn to complexify the discourse on the history and transformations of Harlem. The story of these African communities captures the ever-changing complexity of Harlem.

Thus the objectives of this book are threefold. First, it seeks to render the African presence in Harlem more visible by bringing to the fore the neighborhood's relatively unexplored stories and histories. Even though African communities are visibly present, they are not always part of the Harlem narrative. As the French philosopher and historian of ideas Michel Foucault put it, the absence of archives renders the history invisible.[20] In the case of Africans in Harlem, their absence from the narrative renders them invisible. As a created space, the city can manifest contrasting facets, such as diversity, segregation, and invisibility or anonymity. In this respect, the city can be considered as a complex text, body, and object for study. The challenge of the ambiguity in the city should not, however, deter attempts at understanding the histories and social dynamics of shared urban spaces. In Harlem and other areas of the city, African immigrants inscribe their space with the multilayered motifs of their culture, identity, and sense of belonging. In other words, inscriptions of their embodied experience exemplify the process of transformation for migrants themselves and the space they now inhabit, a space that the Deleuzian term *becoming* well captures.

Second, I hope the book sparks conversation among inner-city communities about ways of facing collective challenges and seizing opportunities that come with having diverse community members. I hope to foster discussions on building local sustainable communities by envisioning and appropriating their futures together. Hopefully, this will also contribute to a more nuanced narrative of immigration in New York beyond the common narratives of European, Caribbean, South American, and Latin American migration waves and communities, complexifying the narrative of New York as an immigrant city. This is particularly important in view of the growing size and presence of the African population throughout New York City; there is need to reflect the changing demographics of the urban landscape.

Third, the African presence and influence in Harlem provide a contained field of study of migration and diaspora that have national and international resonance. The questions of belonging and integration, the growing number of US-born minorities, and the tightening of immigration laws globally are all themes that cut across ethnic and national divides. Cities around the world are diversifying, neighborhoods are being transformed with new arrivals, gentrification is displacing longtime residents, housing affordability is a high-pressure issue, and the differential accessibility of public services creates segregation in urban spaces. As an interdisciplinary book standing at the intersections of migration, diaspora, and urban studies, it adds to the literature and seeks to enrich informed conversation in these areas.

Homi K. Bhabha argues for a conceptual framework that addresses mobility outside of the nation-state, whose borders determine the criteria of exclusion and inclusion. This is particularly important to consider as globalization produces diasporic communities, with Africans of different socioeconomic backgrounds moving across the Atlantic to the United States in pursuit of better opportunities. The quest for a new home, upon arrival in the United States, continues as African migrants often move from one state to another, one city to the next, or resettle in different areas of the city until they find their home. As Bhabha notes:

> Migrants, the unemployed, the poor, and the homeless—among other marginalized communities—search restlessly for a "homeland" within the hegemony of the nation. Theirs is a mobility that moves from one rented home to another, from one job to another, from one part of the country to another, and from one border or frontier to another. The claims for a post-national—or transnational—geography of mobility must be seen in a complex and necessary relation to social mobilities internal to the structure of nation-states and geopolitical regions.[21]

The transatlantic mobility of African migrants to New York City is very often followed by a series of internal mobilities within the five boroughs and increasingly outside the city limits. Gentrification, higher rent, and the desire to reconcile job and community inevitably impel displacement. This mobility of African immigrant communities within national borders remains relatively unexplored. It is accompanied by a circulation of African cosmogonies, transforming spaces inhabited by migrants as they are also transformed by cross-cultural exchanges.

No better way to start the journey than to look at the early history of Black Manhattan. Chapter 1 provides a historical narrative beginning with the first known nonindigenous settler of Manhattan Island (the free Black Juan Rodriguez) and spanning from Little Africa, San Juan Hill, Hell's Kitchen, and Seneca Village to Harlem, offering a historical overview of the space that African immigrants would come to inhabit. This is the type of history that Africans would benefit from knowing about New York City, a history of interest to visitors and residents, and one that still needs to find its way into classrooms and public forums for dissemination. So let us proceed to unearth some of these lesser-known stories.

1

The History of Black Manhattan

From Enslaved Africans to African Immigrants

Harlem, Harlem! Now I've seen Harlem, Harlem!
A green breeze of corn rising from the pavements
Plowed by the Dan dancers' bare feet,
Hips rippling like silk and spearhead breasts,
Ballets of water lilies and fabulous masks
And mangoes of love rolling from the low houses
To the feet of police horses.

—Léopold Sédar Senghor, "To New York"

THE HISTORY OF BLACK New York City extends over four centuries. To offer a full overview of it would be too daunting for the scope of this chapter, yet some key historical markers will provide context for African and African American presence in Manhattan's early history, the exchanges and encounters between Africans and African Americans, and the influx of African immigrants in Harlem since the 1980s. The African presence in Harlem can be further contextualized by looking at African migration trends internationally, thus gaining insight into why, of all the places they might otherwise have chosen in the United States, so many West African immigrants chose to come to New York City. Though few major cities of the world can boast the name recognition of New York's landmarks—the Statue of Liberty, the Broadway theater district, Wall Street, Carnegie Hall, Times Square, and others—surprisingly little is known popularly of the city's history, particularly when it comes to the major contributions of free Blacks and African slaves to the development of New York City. The analysis here focuses on the settling and northward displacement of Black people on Manhattan Island from seventeenth-century Little Africa to twentieth- and twenty-first-century Harlem.

Between the end of the nineteenth century and the 1920s, New York City saw intensifying demographic transformations as a result of the Great Migration, the arrival of European immigrants and people of African descent of the Caribbean and South America.[1] These arrivals laid the foundation for a more diverse New York City population, which is one of its key features as a global city. This historic period of demographic shifts may be regarded as the beginning of the multiethnic and diasporic communities of Harlem.[2] Many working-class migrants and immigrants found in Harlem a socioeconomic environment in which to build communities united by racial, ethnic, and class affinities and by rejection of the racism characterizing white America. Harlem represented hope and the possibility for Blacks to actualize their potentialities and talents in the historical context of systemic discrimination. For many, Harlem projected the image of a Black mecca, even a Black utopia. These pull factors attracted different waves of immigration to Harlem over the decades—a spectrum of Black peoples extending beyond African Americans to include, for instance, African-born immigrants.

Africans in Manhattan's Early History

The free Black named Juan Rodriguez is considered the first known non-indigenous settler of Manhattan Island, which was originally inhabited by Native Americans, the Lenape Indians, who gave the island its name: Manhattan was called Mannahatta (island of many hills) by the Lenape.[3] Juan Rodriguez was a mixed-race freed slave who came from the island of Hispaniola (currently Haiti and Dominican Republic) to Manhattan in 1613 aboard the Dutch ship *Jonge Tobias* as part of a fur-trading company expedition, arriving seven years before the 1620 arrival of the Pilgrims on the *Mayflower*, which is glorified as part of the founding myth of the United States.

Historians have yet to conclude why Rodriguez decided to stay when the ship returned to the Netherlands, but his case raises the question: How does this settler of "New Amsterdam" represent or signify later settlements of Africans (and African descendants) in what would become New York City? Rodriguez helps bring attention to the marginalization of racial and ethnic minorities in the history and space of the city. Unlike certain familiar historical figures whom we have readily come to connect with New York, Juan Rodriguez has yet to enter the mainstream narrative about the city's origins. Likewise, the first African slaves were brought by the Dutch in the mid-seventeenth century—well before the nineteenth- and early twentieth-century European mass migrations to New York City. Yet relatively little research has been done to explore settlements of Africans (and African descendants) in comparison with European immigrants. The history documenting the economic contributions of slaves to the city has yet to gain a lasting place in the public discourse. Moreover, the history and discourse pertaining to the enslavement of Africans need to be reframed, as the predominant approach has been to address the transatlantic slave trade, Indian Ocean slavery, and the trans-Saharan slave trade separately. The resultant schism between them means that each is examined from *either* the experience of the Black Atlantic diaspora *or* within the context of African history. The schismatic treatment of these slave trades points to a larger issue concerning cultural and historical continuity between Africa and the Black diaspora. The works of sociologist and activist W. E. B. Du Bois and anthropologist Melville Herskovits are held to have shaped this separation between African history and African American history at US universities.[4]

In the seventeenth century the Netherlands rose to commercial and naval power, creating trading posts with Native Americans and colony settlements in the Americas. New Amsterdam, one of these colony settlements, was established by the Dutch West India Company. New Amsterdam was renamed New York in 1664 after the Dutch lost their colonies to the British following a series of battles. Captured slaves from Africa were brought across the Atlantic to develop the British colonies, cultivating rice, cotton, and tobacco. In late August 1619, about thirty captured African slaves from the Congo arrived aboard the ship *White Lion* in the British Colony of Virginia; this marked the beginning of the transatlantic slave trade. The first enslaved Africans from Angola arrived in New Amsterdam in 1626. By mid-1800 there were four million slaves in the country. The documentary film *New York Noir: The History of Black New York* (2008), directed by Marino Amoruso, underscores the substantial contribution of African slaves to the construction of early New York: They cleared the shorelines for ships to enter, cleared land for houses and farming, and widened the narrow Native American trails to permit more extensive travel. For the next two centuries New York City and Charleston, South Carolina, became the two main harbors from which African slaves were transported further inland. In New York City, what would later become Wall Street, the world's financial center, was a place where enslaved Africans were bought and sold. According to Anne C. Bailey, "From 1711 until 1762, a slave market operated on Wall Street between Water and Pearl Streets."[5]

African slaves in the early history of New York experienced different severities of subjugation under the Dutch and the English. The former allowed African slaves some relative freedom, particularly to own property on Manhattan Island, whereas the race-based slavery of the English curtailed such freedoms. In 1712, a law was passed prohibiting free Blacks from owning land, setting a pattern for later injustice and legal discrimination. Enslaved Blacks lived predominantly in segregated areas on the west side of Lower Manhattan: in the Tenderloin, Hell's Kitchen, San Juan Hill, and Seneca Village. They began moving to the northern "uptown" parts of Manhattan in large numbers only later, in the second half of the nineteenth and early twentieth centuries. Until then, Harlem was a farming community and retreat for public officials and the wealthy to get away from busy Lower Manhattan, the center of commercial and political power. Alexander Hamilton, founding father and first US Secretary of the Treasury, for instance, built his mansion in what was then a farm community, located in the present-day Harlem on 141st Street between Convent Avenue and St. Nicholas Avenue (now a National Park Service site known as the Hamilton Grange National Memorial). The mansion has been relocated twice, first in 1889 from its original site on 143rd and Convent Avenue to St. Luke's Episcopal Church on 141st Street, where it stayed until 2008, when it was moved across the street into St. Nicholas Park at its current location.

One of the most notable historic sites linked with Africans in colonial New York City is arguably the African Burial Ground in Lower Manhattan, which was discovered in 1991 when bones were found during the excavation to erect a thirty-four-story federal office building.[6] Through its museum and memorial, this National Monument offers a glimpse of the forgotten history of New York as well as of the presence of enslaved Africans in the city in the seventeenth and eighteenth centuries. An estimated 25,000 Africans and people of African descent are buried at the sacred site. The number of people buried at the site shows how Africans have contributed to building "New Amsterdam" (early New York City). The African Burial Ground also provides an early direct connection between Africa and New York City in the formation of the city's African diaspora. Centuries later, waves of African immigrants followed in contributing to the renewal of New York City's creative energies and also inscribing their cultural identities into different spaces across the city. In addition to the burial ground in Lower Manhattan, there is also the 2015 discovery of an

Figure 1. East 126th Street Bus Depot, which sits on the Harlem African Burial Ground. Photo taken in 2021. Courtesy of Boukary Sawadogo and Mira Steinzor.

ancient African burial ground in the East Harlem neighborhood at the East 126th Street bus depot.

This provides further evidence of the African presence in the early history of New York City, specifically in Dutch colonial Harlem in the 1660s. The site of the Harlem African Burial Ground is located on East 126th Street between First and Second Avenues. The Harlem African Burial Ground task force was formed in 2009, and steps for a mixed-use development project have been taken since 2016, including the creation of a memorial and education center, with a targeted completion date of 2023. The history of this burial ground is connected to the Dutch Reformed Church of Harlem, now the Elmendorf Reformed Church, which in 1660 had created separate cemeteries for whites and descendants of African slaves. When the church moved to the Bronx, the bodies of the white parishioners were exhumed and brought there, but the bodies in the African burial ground were left behind. That cemetery was abandoned and later sold to a white farmer who used it as grazing land for his animals.[7] Over the years, several establishments, such as a movie theater, trolley barn, casino, and a bus depot, were erected on the land. So the African presence in Harlem dates back to at least the founding of the Dutch village that the neighborhood once was. It is too early to know how the African immigrants of today will react to the news of this first African presence in Harlem. Ideally, it should inspire them with an even greater sense of pride and belonging as they make their own contributions to the creative energy and diversity of this unique locale.

Little Africa and San Juan Hill

The historical development of Black settlements on Manhattan Island followed a northward trajectory from their beginnings in Lower Manhattan. Blacks first established "Little Africa" in the seventeenth century in what is now Greenwich Village, then moved to San Juan Hill (near the current Lincoln Center), and finally to Harlem. As part of this trajectory from Lower to Upper Manhattan, Seneca Village was created in 1825 at the current location of Central Park, from West 82nd to West 85th Streets between Seventh and Eighth Avenues. The founders of Seneca Village were members of two Black organizations, the African Society for Mutual Relief and the African Methodist Episcopal Zion Church. The formation of this free Black community of Seneca Village was grounded in the principle of racial and personal advancement, which is significant at a historical time when slavery was not yet abolished in the United States. The community was destroyed in 1857 by eviction from the land to make way for the construction of Central Park. This little-known story of Seneca Village holds contemporary relevance for New York City's working poor and immigrants who face similar displacement and gentrification in neighborhoods like Harlem.

In the early days of the slave trade, a community of enslaved Africans and Irish indentured servants lived outside the perimeter of New York City, which ended on Broadway. That community came to be known as Little Africa. Enslaved Africans lived in this shantytown with no sanitation for almost two centuries. Little Africa stretched from what is today Sixth Avenue on the west to the waterfront on the east. The sharing of this space between Africans and whites was difficult at times, particularly during the Civil War when Irish immigrants refused the draft to fight the Confederate army. The lesser-known aspect of Little Africa is that a dynamic arts scene developed there, particularly the theater. In the 1820s, the African American actor and playwright William Alexander Brown founded the African Grove Theater on Mercer and Bleeker Streets in Lower Manhattan, at a time when Blacks in New York City were still enslaved. It was a theater company with Black casts that played for mostly Black audiences, and that showcased Black enterprise and artistic creativity when slavery officially ended in New York City in 1827. The 300-patron capacity African Grove theater had popular success, presenting both original works and productions of Shakespeare plays.[8] This early Black theater may well have contributed to laying the groundwork for the cultural emergence of the Harlem Renaissance in the 1920s through the 1950s, as historian Marcy S. Sacks suggests: "The city's growing Black population sustained a vital artistic core that had made the trek from the Tenderloin to San Juan Hill along with the bulk of the community, and later moved on to Harlem, forming the nucleus of the group forging the Harlem Renaissance in the 1920s."[9]

When Little Africa was incorporated into the municipality of New York City, rising rents and other factors pushed African Americans farther up Manhattan Island in a quest for affordable housing. Some also moved to establish a community where their numbers would help alleviate the pressures of the segregation and racial discrimination they faced in American society. A new, predominantly Black neighborhood known as San Juan Hill was founded on Amsterdam Avenue and 62nd Street. Sacks documents the uptown march of the Black community from the lower tip of the island, noting that by the end of the nineteenth century the greater San Juan Hill district—stretching between 60th and 64th Streets and Tenth and Eleventh Avenues—claimed the bulk of the city's Black population.[10] This neighborhood lasted from the late nineteenth century to the first half of the twentieth century before being demolished for housing developments; eventually it became the site of Lincoln Center.

Even before the decline of the San Juan Hill neighborhood, Harlem had begun attracting African Americans from Lower Manhattan, as well as migrants from the post-Reconstruction South. The flow of population known as the Great Migration commenced in the wake of the Civil War as Blacks left the Jim Crow South for better economic opportunities and social advancement in the North.[11] According to Sacks, the fall of Reconstruction and the rise of Jim Crow legislation in the South "helped precipitate a sharp increase in the number of southern black people seeking friendlier environs in the North."[12] Isabel Wilkerson's award-winning historical study *The Warmth of Other Suns: The Epic Story of America's Great Migration* (2011), for example, documents the Great Migration through the journeys of three African Americans. The notable series of paintings titled *The Migration of the Negro* (1941) by American painter Jacob Lawrence, a longtime resident of Harlem, likewise provides insights into the Great Migration. Blacks were drawn to industrial cities such as Detroit, Chicago, Philadelphia, and New York, and particularly to Black neighborhoods in such cities in the hopes they would have fewer issues with discrimination and assimilation. Several factors made Harlem an attractive destination for African Americans in the early twentieth century: the construction of new subway lines, more affordable housing as Lower Manhattan became increasingly expensive for Blacks, businesses catering to Blacks and Black immigrants, and Harlem's growing reputation as a cultural center for the brightest and most talented Black artists. With the completion of the New York subway's Number 2 and 3 lines in 1904, Harlem was only a ten- or fifteen-minute train ride from Times Square and Wall Street.

Prominent Harlemites:
Madame Walker, Madam St. Claire, Marcus Garvey

The Black real-estate entrepreneur Philip Payton greatly contributed to opening up Harlem to Blacks from 1904 through the early 1920s by way of his Afro-American Realty Company.[13] Payton started out as a janitor for a real-estate firm before eventually setting up his own company, which purchased vacant apartments from the mostly white landlords and rented them to Black tenants. Harlem became a far more affordable alternative to the high-rent apartments in Lower Manhattan, where commercial development made living downtown particularly costly. Payton's company allowed Blacks to rent apartments in Harlem in greater numbers than would have otherwise been possible at the time. Although Payton is generally lauded for his business acumen, criticism was leveled at his company for his practice of charging Black tenants relatively higher rent. Yet Payton's economic activism earned him a legacy in the history of Harlem, alongside that of entrepreneur Sarah Breedlove.

Breedlove, better known as Madam C. J. Walker, was the early twentieth-century equivalent of Oprah Winfrey. A Black businesswoman who gained prominence for creating haircare products and cosmetics developed specifically for Black women, Walker was the first Black female self-made millionaire in the United States.

Walker's life, achievements, and pioneering business in Black haircare products are the subject of numerous books and audiovisual productions, including the original Netflix series *Self Made: Inspired by the Life of Madam C. J. Walker* (2020), starring Academy Award winner Octavia Spencer and Tiffany Haddish, with NBA star LeBron James listed as an executive producer.[14] A lesser-known yet equally significant figure is Stephanie St. Clair, later known in Harlem as Madam St. Clair, who moved in the 1910s to Harlem's Sugar Hill, then the neighborhood of the Negro elite in Harlem, from her native Martinique in the French West Indies. Further research

Figure 2. Portrait of Madam C. J. Walker, circa 1914. With permission of the Schomburg Center for Research in Black Culture.

may illuminate whether the paths of Walker and St. Clair ever crossed, and how the former might have inspired the latter in her own success in Harlem. St. Clair arrived in New York City at age twenty-six via the port of Marseille in France. This young Black French woman would become Madam St. Clair, "Queenie, the queen of Harlem's illegal lottery."[15] The significance of Madam St. Clair's trajectory should be situated within the broader historical context of segregation and the lynching of Blacks in the South. The journey of a foreign single Black woman with little command

Figure 3. Group of men holding a banner in a Marcus Garvey Day parade in Harlem. 2008. Photo by Daoud AbuBakr.

of the English language in this historical context is quite extraordinary. The book by Martinican writer Raphaël Confiant titled *Madam St. Clair, Queen of Harlem* (2020) offers a larger context for the story of the gangster lady in Harlem during Prohibition, including the activism of Marcus Garvey and the Harlem Renaissance through its iconic poets Langston Hughes and Countee Cullen.

Indeed, Marcus Garvey's Universal Negro Improvement Association (UNIA), the Harlem Renaissance movement, and the Negritude literary movement all contributed immensely to the political and socioeconomic emancipation of Blacks through their portrayal of Black identity in positive terms. Whereas the Harlem Renaissance writer W. E. B. Du Bois developed the concept of "double consciousness" in his seminal book *The Souls of Black Folk* (1903) to express the internal conflict of identification experienced by African Americans, Garvey, through the UNIA, advocated for African Americans to return to Africa.[16]

The UNIA is an international Black nationalist movement founded in 1914 in Jamaica by Marcus Garvey which advocated for Pan-Africanism— Black unity based on shared African heritage, self-reliance, and Africa

Figure 4. Marcus Garvey Day parade in Harlem: a crowd procession in the streets. 2008. Photo by Daoud AbuBakr.

controlling its resources. UNIA gained tremendous visibility and influence after Garvey moved to New York City in 1916. UNIA had branches in cities in the United States and abroad. The deportation of Marcus Garvey in 1927 after his indictment on fraud charges led to the gradual dissolution of the organization. The UNIA, like the Harlem Renaissance, was born out of the African diaspora—those dispersed from their homeland—questioning the effectiveness of their civil and political rights and their place in post-Reconstruction American society. This was especially prudent in the wake of Black participation in the First World War. Despite the heroic performance of the 369th Infantry Regiment known as the Harlem Hellfighters during both World Wars, these Black servicemen returned home to a sociopolitical and economic environment that remained stubbornly segregated. This became known as the "two battlefronts" for African Americans: fighting fascism in Europe while facing racism in America. In other words, Black soldiers were engaged in the Second World War to free the world from tyranny while Jim Crow segregation at home in the South was the law of the land. Blacks were drafted into the army and fought in Europe and the Pacific in segregated units. The renowned African American poet

Langston Hughes underscored the issue of the two battlefronts in his 1943 poem "Beaumont to Detroit," which ends by asking, "How long I got to fight/Both Hitler and Jim Crow."

Harlem Renaissance and Negritude Movement

Harlem was quickly becoming between late 1910s and early 1920s the capital of Black culture as the Harlem Renaissance movement brought together Black artists, musicians, writers, and entertainers of different backgrounds. The dancer and trained opera singer Assadata Dafora (1890–1965), for example, was born and raised in Sierra Leone and moved to Europe to study opera before immigrating to New York City in 1929. His musical drama *Kykunkor* (The witch woman) was a success on Broadway in the 1930s and contributed to a long history of African dance on Broadway.[17] Dafora was a renowned dancer and creative talent on Broadway who regularly performed at community events in Harlem, including at Mother African Methodist Episcopal Zion Church on January 26, 1931. As a church that hosted African leaders and provided a place for student activists from Africa to meet in the 1960s and 1970s, it has historical ties to both Africa and Africans living in Harlem. Other influential literary figures of the Harlem Renaissance include Zora Neale Hurston, Countee Cullen, and Alain LeRoy Locke. Locke's book *The New Negro* (1925) helped popularize the concept of the "New Negro," which called for dignity for Blacks and rejection of racial discrimination and segregation. Léopold Sédar Senghor, one of the founding members of the Negritude literary movement, wrote the poem "To New York" upon his visit to Lower Manhattan and Harlem in the 1950s to share his impressions of and feelings about those two areas of the island. This poem and many others by poets from different African countries were edited and published together in *Poems from Black Africa* (1963) by Langston Hughes.[18]

Whereas Lower Manhattan is dominated by mostly steel and concrete structures, Senghor's poem describes Harlem as full of life, representing the type of energy that New York City needs.

> New York! I say to you: New York! Let black blood flow into your
>   blood
> That it may rub the rust from your steel joints, like an oil of life
> That it may give to your bridges the bend of buttocks and the
> suppleness of creepers.
>   —Léopold Sédar Senghor, "To New York"

The situational circumstances between Blacks in Harlem and those in colonized Africa may have been different at the time, but the two groups were brought together in Harlem through an intellectual exchange focused on Black dignity, pride, and liberation from systemic forms of oppression.

The Harlem Renaissance was a source of inspiration to the Negritude movement as it was taking form under the leadership of the Paris-based students Léopold Sédar Senghor from Senegal, Aimé Césaire from Martinique, and Léon-Gontran Damas from French Guiana. They interacted with African American writers, artists, and entertainers in Paris while attending school there. These Negritude theorists would form the beginnings of the intelligentsia in the late 1930s and early 1940s that denounced the French colonial system in Africa and the Caribbean, paving the way for political independence. The solidarity between the two groups was instrumental in fostering transatlantic ties in the struggle for freedom and racial justice, specifically after Africans and African Americans had seen whites at their worst during the two world wars. As a result, this experience demystified white people in their eyes. The cross-Atlantic Black encounters through their writings or activist measures in Paris, coupled with the eye-opening experience of fighting alongside Allied troops during the Second World War, helped strengthen the commitment of Negritude members to demand an end to the exploitative system of colonialism. The militant undertones of Negritude were not only political but also cultural, promoting and attempting to restore pride in Blackness after centuries of degrading treatment.[19]

Negritude also had its critics, however. The essentialist approach to African-ness or Blackness was vehemently questioned by the 1986 Nobel laureate in literature, Wole Soyinka; the cultural theorist and psychiatrist Frantz Fanon; and the writer and theorist Édouard Glissant. In his play *A Dance of the Forests* (1963), Soyinka rejected the essentialist tendency of Negritude through his now-famous quote: "The tiger does not proclaim its tigritude, it leaps and devours its prey." Frantz Fanon, the critical race theorist from Martinique, objected to the essentialism of Black experience across continents and the tendency to constantly fall back on the past as a way to reclaim Black identity. Although Fanon's writings drew on the Black consciousness of Negritude, he described the long-lasting psychological effects of colonization. In *Black Skin, White Masks* (1952), Fanon theorized that colonialism leads to the development of an inferiority complex. This emphasizes that colonialism, as with other forms of oppression, is more about mental control than the occupation of territory and the sheer physical violence inflicted on the oppressed. He argued real liberation can come only from mental liberation.

Édouard Glissant, professor of literature at City College of New York (CUNY) in Harlem, then later at CUNY's Graduate Center in Lower Manhattan from 1995 to 2011, posited that identity in the Caribbean does not have a single African root. Rather, it draws on multiple roots depending on one's milieu. The works of Glissant and other Caribbean thinkers have helped conceptualize the creation of identity out of fragmentation. Generally, the criticisms leveled at Negritude by Soyinka, Fanon, Glissant, and many others helped it evolve toward universalism not only to address the condition of the disenfranchised but also to be a lens through which to help understand the complex construction of cultural identity within the context of migration. This (re)definition of identity, Blackness, or Africanness is still faced by African immigrants in Harlem as they have lived and work alongside African Americans and immigrants from the West Indies since the 1970s and 1980s.

Just as the African presence in Harlem merits more public and scholarly attention, so does the historical presence there of Blacks of Caribbean background. Marcus Garvey's Jamaican roots are almost completely omitted from discussions of his political activism in Harlem in the 1910s as a proponent of the "Return to Africa" movement. Also, that Malcolm X's mother immigrated to the United States from the Caribbean is largely ignored. Other Harlemites, such as Sidney Poitier and Harry Belafonte, share West Indian connections. In the 1960s and 1970s, large numbers of Haitians and Jamaicans moved to Harlem as part of the larger migration of West Indians to New York City, where they worked in health care, education, and service industries.

In the 1960s, other African writers visited New York City and Harlem, which they reported on in fictionalized accounts of the city, addressing the place of Blacks in American society. Bernard Binlin Dadié from Côte d'Ivoire was one of those writers, though it should be noted that he was not part of the Negritude literary movement. He published *Patron de New York* in 1964, later translated into English as *One Way*, which offers an African take on American society in New York City as part of a trilogy examining the human condition in contemporary big cities (New York, Paris, and Rome).[20] The images and caricatures of locals are seen through the eyes of the traveling Other and conveyed in epistolary form. Like Senghor, Dadié viewed the highly mechanized city of New York as dehumanizing at times: Harlem is suffering, and who will hear and respond to "those heart-rending cries rising from this African village in the heart of New York?"[21] In his poems "Harlem" and "Jour sur Harlem," published in his collection *Hommes de tous les continents* (Men of all continents, 1967), Dadié also reinforces the image and portrayal of Harlem as a site of suffering for Black people in the middle of New York City.

The New Black Mecca

From the 1920s to the 1950s and beyond, Harlem flourished as the global center of Black politics and culture, drawing the brightest minds of the time to tackle the most difficult issues facing Blacks around the world: subjugation, segregation, and identity. In addressing Black identity and politics during the first half of the twentieth century, those living in continental Africa and those dispersed from their homeland were in continual dialogue about the role of Blacks in their respective societies, an intellectual and political dialogue whose substance and intensity were unmatched by later generations until the early twenty-first century. In the historical context of racial discrimination, African Americans who were not treated as full-fledged citizens faced the question of what their place was in American society, a question that was later underlined during the civil rights movement of the 1960s. While African Americans were fighting systemic racial discrimination in the United States, independence movements against colonial rule in Africa started claiming sovereignty over their peoples' destinies. As we shall see in the next chapter, pan-Africanism, an ideological and political movement aimed at unifying people of African descent beyond cultural differences or geographical locations, was never more active and compelling than it was in Harlem, given the existential challenges and identity issues faced by Blacks. Moving on from the history of Black New York City to contextualize the spatiotemporal space in which African-born immigrants came to inhabit, I now turn our attention to the relations between Africans and African Americans during the Cold War era. This period was fraught with transformative changes for Black people, specifically Third World liberation and civil rights movements, and through it Harlem acted as a creative and activist center for the Black world.

2

···

Black Radical Politics and African Awakening in the Cold War and Beyond

We have to keep in mind at all times that we are not fighting for integration, nor are we fighting for separation. We are fighting for recognition . . . for the right to live as free humans in this society.

—Malcolm X, in Harlem, April 6, 1964

Harlem is the "Soweto of America."
—Nelson Mandela, during his first visit to Harlem after twenty-seven years in prison, June 21, 1990

EXCHANGES AND DIRECT CONTACTS between radical movements in the Black Atlantic world and in Africa over the twentieth century led to the awakening of Africans, which inspired them to fight for liberation from colonial rule and against corrupt and autocratic regimes. In the development of these liberation movements, Harlem has often been a source of inspiration and also a nexus of exchanges and encounters. Anti-colonial struggles in Africa and the civil rights movement in the United States brought Blacks together in their opposition to exploitative and dominant political structures that denied them their humanity. In the larger context of the Black radical tradition in this country W. E. B. Du Bois, Frantz Fanon, Malcolm X, and Angela Davis, to name a few, became known as revolutionary voices as they spoke out against racism, discrimination, colonialism, and inequality. The Black Lives Matter movement may be regarded as a continuation of that Black radical tradition.

From the early twentieth century to today, Africa underwent four periods or waves of radical tradition that will be traced in this chapter: The first period of radical political awakening occurred from the 1920s to the 1940s with the arrival of some of the first African students to study in the United States; the second occurred between the 1950s and 1970s with the rise in anti-colonial struggles and nationalism in Africa, the Caribbean, Latin America, and Asia; the third occurred in the early 1980s, with the emergence of young revolutionary figures such as Thomas Sankara in Burkina Faso and Jerry John Rawlings in Ghana; and the fourth wave has seen the rise of youth civic and democratic movements since the 2010s, born out of frustration over the lack of opportunities for social mobility and democratic change, corruption, rigged elections, and unequal distribution of national wealth. From the 1940s to the late 1980s a solidarity movement formed from the transatlantic cooperation and mutual support between Africa and the African diaspora in their struggles against various forms of systemic oppression.

The First and Second Waves: 1920s to 1970s

The first of the four awakening movements occurred in Africa from the 1920s to the 1940s, with the arrival of some of the first African students to study in the United States. Among those students were the future first president of Nigeria, Nnamdi Azikiwe; the future president of Ghana, Kwame Nkrumah; and the intellectuals and activists from Sierra Leone, Alfred T. Sumner and his son Doyle L. Sumner. Azikiwe and Nkrumah are known to have been Harlem residents during their student years in the United States. This first generation of African students attended religious-affiliated schools: Nkrumah attended Lincoln University, Alfred T. Sumner attended the Quaker school Lebanon Valley College—both located in Pennsylvania. These African students forged strong ties with W. E. B. Du Bois and a founding figure of the Harlem Renaissance, Alain Locke. Kwame Nkrumah was known to have directly engaged with Black Americans about his pan-Africanist ideas. Historically, Africans had not had direct encounters with African Americans until the post-Reconstruction era when Black Americans were still not enjoying full citizenship, even though slavery had ended decades earlier. Du Bois's notion of "double consciousness" and Marcus Garvey's "return to Africa" movement attest to the delicate situation of Black Americans at the time.

The second wave of radical African politics occurred on the heels of the first, between the 1950s and 1970s, with the rise in anti-colonial struggles and nationalism in Africa, the Caribbean, Latin America, and Asia. Kwame

Nkrumah, Patrice Lumumba, Gamal Abdel Nasser, and Julius Nyerere were key figures of this wave, which came to an abrupt end with military coups in most cases—such as that in Guinea with the rise to power of Ahmed Sékou Touré, as well as in Ghana and Congo. These figures, much like Robert Mugabe of Zimbabwe, were nationalist leaders who were well regarded within the Black American activist community, but Touré and Mugabe remain divisive figures among Africans because of the autocratic turn that their regimes often took. Thousands of dissidents against Sékou Touré died in detention at the infamous Camp Boiro.

Between the first and second waves of radical African leaders and Black revolutionaries in the United States, multifaceted exchanges and support took place to advance mutual causes. Those exchanges should be understood within the larger context of anti-colonial struggles, the civil rights movements, and the Cold War. A number of Black leaders visited the continent, including the two prominent figures of the civil rights movements—Martin Luther King Jr. and Malcolm X—as well as certain members of the Black Panther Party. Some Black revolutionaries from the United States and the Caribbean also found a home in Africa, away from persecution in their own countries. Malcolm X's visits to several African countries, following his transformative pilgrimage to Mecca, showcased the convergence between the Black nationalism that he promoted and the pan-Africanism that Africa's newly independent countries sought to establish. One of these pan-Africanist efforts led to the creation of the Organization of African Unity in Addis Ababa, Ethiopia, on May 25, 1963. In his address delivered to African leaders gathered for the summit of the Organization of African Unity in July 1964, in Cairo, Egypt, Malcolm X radically advocated for Africa to take a stance against racial discrimination suffered by African Americans. "Our problem is your problem. This is not a civil rights issue but a human rights issue," said Malcolm X. In response, the Organization of African Unity showed solidarity by adopting a resolution condemning racial discrimination in South Africa, Rhodesia (the present-day Zimbabwe), and the United States. Malcolm X's address also underlined how racial discrimination and prejudice in America make no distinction between Africans and African Americans—for they are all considered Black in the eyes of the oppressive system.

Solidarity was already a reality and an underlying principle in the relations between Africans and African Americans in the highly politically charged environment of the 1960s—with the emergence of liberation struggles and the civil rights movement. In the solidarity movement for liberation, Ghana, for instance, under Nkrumah, became a refuge for

Black activists. At the invitation of Ghana's new prime minister, Kwame Nkrumah, Martin Luther King Jr. traveled to Ghana (formerly known as the Gold Coast) in 1957, March 4–12, to attend the new country's independence ceremony. Witnessing Ghanaians celebrating their independence after years of struggle renewed King's convictions for justice for the segregated Blacks in the United States, particularly after the success of the Montgomery bus boycott of 1955–1956. The civil rights activist A. Philip Randolph (1889–1979) and the congressman Adam Clayton Powell Jr. (1908–1972), both from Harlem, also attended Ghana's independence ceremony. A parallel was there for Africans and their diaspora to consider in their struggles against oppression and injustice. Nkrumah returned to Harlem first in July 1958, then again in October 1960, during his visit to the United Nations General Assembly.[1] These exchanges and encounters mutually benefited Africans and African Americans, such that the historian Kevin K. Gaines wrote about the welcoming relationships that Ghana maintained with the diaspora: "Ghana was unrivaled among African nations in its willingness to provide sanctuary to Black (and non-Black) radicals from the United States, the Caribbean, Africa and Europe unable to function politically in their countries of origin."[2] Decades after Nkrumah's official visit to Harlem, another Ghanaian revolutionary leader visited the neighborhood in 1995 at the invitation of the Lumumba Coalition, Jerry John Rawlings, who served as president of Ghana from 1981 to 2001. In addition to Ghana, Guinea in the 1960s under Sékou Touré was welcoming to Black activists. The political activist Stokely Carmichael spent time in Conakry, the capital, working for the National Ballet of Guinea. While there, he met the exiled South African singer and activist Miriam Makeba, who lived in the country between 1968 and 1986. She alternated between living in Guinea and the United States, specifically in New York City and Philadelphia.

Algeria, like Ghana and Guinea, was a meeting place in the 1960s for activists and revolutionaries coming from the United States and the Caribbean as the country was fighting for its political independence from France. The role of Algiers as a center of liberation is well documented in the 2018 memoir of American activist Elaine Mokhtefi, *Algiers, Third World Capital: Freedom Fighters, Revolutionaries, Black Panthers*, and in the documentary film by Stanley Nelson, *The Black Panthers: Vanguard of the Revolution* (2015). Eldridge Cleaver of the Black Panther Party took exile in Algiers, where the West Indian writer and revolutionary Frantz Fanon actively participated in the Algerian liberation war. Ulric Cross from Trinidad and Tobago is a lesser-known yet important figure from the

Caribbean who also contributed to African independence struggles. His trajectory was different from that of most West Indian activists, whose involvement on the continent went from the Caribbean to Paris and then to Africa. London, rather than Paris, served as the nexus of Cross's involvement in the fight for African countries' liberation. Frances-Anne Solomon's documentary *HERO: Inspired by the Extraordinary Life and Times of Mr. Ulric Cross* (2018) details his contribution to nationalist liberation movements in West, Central, and East Africa.

While violent and nonviolent means were used to win the fight for political independence, audiovisual images galvanized support by telling the story from an insider perspective. These independent productions brought international attention to liberation struggles that might not have otherwise received coverage beyond that of Western-based mainstream outlets. The African American director Robert F. Van Lierop, from New York City, traveled to Mozambique and made two documentaries about its liberation struggle: *A Luta Continua* (The struggle continues, 1972), was named for the rallying cry of the Mozambique Liberation Front (FRELIMO) in its struggle for independence from Portuguese colonial rule, and *O Povo Organizado* (The people organized, 1976), depicted post-revolution life in Mozambique. The Guadeloupean director Sarah Maldoror made the film *Sambizanga* (1972) to depict the realities of the independence movement in Angola. Maldoror had previously been an assistant to Gillo Pontecorvo on his movie *The Battle of Algiers*. Nonfiction film productions, specifically documentaries, have played a significant role in independence movements in Lusophone (Portuguese-speaking) countries such as Mozambique and Angola. This has led to a strong and distinctive tradition of documentary practice in Lusophone African cinema in comparison with other cinematic practices on the continent.

In another notable moment of solidarity, the African American Students Foundation played a key role in what is now referred to as the "airlift of East African students to America" in 1959 and 1960. It all started with Tom Mboya, an active Kenyan liberation movement leader who served as secretary-general of the Kenya Federation of Labor. He had toured the United States a few years prior, giving lectures about the independence of Kenya and seeking scholarships for East African students to improve their access to higher education, given that their countries were still under colonial rule. Once independent, these countries would need a well-educated and trained workforce to realize their political independence and begin economic development. The businessman William X. Scheinman encouraged Mboya to visit Harlem in 1956. Key African American figures were

Figure 5. East African students on US bound flight. With permission of Cora Weiss. Photograph was provided by the African Activist Archive Project at Michigan State University.

actively involved in fundraising for the project, including US Representative Charles Diggs, a great figure of Black internationalism and one of the founders of the Congressional Black Caucus; Jackie Robinson, the first African American major league baseball player and a civil-rights activist; the civil-rights leader Malcolm X; actor Sidney Poitier; and singer Harry Belafonte. The African American Students Foundation organized chartered flights from Kenya to New York City thanks to a $100,000 gift from the Kennedy Foundation. In total, about eight hundred African students were brought in to study at US colleges and universities. Among them were the father of President Barack Obama and the 2004 Nobel Peace Prize laureate Wangari Maathai.[3]

The anti-colonial and anti-apartheid fights of the 1970s and 1980s were a catalyst for bringing African and African American students into pan-African student organizations that campaigned to end oppressive systems in Africa, such as the African Student Association, numerous South Africa boycott and disinvestment committees across US university campuses,

Figure 6. Malcolm X welcoming and speaking with students from the East African airlift, New York City, 1960. With permission of Cora Weiss. Photograph was provided by the African Activist Archive Project at Michigan State University.

and local support committees for SWAPO (the South West Africa People's Organization) and ZANU-PF (Zimbabwe African National Union-Patriotic Front) liberation struggles. Some members of these groups still reside in Harlem in 2021, such as Ed Sherman, Wodajo Mogues, and Rashidah Ismaili AbuBakr. Spaces of exchange and interaction were created thanks to the active involvement of Black students in liberation struggles in the Black Atlantic world. In addition, the Abyssinian Baptist Church in Harlem helped African students in the 1960s and 1970s by providing space to meet and connect with the neighborhood. Interactions between African and African American students in Harlem not only manifested the solidarity within the movement but also significantly contributed to furthering understanding between Africa and the diaspora. In certain situations, it was African American jazz musicians who fostered connections with the New York City–based African student population. Jazz icons Charlie Parker and Dizzy Gillespie held concerts at Diplomat Hotel in the 1940s for African Students and the African Academy of Arts and Research, which was founded by the future Nigerian minister Kingsley Ozumba Mbadiwe.[4] In this context, as in countless other moments of the twentieth and twenty-first centuries, jazz brought Africa and the diaspora together.

Beyond the geographic confines of Harlem and New York, other pan-Africanism initiatives were developed to forge ties between Africa and the diaspora. World Black festivals were created as spaces of solidarity and exchange. These festivals, held in Europe and Africa, enabled Black people to imagine and celebrate Blackness on their own terms. The list of world Black festivals includes:

1956 in Paris: First International Congress of Black Artists and Writers

1959 in Rome: Second Congress of Black Artists and Writers

1966 in Dakar: World Festival of Black Arts

1969 in Algiers: Pan-African Festival of Algiers, attended by entertainers Miriam Makeba and Nina Simone, Black Panther activists, and representatives of national liberation movements

1974 in Kinshasa: Music Festival featured entertainers from the continent such as Miriam Makeba, Franco & L'OK Jazz, Tabu Ley, and Abeti Masikini. The line-up of great stars of the diaspora included Bill Withers, James Brown, B. B. King, and The Spinners.

1977 in Lagos, Nigeria: World Black and African Festival of Arts and Culture (FESTAC '77)

2010 in Dakar: World Festival of Black Arts

With the exception of the 2010 festival, all took place during the Cold War era. These festivals were often sites of Cold War contestations and suspicions between the United States and the Soviet Union. There were reports of the Central Intelligence Agency meddling in different editions of the festivals, either through infiltration or the funding of US-based cultural organizations such as the American Society for African Culture.[5] Founded in 1957, the American Society for African Culture is an organization of African American scholars, writers, and artists with the goal of (re)connecting them with their African heritage. African American writers and artists participated in editions of the Pan-African festivals individually or affiliated with organizations; for instance, African American historical figures such as Langston Hughes, Duke Ellington, and Josephine Baker participated in the 1966 festival in Dakar, and the 1974 music festival in Kinshasa saw the fight between professional heavyweight boxers Muhammad Ali and George Foreman.

In the international context of the era, David Murphy rightly notes that these events were "organized against the backdrop of African decolonization and the push for civil rights in the USA."[6] There was a chain of solidarity connecting Blacks across the Atlantic because of racism and oppression. During the Cold War, Harlem was the prime place for African and other progressive leaders to visit in New York when they traveled to attend the annual United Nations General Assembly meetings. Both Jawaharlal Nehru and Fidel Castro visited Harlem on these occasions. Castro's stay at Hotel Theresa is one of those visits that Harlemites remember fondly, probably because of its special circumstances: Castro arrived in New York in September 1960 to address the General Assembly of the United Nations, and upon checking in to the Shelburne Hotel in midtown Manhattan, he felt unfairly treated when the hotel management requested a $10,000 advance in cash to cover any damages by the Cuban delegation. Castro refused to pay the damage deposit and instead headed uptown to Hotel Theresa, where he was warmly welcomed by Harlemites. In her 1981 autobiography *The Heart of a Woman*, the African American writer and civil-rights activist Maya Angelou described the enthusiasm of members of the Harlem Writers Guild upon learning that the Cuban revolutionary leader was moving out of the Shelburne Hotel to stay instead at Hotel Theresa in Harlem.[7] To contextualize matters, in 1959 Castro had nationalized American companies operating in Cuba without compensation, and he considered the Shelburne Hotel incident to be harassment by the US government.

Harlem International Trade Center: A Project of the 1970s

Harlem's role in the liberation and nationalist struggles of Third World countries in Africa, Asia, the Caribbean, and Latin America in the 1960s and 1970s is well documented. Harlem occupied a significant geopolitical place for these countries during the Cold War. The neighborhood offered a militant platform for visiting leaders from developing countries who attended the annual United Nations General Assembly meetings in September to make their voices heard on international matters. Because these countries do not have veto power in the UN Security Council—and therefore are not in a position to significantly shape world affairs—the annual UN General Assembly meetings were, and still are, an important forum for them. Whenever these countries' leaders came to New York City, they put on their agendas a visit to their respective diasporic communities in Upper Manhattan, and this practice continues today. Another agenda item was meeting Black leaders and addressing the Harlem community to build ties and international coalitions. This was particularly important after the Bandung Conference in 1955, the first large-scale Asian-African conference to discuss peace and economic development, which led to the creation of the Non-Aligned Movement, whose member countries sought to remain unaligned and independent of both sides during the Cold War: both the Western capitalist bloc and the Eastern socialist bloc.

A lesser-known connection between Harlem and the so-called Third World, however, is how the neighborhood developed plans to become the trade center of the Third World in Harlem in a way that the World Trade Center in Lower Manhattan would be for the rest of the world. Indeed, the impetus for the Harlem Third World International Trade Center first originated from unsuccessful attempts by Harlem leaders to have the World Trade Center be built in Harlem instead of Lower Manhattan. Under pressure of the advocacy of Harlem leaders, New York Governor Nelson Rockefeller promised resources for renewal and socioeconomic development of the neighborhood, given that Harlemites felt left behind in terms of resources and investment. Governor Rockefeller proposed the creation of the Harlem Urban Development Corporation (HUDC) and a state office building in 1966. The nineteen-story Harlem State Office Building was completed in 1971 and renamed in 1983 as the Adam Clayton Powell Jr. State Office Building; located at the corner of 125th Street and Adam Clayton Powell Jr. Boulevard, the African Square is part of its plaza. The location of the building in central Harlem is historically meaningful because the Hotel Theresa stood nearby, where Fidel Castro stayed during his 1960 visit and where Malcolm X had an office (today it is an office building known as Theresa Towers). Louis Michaux's African National Memorial Bookstore was in the vicinity (on Seventh Avenue between 136th and 137th Streets) before moving to its current location on 125th Street; a landmark cultural institution in Harlem and beyond, the bookstore hosted prominent Black figures such as W. E. B. Du Bois, Marcus Garvey, Langston Hughes, Malcolm X, and Kwame Nkrumah.

This initiative should be understood in the larger context of efforts to redevelop and revitalize Harlem. The neighborhood had been suffering neglect and economic distress, with race riots and drug-use epidemics as visible signs of a deep-seated malaise. The good times of Harlem's prominence during its renaissance in the 1920s had faded into history by the 1970s.

With the mission of economic development and urban renewal of Harlem, the HUDC established the Harlem Third World Trade Institute (HTWI), which, as part of its initiative, worked from the late 1970s to the late 1980s to bring to fruition the Harlem International Trade Center. The

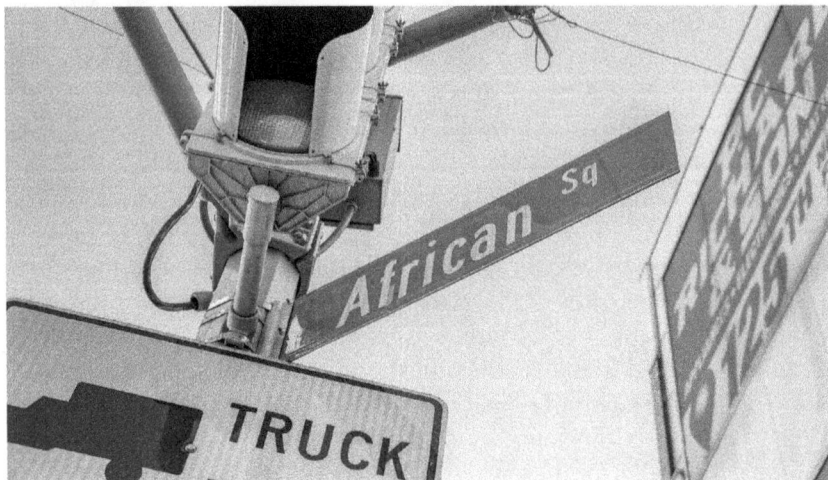

Figure 7. African Square sign at the intersection of Adam Clayton Powell Jr. Boulevard and 125th Street. Photo taken in 2019. Courtesy of Boukary Sawadogo and David A. Sawadogo.

Trade Center was to be built to the east of the African Square at the corner of West 125th Street and Lenox Avenue and was to comprise a forty-four-story office tower, a shopping center, a hotel, and an educational and cultural center where African languages and cultures would be taught.[8]

In 1982, community organizer Robert Alexander "Balozi" Harvey was appointed executive director of both the HTWI and the Harlem International Trade Center. The latter was conceived and developed with the goal of making Harlem the global trade center of the Third World, specifically to foster economic ties between Harlem and countries in Africa and the Caribbean. Because New York City was already a major economic hub, Harlem would be an entry point for those countries into the US market. Other initiatives of the early 1980s to make Harlem the trade center of Third World countries included the creation of the Caribbean Basin Institute for Education and Culture after the US Congress voted on the Caribbean Basin Initiative. Initiated by Congressman Charles Rangel, and sponsored by the HUDC, the Harlem Caribbean Trade Conference was held on January 30–31, 1984, to expand trade opportunities between the United States and the Caribbean. State and government leaders and business delegations from Africa, the Caribbean, and South America visited the HTWI on their trips to New York City. In general, making a stop in Harlem has become a tradition for African government officials visiting the United States, making Harlem the third most-visited place in the

Figure 8. Space next to Harlem State Office Building where the Harlem Third World International Trade Center was supposed to have been built. Photo taken in 2019. Courtesy of Boukary Sawadogo and David A. Sawadogo.

country after Washington, DC, and the United Nations for African leaders. More than twenty heads of state have visited the HTWI including the presidents Joseph Momoh (of Sierra Leone), Yoweri Museveni (Uganda), Moussa Traoré (Mali), Denis Sassou-Nguesso (Congo), Ali Hassan Mwinyi (Tanzania), Robert Mugabe (Zimbabwe), Thomas Sankara (Burkina Faso), Jean-Baptiste Bagaza (Burundi), and the former prime ministers Justin Metsing Lekhanya (Lesotho) and Pedro Pires (Cape Verde).[9] Likewise, African American business delegations in turn have traveled to Africa over the years under the aegis of the HTWI to explore and propose investment opportunities.

The meetings with African leaders at the HTWI typically consisted of a three-step routine: First, the visiting leader would hold a press conference and take questions on national and international affairs. For instance, President Moussa Traoré took questions on the war that broke out in late December 1985 over a border-demarcation dispute between his country, Mali, and neighboring Burkina Faso. President Joseph Momoh had to defend himself against allegations that his rule was growing authoritarian, forcing critics of his regime into exile and expatriates fearing for their safety if they returned to Sierra Leone. The second step—the main event—was a reception lunch, followed by the guest's speech. African leaders usually laid out the investment needs of their countries, highlighting priority economic sectors such as agriculture, mining, telecommunications, and fishing. They would then appeal to attending Black American businesspeople to invest in their countries. In the third step of the visit, invariably, the host would present a replica in miniature of the proposed HITC to the visiting dignitary. Commitments were made by both sides to pursue pan-African solidarity and economic development, which a diverse crowd of community leaders, elected officials, diplomats, and business representatives usually attended. Noted guests from the Black community also attended; they included filmmaker and political activist Robert Van Lierop, the Black nationalist and civil-rights leader Audley Moore (aka Queen Mother Moore), the boxer and activist Muhammad Ali, and members of the band Kool & the Gang.

Investment from the Black diaspora would not only contribute to building ties with Africa but more importantly would help alleviate the burden of debt suffered by most African countries as a result of loans from bilateral and multilateral partner countries. African countries were often obliged to rely heavily on loans and development aid as funding mechanisms for economic development, and this dependence proved untenable for the long term, leading to the debt crisis that confronted the continent during the 1980s and early 1990s.[10] African leaders were actively seeking private investors outside the framework of institutional lending by the Washington, DC–based World Bank and the International Monetary Fund. As a platform to establish and facilitate business relationships between representatives of the African and African American business communities, the HITC helped African countries diversify funding sources. As much as the HITC was about investment and economic development, it was also about Black nationalism in its attempts to forge understanding and common ties between Africa and the diaspora. This was in line with the ideals of the century-old pan-Africanism movement to unite Africans with the Black peoples of the diaspora and vice versa.

The Harlem International Trade Center project needs to be understood in three ways. First, it was an example of Black internationalism and twentieth-century New York City, specifically with Harlem as a world capital of freedom for Black people. That militant dimension of Harlem is not present today as it was in the past. With the end of Cold War politics and the gradual shift in focus from Black nationalism to world economic matters, Harlem no longer plays the historic role it once did. Second, although the transatlantic dimension of the HITC is indisputable, the argument can be made that the project was a case of urban politics internal to the United States. The creation of the Harlem Urban Development Corporation may be viewed more skeptically as a way officials sought to mitigate and de-radicalize Black activism in the 1960s and 1970s, shifting attention away from political demands—such as full-fledged citizenship and effective rights for Blacks—to economic programs for the renewal of poor Black neighborhoods in New York, Chicago, and Los Angeles. Third, the Harlem International Trade Center demonstrates how Harlem was, and still is, a nexus of people and ideas within New York City. The Afro-Atlantic heritage is celebrated, and multifaceted exchanges are made between Africa, North America, and the Caribbean. All three aspects of the Harlem International Trade Center should be regarded as indicative of the complex nature of any transcontinental exchange and connection. Harlem is itself a complex neighborhood that is constantly evolving. Even though the trade center never materialized, the Institute headed by Balozi Harvey did in fact function and sponsor numerous events and meetings to try to build bridges between Africa and the diaspora in Harlem.

The Third Wave: Focus on Thomas Sankara

The third period of African radical activism occurred in the early 1980s, particularly with young revolutionary figures such as Thomas Sankara in Burkina Faso and Jerry John Rawlings in Ghana. These two Marxist revolutionaries came to power in military coups—which most African countries had been experiencing since the mid-1960s—only to end the continuation of the status-quo political alignment with former colonial powers; the neighboring countries of Côte d'Ivoire, Togo, Mali, and Senegal were still strong spheres of French influence in West Africa at the time, and this remains the case in many of these countries today. Sankara's and Rawlings's revolutions aimed to rid their countries of neocolonialism and work toward effective socioeconomic development by introducing progressive social programs. The principled stance of self-reliance advocated by nationalist leaders and African unity by pan-Africanists of the 1950s and 1960s found new life in these movements. But for how long? Forces both within and outside of Africa would conspire against the revolution led by Thomas Sankara, resulting in his assassination on October 15, 1987. His revolution lasted only four years after he came to power on August 4, 1983, at the age of 33.

In Africa and around the world Sankara, the radically anti-imperialist and pan-Africanist leader, is well known and regarded as the Marxist revolutionary and pan-Africanist who fought for freedom, unity for oppressed people, and resistance to French neocolonialism. The legacy of Thomas Sankara endures today in Burkina Faso and well beyond. He became the "African Che Guevara" in the eyes of youth who were resisting continued exploitation of the continent by the West and fighting for democracy and good governance. He brought several changes to his country, among them the country's name change from Upper Volta to Burkina Faso, which means "land of upright people" employing a combination of the indigenous languages of Mooré and Jula. The name change symbolically represented Africans' agency and self-determination in the wake of colonialism and neocolonialism. Other progressive social changes introduced by Sankara were a sense of pride in being a Burkinabe, an African, and Black, the empowerment of women, environmentalism (millions of trees were planted to fight desertification), food sufficiency, vaccinations for millions of children, and construction of infrastructure for schools, housing, and a national railroad. During his stint as the nation's president, Sankara lived modestly and became an example of integrity and self-sacrifice to his people. His legacy has been the focus of numerous books including *Thomas Sankara: An African Revolutionary* (2014) by reporter and scholar Ernest Harsch, and *A Certain Amount of Madness: The Life, Politics and Legacies of Thomas Sankara* (2018), edited by Amber Murrey.

As young progressive revolutionaries, Thomas Sankara and Jerry Rawlings addressed Harlem at public events sponsored by the Patrice Lumumba Coalition. Their anti-imperialist and nationalist stances resonated strongly in a neighborhood known for its role in Black world politics. Like other African leaders visiting Harlem, Sankara and Rawlings were drawn to the militant dimension of a predominantly Black neighborhood resisting the oppression of majority structural forces. The sociopolitical situation of Harlem, in other words, reflected the liberation struggles that Third World countries were facing on the international scene. The Black experience in America was similar to that of African countries still striving to assert their newly gained political independence and to end apartheid. On his visit to Harlem on June 21, 1990, Nelson Mandela referred to Harlem as the "Soweto of America," drawing a parallel between the famed Black township in the anti-apartheid fight and Harlem of that time as a disadvantaged racialized ghetto.

There were many direct witnesses to and participants in Thomas Sankara's famous visit to Harlem who still live in the neighborhood in 2021 or elsewhere in New York City. Here is a written statement by the journalist and writer Ernest Harsch, an eyewitness to Sankara's Harlem visit in 1984:

Thomas Sankara's meeting in Harlem has left a politico-historical legacy and fond memories of a charismatic African president who came to address his African American brothers and sisters on the struggle for the liberation of black people. As the revolutionary leader of Burkina Faso was planning to address the UN General Assembly in New York in late 1984, it soon became apparent that President Thomas Sankara would not be invited to stop by the White House. That was not surprising, given his sharp denunciations of US military intervention in Central America. So, he decided to go to Harlem instead. "Our White House is in Black Harlem," Sankara famously told the people who turned out to greet him.[11]

The meeting in Harlem on the evening of October 3, 1984, was hastily organized by a loose network of African and African American organizations and activists—the Patrice Lumumba Coalition, All African People's Revolutionary Party, Caribbean People's Alliance, and other groups—converging in the auditorium of Harriet Tubman High School (250 West 127th Street). The high school auditorium, which seats four hundred, was packed beyond capacity, with people filling the aisles and overflowing out the doors. A Guinean dance troupe and several local speakers introduced the event. When Sankara stepped onto the stage, the crowd broke into wild applause. The Burkinabe leader knew how to work the audience; with the help of an interpreter, he opened and closed his relatively brief address with a series of call-and-response chants: "Imperialism," to which the audience replied, "Down with it!" "Racism," followed by "Down with it!" And then "Power . . ."—"to the people!" During his speech, which focused on the need for Africans and African Americans alike to support anti-imperialist struggles around the world, Sankara lifted high his holster and pistol, declaring, "I am ready for imperialism!" While a handful of white Secret Service agents on the edge of the stage tried to remain stoic, the crowd erupted in cheers, laughter, and applause.[12] Although other African presidents have made public appearances in Harlem before and since Sankara, that visit demonstrated an especially vital connection between the neighborhood's people and an African leader who knew how to stir their hearts.

Thomas Sankara's visit to Harlem was not concerned with ideological posturing or alignment in the polarized world of the Cold War but rather revealed his staunch support for the Black cause as a global question of race and class, a forerunner to the way the Black Lives Matter racial-justice movement has ignited the global resonance of the cause of minorities. In 1985, after his Harlem visit, Sankara launched the idea of the pan-African organization of the Institute of Black Peoples (IBP), which was soon followed by an international symposium of Black figures in Ouagadougou,

Burkina Faso, April 20–26, 1986. The creation of the IBP under the initiative of President Sankara, headquartered in Ouagadougou, was intended to "enable Black People to commit themselves more fully to their history and to play their part in that Promethean history of which the West claims to be the sole possessor."[13] The convention establishing the IBP was held April 7–10, 1990, concluding four years of preparatory work by the International Technical Committee charged with formally launching the institute. Since then, for at least two decades after the assassination of Sankara, the pan-African institute has experienced some lethargy in its activities because of limited financial backing from international partners. In August 2020, the government of Burkina Faso decided to resurrect the Institute of the Black Peoples with a five-year plan to return it to its pan-African standing. As a brainchild of president Thomas Sankara, the idea of IBP was birthed from the encounter in Harlem of Africa and the Black diaspora.

Today African heads of state and other government leaders visit Harlem not only for what it has represented historically in Black people's struggle for liberation but most significantly because Harlem is home to some of the largest African immigrant communities in New York City. The immigrant communities are informed of the arrival of visiting delegations through various means of communication: Flyers are posted on street corners, email blasts are sent to members of associations or professional organizations, and messages are posted on social media. The visits are often driven by political motivations. Because the voices of the diaspora can more easily get international attention for issues in their countries of origin than can the citizens inside the country, government officials are quick to court them in order to avoid dissenting voices being heard on the international scene. Immigrants have also become sought-after voters ever since several countries passed voting laws allowing émigrés to vote in parliamentary and/or presidential elections from abroad. This is the case, for instance, of Burkina Faso, Mali, and Senegal.

Fighting Apartheid in the 1980s: The Riverside Church

In the late 1970s, the Riverside Church—an interdenominational church located in Morningside Heights (near Columbia University in Upper Manhattan)—under its ministry for social justice, established an internal South Africa task force to spearhead initiatives and campaigns in the anti-apartheid movement.[14] Riverside Church's commitment to anti-apartheid struggles is based on its principled stance against racial segregation as a policy and practice; its active involvement concerns not only the anti-apartheid movement but also post-apartheid South Africa. The task force has been known by different names in internal documents, marking its evolutionary development, but since 1995 it has been known as the South Africa Initiative. The makeup of the task force has evolved over the years and has included church members and interested outside stakeholders, overseen by an executive director. The task force worked in close collaboration with its partner organization, the South African Council of Churches, in implementing education, community health, and reconciliation projects in South Africa.

The Riverside Church developed different initiatives as part of the anti-apartheid movement, such as lobbying elected New York City and national officials, pushing for the boycott of US companies doing business in apartheid South Africa, conducting letter-writing campaigns, and protesting at the South African consulate in New York City.[15] As part of the larger anti-apartheid movement of other community and faith-based organizations, it helped set up the education-focused Liberation Fund. Established on January 8, 1987, the fund aimed to support projects working toward the liberation of people in southern Africa, and to support education for South Africans at home and those exiled in the United States.

Projects developed by the South Africa Initiative have been guided by four main objectives: to support educational, social, and health programs in South Africa; to nurture new generations of leaders; to invest funds from the Riverside Church's portfolio in South Africa; and to promote reconciliation and healing. These objectives should be understood within the larger framework of the healing of hearts and minds to enable the advent of a "rainbow nation" that anti-apartheid leader Nelson Mandela had envisioned and worked to realize. After the end of apartheid, Riverside Church continued its South Africa Initiative under the directorship of Stephen Karakashian. One example was the establishment of the Kwa Thema Healing and Reconciliation Center, a healing and reconciliation center for the Kwa Thema community in the East Rand region outside Johannesburg. The center was designed to provide counseling services to victims of trauma and violence, which was particularly critical in the context of bringing about social cohesion in the post-apartheid era.

Another initiative was Shared Interest, a US-based organization established in 1994 to mobilize resources for the development of poor communities in southern Africa. The year 1994 marked an important historical date: South Africans elected Nelson Mandela as their first truly democratically elected president. But the political freedom achieved with the end of apartheid would be durable only if economic freedom is also attained; thus calls for new investment in South Africa increased after years of divestment campaigns by activists and organizations. In its newsletter to church members, *Carillon,* the Riverside Church explained that capital raised in the United States through Shared Interest would serve to guarantee loans made by South Africa's banks to community-based intermediary organizations in townships. These intermediary organizations were the only source of capital for poor Black communities during apartheid. The guaranteed capital raised by Shared Interest secured the loans so that banks could lend money with minimal risk. At its July 1996 meeting, the Riverside Church Council approved $300,000 as a social investment fund in Shared Interest over a five-year period. By September 15, 1996, Shared Interest had raised more than $1.5 million to invest in South Africa, according to its own estimates.[16]

Anti-apartheid South African leaders regularly visited Riverside Church and gave talks. Nelson Mandela gave a speech there on June 21, 1990, during his first visit to the United States. He made another visit on May 14, 2005. In 2001, the opera by Chandler Carter, *No Easy Walk to Freedom,* based on the life of Nelson Mandela, premiered at the Riverside Church. Other notable South African leaders who visited the Riverside Church were Bishop Desmond Tutu and the clerics and activists Allan Boesak and Beyers Naudé. Many other institutions and individuals were actively involved in the anti-apartheid campaigns in the United States.[17] The American Committee on Africa, for example, created in 1953, worked in the United States and on the continent to support African struggles against colonialism and apartheid. In New York City, the Harlem-based Patrice Lumumba Coalition—led by Elombe Brath, the American Committee on Africa, and the Riverside Church—stands out for its consistent work to bring public attention and support to the fight to end apartheid in South Africa. The coalition was founded in 1975 to support liberation movements in southern Africa to gain freedom and political independence. Although most African countries gained independence in the 1960s, minority-white-ruled territories and Portuguese colonies continued to deny African populations the right to self-determination through the 1970s and 1980s. As part of broader coalitions, the Patrice Lumumba Coalition organized demonstrations and boycotts in support of the People's Movement for the Liberation of Angola (MPLA), the Mozambique Liberation Front (FRELIMO), the South West Africa People's Organization (SWAPO, in Namibia), the Zimbabwe African National Union (ZANU), and the African National Congress (ANC) in South Africa. The anti-apartheid struggle had universal appeal in its fight against systemic oppression, which was also the case elsewhere in Africa, Latin America, and Asia. But this struggle had specific resonance for Harlemites through the Patrice Lumumba Coalition, which aided struggles for civil rights and provided basic public services in de facto segregated Black communities. Participation in the anti-apartheid struggle was not only about solidarity with Black South Africans; it also reflected how minority groups felt in their own struggles against oppressive systems of power.

The example of the Riverside Church illustrates well the role that institutions can play in building communities, creating links of solidarity, and forging a sense of belonging across differences. Other such institutions are themselves identity markers, cultural markers, and repositories of the history for neighborhoods like Harlem.[18] Religious, cultural, and educational institutions in the neighborhood include the Abyssinian Baptist Church, the Schomburg Center for Research in Black Culture, the City College of New York, and the Africa Center (formerly known as the Museum for African Art). Beyond their historical place and role in the community, however, the question today is what these institutions are willing to do to address challenges facing present-day Harlem—issues such as the gentrification that is displacing longtime residents and erasing cultural identity. How can community institutions continue their mission to educate, raise awareness, and mobilize to preserve Harlem's historical legacy as a mecca of Black politics and culture while also mitigating the effects of gentrification on the neighborhood? This question is premised on the idea that institutions may have a role in safeguarding communities against gentrification. An alternate view on gentrification is that it is an irreversible process in urban development, as low-income areas are transformed into better spaces of living and working conditions. Betterment is not bad in itself, but gentrification uproots longtime businesses and eliminates affordability for low-income minorities in such areas. This holds particularly true for decades-old African immigrant communities in Harlem, which face dislocation as higher residential and commercial rents force many Africans out. The complex and thorny issue of gentrification in Harlem is addressed more extensively in Chapter 4.

The Fourth Wave:
Youth Civic Movement and Black Lives Matter

The fourth wave of radical movement in Africa has been the rise of civic and democratic youth movements since the 2010s, born of frustration over lack of opportunity for social mobility and democratic change, corruption, rigged elections, and unequal distribution of national wealth. These youth movements are resisting autocratic regimes, austerity, and neocolonialism. As the future appears to lead to nowhere, millions of young people risk their lives crossing the Sahara Desert and braving the Mediterranean Sea to immigrate to Western countries, regarded as lands of opportunity. But not all youth are taking the treacherous road to immigration; some young people are choosing to remain in their home countries and challenge the political and economic situations that have kept them on the periphery. This has led to the rise of youth movements demanding accountability and political and socioeconomic reforms from governing bodies. Such movements include Y'en a Marre (Fed Up) in Senegal, Le Balai Citoyen (The Civic Broom) in Burkina Faso, Filimbi (Whistle) and Lutte pour le Changement (La LUCHA, or Fighting for Change) in the Democratic Republic of Congo, and the Economic Freedom Fighters (EFF) headed by Julius Malema in South Africa. Malema was previously the African National Congress Youth League president until his falling out with the party establishment. The Economic Freedom Fighters are now represented in South Africa's parliament. As the Brazilian director Iara Lee highlights in her documentary *Burkinabè Rising* (2018), young activists and artists were at the center of the popular uprising on October 30, 2014, that forced President Blaise Compaoré into exile in Côte d'Ivoire after his twenty-seven-year rule over Burkina Faso.

In the protests and demands of these young activists questioning inequality, capitalism, racism, and exclusion from decision-making power there is some continuity with the global liberation struggles of the 1960s and 1970s. Youth activism is particularly essential to how the African continent imagines its future, with a majority youth population and high youth unemployment. How can youth be an asset in the continent's economic development by drawing on and promoting their creative energies and entrepreneurship? This is the problem for both youth and ruling parties to solve. Though it may be anachronistic to talk about the future of the Third World today, the fight for full citizenship, freedom, and dignity for the disenfranchised is even more relevant than it was in the past. The end of the Cold War brought down socialist governments in Africa, thus accelerating the spread of neoliberal regimes. Progressive and social agendas were stalled in their execution; neoliberal economic policies have widened socioeconomic inequalities and brought into focus the driving force behind governmental policies. On the one hand, trade unions and student movements have generally acted as counterpowers in demanding accountability from political leadership or pushing for reforms that have often resulted in the enactment of progressive policies by governments, but on the other hand, political opposition parties have been weakened by ruling parties co-opting their leaders by offering them privilege and material comforts through desirable advancements and perquisites. Thus, the power of trade unions and student movements has been eroded by the widespread neoliberal policies dictated by the World Bank and the International Monetary Fund.

With the end of socialist governments and the declining power of trade unions and student movements, what social or political entity will carry progressive politics? The answer appears to lie with civic youth organizations, equipped with the mobilization potential of new means of communication, which are pushing for democratic reforms, accountability, and fair use of national resources for development. Y'en Marre, La Balai Citoyen, La LUCHA, and Filimbi are examples of grassroots movements for progressive change. The revolt of Sudanese youth and the Sudanese professionals' association that ended the thirty-year-rule of President Omar al-Bashir in 2019, for example, demonstrates the reconfiguration of progressive forces. Sociopolitical changes are certainly underway in Africa spearheaded by politically conscious youth.

Although these youth movements can to some extent be viewed in parallel with the Black Lives Matter movement in the United States, these are not transatlantic movements as the above-mentioned first and second periods of radical politics in Africa were. The era of Black activism at the international level—such as the anti-apartheid movement that brought Africans and African Americans together, building bridges across the Atlantic—appears to be on the decline today. It is as if the more globalized the world has become, the more we have retreated to narrower identities; ethno-nationalism is on the rise in several countries. Issues around race and full-fledged citizenship tend nowadays to be contextualized and addressed within national boundaries. Today's global connectedness seems to have paradoxically led to some form of withdrawal from international engagement. Counterarguments are often made by pointing to a different kind of activism that social media has ushered in by mobilizing attention on transnational issues. In this respect, activism occurs in the digital space where cultural and entertainment icons, and social media and YouTube personalities—known as "influencers" in certain instances—wield formidable power in shaping opinions. Neither approach is deemed inappropriate but rather prompts the question as to how best to connect the digital space, the streets, and the corridors of power to bring about change.

Yet a new sense of solidarity may be emerging today in the American diaspora where police brutality, Black profiling, and racism do not discriminate between Black immigrants and Black Americans.[19] In the wake of the killing of George Floyd, African immigrants joined protests of the Black Lives Matter movement that took place in late May and early June 2020 across the United States and internationally. In Minneapolis, where a large number of East African immigrants live, Somalians took part in the protest marches against police violence toward Black Americans. This can be read as an indication that Somalians recognized that any one of them could be a subject of disproportionate police violence and racism because of their Blackness. They are all too aware that what happened to George Floyd can happen to them. For Somali refugees, the violence brings back memories of trauma they fled in leaving the war-torn, failed state of Somalia in the Horn of Africa; thousands of Somalians have come to live in the state of Minnesota since the 1990s, with large concentrations in the Twin Cities of Minneapolis and St. Paul, through refugee settlement programs. Police violence on Black bodies makes no distinction between African-born migrants and African Americans. Solidarity is what is called for; above all, it is about living up to the expectations and responsibility of our common shared humanity—the respect for the value of human life beyond any lines of differentiation or othering. The Black Lives Matter movement, made of diverse racial and ethnic participants in the protests, showed the power of solidarity as a catalyst for demands of policy change and overcoming the long legacy of transatlantic racism.

3

⠿

Push and Pull Factors in African Immigration to Harlem

The immigration experience is not only shaped by the characteristics of immigrants; it is equally determined by the context of reception
—Ousmane Oumar Kane, *Homeland Is the Arena: Religion, Transnationalism, and the Integration of Senegalese Immigrants in America* (2011)

THE HISTORY OF THE FORMATION of the first overseas ethnic, racial, working-class communities in Harlem shows how this neighborhood of color represented a beacon of hope for change. Resistance to racism and colonialism spurred the formation of alliances and communities of the oppressed across continental boundaries, turning Harlem into a space of rebirth and growth. These first ethnic communities in Harlem—arriving from the West Indies, the Indian subcontinent, and Africa (Somalia)—were motivated to migrate in part as a consequence of British colonial rule in their homelands. Much like the Great Migration of African Americans from the South to the North to flee segregation and gain opportunities of upward social mobility, West Indians and Africans found in Harlem a space away from colonial rule and racism. Historian Irma Watkins-Owens notes in *Blood Relations: Caribbean Immigrants and the Harlem Community, 1900–1930* (1996) that between 1900 and 1930 some 40,000 immigrants of African descent, most from the British-held colonies of the Caribbean, settled in Harlem as it was emerging as a Black community. She demonstrates the multilayered contributions of Caribbean immigrants to the "multiethnic African American Harlem whose contours took shape in the early twentieth century."[1]

Vivek Bald, a scholar of migration and diaspora, provides further insights on the formation of early ethnic communities in Harlem in *Bengali Harlem and the Lost Histories of South Asian America* (2013), a history of South Asian migration to the United States in the late nineteenth and early twentieth centuries. Bald explores the Indian presence especially in the Lower East Side and Harlem from the 1910s to the 1930s, a working-class community that was started by an ex-seaman who jumped ship from a British steamship in search of better life opportunities. Around the time of the First World War, hundreds of Indian maritime workers who labored in the engine rooms and kitchens of British steamships "escaped into the crowded waterfronts of New York, Philadelphia, and Baltimore in search of less brutal and captive work and better wages onshore."[2] A parallel to this could be established with the formation of the first African community in Harlem that was started, according to the Harlemite Wodajo Mogues whom I interviewed, by Somalis who jumped ship in New York City after the end of the Second World War. Somalis were the first to open African-owned and -operated stores at the corner of 116th Street in Harlem, the current location of Little Senegal. Mogues remembered interacting with these Somalis when he first moved to the neighborhood in 1968 from Ethiopia as a seventeen-year-old student on a scholarship to attend college in Minnesota; he then ended up staying in Harlem because of the affinities he felt with the neighborhood. He later became active in the Pan-African Student Association of New York.

Watkins-Owens's and Bald's documentation of ethnic minorities settling in Harlem underlines the interracial diversity there in the 1930s, consisting of several diasporic communities. Bald notes that the neighborhood's inhabitants shared similar pasts and similar circumstances: "They came to Harlem in the wake of anti-black violence in the South and the disruptions of British and US rule in the Caribbean" (163). Harlem was then a hub of diasporas. Still in 2021 Harlem is home to diasporic communities, though gentrification is causing the displacement of some of these residents (to be discussed in Chapter 4).

A Snapshot of the New African Diaspora in Harlem

The new African diaspora has enriched and complexified the narrative and representation of Harlem. Mass migration from Africa to Harlem since the middle of the twentieth century has displayed two main patterns. The

1960s and 1970s predominantly saw Africans from anglophone countries moving to Harlem, whether they be artists and activists finding refuge from the persecution in their home countries or middle-class professionals in search of better opportunities. The second, larger mass movement, occurring in the late 1980s and early 1990s, concerns the mostly French-speaking West Africans. The scholar Zain Abdullah comments on this migration trend in his *Black Mecca: The African Muslims of Harlem* (2010): "While most West African immigrants to the United States have come from English-speaking nations with Christian leanings such as Nigeria and Ghana, the recent surge of African immigrants into Harlem originates in French-speaking countries. As a result of major changes in the US immigration laws of 1965, which allowed an unprecedented arrival of new immigrants from Asia, Latin America, the Caribbean, and Africa, scores of Muslims from African nations were allowed to enter the United States."[3] Though the first major wave of contemporary African migrants carried out tremendous work in preparing the space for later immigrants, in this chapter I especially focus on the second and larger mass migration because of its high-impact cultural and economic presence in Harlem through the first two decades of the twenty-first century. It has contributed to changing Harlem from a neglected neighborhood in the 1980s to a more attractive place, which eventually paved the way for the current gentrified space. The cultural diversity infused in the neighborhood by the arrival of West Africans is evident in the live music venues, restaurants, stores, places of worship, and the visible array of immigrants of different African nationalities.

As of 2020, there are about 175,000 sub-Saharan Africans living in the metropolitan New York–New Jersey area. This number has doubled each decade from the 1980s through 2010. As Sam Roberts describes in his *New York Times* article, as of 2014 about a third of Black New Yorkers were born abroad, mostly in the Caribbean, and Africans constitute about 4 percent of the city's foreign-born population but as much as 10 percent in the Bronx.[4] Immigration to New York City has resulted in demographic shifts in the boroughs and neighborhoods. African immigrants generally settle into neighborhoods that already have some African presence through kin or people from their homeland. Recent immigrants tend to stay with relatives or friends, sharing rooms and apartments while they build their own social networks in the community, which will enable them to seek jobs and housing on their own. "Little Egypt," on Steinway Street in Astoria, Queens, is home to immigrants from North African and Middle Eastern countries. There exists a large Nigerian community in Rosedale, Queens. The concentrated presence of Africans in New York City's boroughs also include communities of Liberians (Little Liberia) and Sierra Leoneans on Staten Island, and the Ghanaian enclave in the Bronx around East 167th and McClellan Streets on Grand Concourse and College Avenue.

Harlem is home to some of these African immigrant communities, which are predominantly French-speaking West Africans such as Senegalese, Malians, Guineans, and Burkinabe. Anglophone Africans are also present, though in relatively lesser numbers. The Senegalese are arguably the most visible community through their cultural and economic presence in the neighborhood, with the iconic Little Senegal strip. About 10,000 Burkinabe immigrants live in New York City, with the highest concentrations in Harlem, the Bronx, and Brooklyn—though the nearby city of Newark, New Jersey, is home to the highest concentration of Burkinabe in the United States. The immigrant communities in Harlem are composed of asylees, resettled refugees, and economic immigrants. The latter group, when it started in the 1980s, was made up of single men who would later be joined by their families. In contrast to the 1980s, newly arriving Africans in the neighborhood since the 2010s are both single males and females.

The two main push factors in the migration from the mid-1960s to the 1980s were political instability and economic distress. The political instability was the direct result of repetitive coups d'etat and military regimes in many African countries for more than twenty years after gaining independence from colonial powers. Economic deterioration was marked by droughts in the 1970s, slow economic growth, and the debt crisis in the 1980s, which led to structural adjustment programs imposed by the International Monetary Fund. In his memoir *My First Coup d'Etat, and Other True Stories from the Lost Decades of Africa*, John Mahama Dramani, who was president of Ghana in the years 2012–2017, refers to the lost decades as a marked period of stagnation in economic development and the arts from the 1970s through the early 1990s.[5] Politically, this period marked the rise of the post-independence military regimes in Africa. The book unveils segments of the postcolonial history of Ghana—and by extension of Africa—from the perspective of a child growing up in the context of his country's first military coup in 1966, an experience which contributed to shaping his political awakening and consciousness. As Dramani notes, driven by military regimes, hunger, and civil wars, the lost decades led scores of Africans to forced migration or self-imposed exile.[6]

In addition to the migratory trend of African activists and intellectuals who fled political persecution and instability in their home countries in the 1960s and 1970s, another trend occurred in the 1970s and 1980s, when middle-class professionals began immigrating for better economic opportunities. The severe multi-year cycles of drought that the Sahel region in Africa suffered in those years forced populations to migrate in search of better opportunities, both within and outside of the continent. The compounding effects of extremely low crop yields and mass cattle deaths made living conditions untenable for the predominantly rural populations of the Sahel, and those who relocated across West Africa. The film *The Man Who Stopped the Desert* (dir. Mark Dodd, 2012), which features the inspiring life story and achievement of the farmer Yacouba Sawadogo from northern Burkina Faso, shows how villages were emptied of their populations in the 1970s and 1980s. They left the dry and barren lands for cities or for the southern areas of Burkina Faso where rainfall was life-sustaining. The case of the north of Burkina Faso portrayed in the film is an example of what happened across the whole Sahel region, stretching from Senegal, Mauritania, Mali, Niger, Chad, Cameroon, and Sudan, to the north of Ethiopia. Now, in 2022, the larger question is whether there might be a repetition of history because of the effects of climate change, which would create out-migration movements of farmer communities. Climate change and terrorist attacks have already forced people out the Sahel's rural areas onto the paths of migration, which will shape global migration patterns as other parts of the world also face similar challenges of extremist violence and food insecurity. Migration—whether internal or transnational—appears a necessary choice for those who would meet certain death if they were to stay without having a livelihood.

In the larger context of global West African migration in the postcolonial era, it is also important to underline clandestine migration trajectories from the cities of Dakar and Abidjan to Europe from where African migration routes would redirect to North America due to economic crisis and the tightening of immigration rules in Europe. In the 1950s, West Africans' migration to France departed from Dakar by sea, at a time when Senegal was still home to the capital of a federation of eight colonial territories which were known as French West Africa. The growing clandestine migration of Senegalese, Malians, and Mauritanians in the 1960s started alarming French authorities, who demanded tougher control measures from the departing country of Senegal. Gradually, it shifted to Abidjan, the capital of Côte d'Ivoire and also a city of emigration for large numbers of nationals from West Africa, became a departing point of African illegal immigration to Europe from 1960 to 1975.[7] Illegal migrants, often untrained professionally, sought better life opportunities in the lands of former colonial powers—but only for a certain time until they felt unwelcome and had to make the transatlantic journey to the United States.

African Migration to and from France

The strong presence of French-speaking West Africans in Harlem since the late 1980s is in part due to re-routing migration from France and other European countries that closed off their borders to a labor force they had once used during post–World War II economic reconstruction. France encouraged that labor migration from its former colonies to help rebuild the country, as did Britain with what is referred to as the Windrush. The history of African migration to France should also be understood in the context of then newly independent African countries needing trained professionals for their economic development; France was an obvious choice for those seeking to pursue higher education or receive professional training. Thousands of young francophone Africans were sent on government scholarships to study in France from the 1960s to the 1980s with the intention of returning to their home countries to work; ultimately some African students decided to stay in France. They, along with the residents of French overseas territories who migrated to mainland France, faced enormous challenges not only to land decent jobs on par with their credentials and training but also to integrate into French society. As the years went by, France and other countries became increasingly unwelcoming to immigrants.

The deportation of large numbers of West Africans from France—particularly nationals from Mali, Senegal, and Guinea—came to public attention in the 1990s as undocumented immigrants went on hunger strikes while chartered planes of undocumented sub-Saharan African immigrants were deported. The highly publicized incident of undocumented West African immigrants squatting at the Church of Saint-Bernard in Paris in 1999, demanding the right to stay in France, was a watershed historical moment. In his semi-autobiographical book *We Won't Budge* (2003), the cultural theorist and African cinema scholar Manthia Diawara describes how rising racism led francophone African immigrants in France, himself included, to consider emigrating to the United States:

> In the 1960s and 1970s, it was radical for those of my generation from the former French colonies of Cote d'Ivoire, Guinea, Mali, and Senegal to use America as a dream space for emigration. We dreamed of going to France—the land of Liberty, Equality, and Fraternity—in order to rise above what we considered our miserable condition in Africa. . . . But as soon as our members grew larger, the National

Front and other racists raised their ugly heads against immigration and homeboy cosmopolitanism as threats to public safety and as a danger to French culture.[8]

Patterns of immigration involving Africa and Europe often reflect historical and cultural ties between the departing and the receiving countries. Colonial history shaped those immigration patterns in the second half of the twentieth century, such as Windrush—the postwar immigration of people from the West Indies to the United Kingdom. This is no different from individual migrants within continental Europe seeking to better their lives, with France, Italy, Germany, Belgium, and Spain being the top destinations.

In the wake of the 1974 economic crisis, laws governing migration to and stays in Western European countries were tightened, particularly for non-Europeans. Prior to the economic crisis, Europe had recruited North Africans in massive numbers for many years to help rebuild after World War II, which led to an unprecedented economic boom in France known as *Les Trente Glorieuses*, or "The Glorious Thirty," referring to the years 1945–1975. In the aftermath of this post–Second World War boom, the economic downturn has led to a shift from the recruitment of foreign workers to entry and stay policies focused on family reunions as part of restrictive immigration measures in France. The film *Inch'Allah Dimanche* (Sunday God willing, 2001), directed by Yamina Benguigui, for example, focuses on these family reunions in the 1970s, depicting the different challenges faced by an immigrant Algerian family integrating into French society. As the French cultural-diversity scholar François Durpaire indicates, other restrictive policies included the introduction in 1974 of residence permits, deportations, and financial assistance to provide incentives to undocumented immigrants to return to their home countries.[9] Although the Socialist president François Mitterrand made some small-scale mitigations to the regulations of undocumented immigrants in 1981 and 1982, their limited scope did not bring significant changes to the immigration laws that were making entry and stays increasingly difficult. The Pasqua Decree of 1994, named for France's minister of the interior at the time, Charles Pasqua, further tightened the conditions of entry and stay while allowing for expedited deportations. In describing these hard-line immigration policies, Manthia Diawara asserts, "Pasqua is to French immigration what the most conservative Republicans are to the immigration of Mexicans into the United States."[10]

The situation was no better in Italy, Germany, and Spain. These other economic powerhouses of Europe started closing their borders to immigrants and tightening the rules of stay for those already residing there. Under these circumstances, West African immigrants began shifting their attention to the United States. The "American dream" that everyone can succeed and be prosperous through hard work and determination was a big draw, as was the advent of satellite television, which helped expand would-be immigrants' worldviews. But the reality could be different: the newly arrived immigrant soon found out that it took more than just hard work, as language barriers and hidden or institutional discrimination presented the real challenges for those looking for upward social mobility. In selecting the United States, West African immigrants did not assume there was no racism, discrimination, or violence against immigrants.[11] But they believed they would be afforded more opportunities for social mobility in this country than Europe. Although opportunities for advancement were available to newly arrived immigrants, they often were confronted early on with identification challenges in integrating into American society, specifically related to how they define themselves: for instance, are they Burkinabe, Senegalese, Guinean, Malian, Nigerian, African, Black, African American, or American? These newly arrived immigrants soon found out that they would have to identify with a particular community based on national origin, ethnicity, or other parameters. The formation of such ethnic communities, interestingly, runs counter to the very idea of a "melting pot" as a guiding principle of American society, but for now identity politics were a lesser concern for these immigrants than their search for better opportunities.

The financial and economic crisis of the 1980s and early 1990s led to the mass migration of young and able Africans to the global North for better economic prospects. The CFA franc, the currency of eight French-speaking countries in West Africa and six countries in Central Africa, was devalued by 50 percent on January 1, 1994. This devaluation tremendously eroded the purchasing power of residents of these countries, and it also curtailed governments' financial power to make major economic, social, and infrastructure investments to meet the development needs and expectations of their populations. The profound socioeconomic impact on the poor of this overnight currency devaluation is rendered in the Senegalese director Djibril Diop Mambéty's comedy film *Le franc* (1994), in which the musician protagonist Marigo is struggling financially to pay rent and buy groceries. Marigo wins the lottery, securing a path to financial stability.

The plot shows that path is shaky, however, when the protagonist has to remove the door of his room on which the lottery ticket is glued and carry it for miles to claim the money. Anything might happen to him or the door along the way. The devaluation had worsened the condition of the most vulnerable, like Marigo, so that sheer luck became their last hope for socioeconomic mobility or a social safety net in the absence of government measures to mitigate its impact on poor people.[12]

Economic downturn affected countries such as Côte d'Ivoire, which had historically been a land of economic migration for nationals of other West African countries, making immigration to destinations outside the subregion inevitable. In this respect, the United States became a viable destination as France itself was experiencing an economic downturn and had already started enforcing tougher policies on the entry and stay of African immigrants. Thus, the presence of francophone West Africans in Harlem signals the global migration of Africans beyond the traditional colonial and linguistic links to former colonial powers. David Styan has examined a similar trend, documenting how tens of thousands of French-speaking Africans—particularly Congolese, Ivorians, Cameroonians, Togo-lese, and Rwandese—have settled in London since the 1980s and 1990s, most of whom came to London through the process of political asylum.[13] How much does the francophone influence still define the identity of these Africans in global cities such as New York and London? This remains very much an open question.

Challenges of Integration in France

France has a long-established tradition as a country of "enlightenment" marked by cultural tolerance and vibrancy. Numerous African American cultural icons moved to France from the 1920s through the 1960s, including entertainers Josephine Baker and Ada "Bricktop" Smith, writers James Baldwin, Chester Himes, and Richard Wright, and several notable jazz musicians, when segregation and racial tensions were high in the United States.[14] This tradition, coupled with historical colonial ties, led thousands of African students to pursue their studies in French universities, as the newly independent African countries needed a well-trained national work-force to fill positions in the public administrations. And yet this image of tolerant France may be increasingly ideal rather than real. The volume *La France Noire* (2012), edited by Pascal Blanchard, documents the his-tory of Black people in France over the last three hundred years with the underlying idea of the invisible[15] presence of Black people within the history of mainstream France. In sum, it points to French society's resistance to fully embrace Blacks.

In many instances, the chance for professional success in careers for African graduates from French universities lay outside of that country. Academics trained in France who established successful professional trajectories outside of France include Manthia Diawara of New York University, Souleymane Bachir Diagne and Mamadou Diouf of Columbia University, Alain Mabanckou of the University of California, Los Angeles, and Achille Mbembe of Witwatersrand University in South Africa. It is unlikely that these individuals would have experienced similar opportunity to succeed in academia in France, where the road to professional accomplishment is steeper for racial minorities from former colonies in Africa and the Caribbean. Of course, the path to self-realization for many French nationals leads beyond the confines of metropolitan France, even for reasons unrelated to race and ethnicity; this is the case, for instance, for French academics working as teacher-scholars at American universities, and for the long list of prominent French intellectuals who have been recruited by academic institutions in the United States.[16] Personally, whenever I travel to France, I tend to speak English in public spaces, reserving my conversations in French to private circles, because as a Black West African I have learned that speaking English earns one more respect and consideration as an ethnic minority from Africa. One is often better treated as an African American in Paris than a French-speaking West African. The larger point here concerns how the inferiority complex has been reversed: Europe is now increasingly envious of North American culture, whereas the US formerly experienced a "complex" toward the refined, centuries-old culture of Europe. Times have changed.

While the presence of African-immigrant talents can be viewed within the larger pattern of individual pursuits of professional careers, they can also be understood as part of the United States's post–World War II policy of developing area studies. After the war, the United States wanted to develop knowledge about different parts of the world, which led to the birth of area studies under Title 6 of the Higher Education Act: African Studies, Asian Studies, Middle East Studies, and Latino/Hispanic Studies. Initially oriented toward the social sciences (economics, history, and political science), these area studies began intersecting with the humanities in the 1960s and 1970s. African Studies programs, literature, and language departments have attracted some high-profile African intellectuals and recent PhD graduates. The same holds true for Asian Studies, Middle East

Studies, and Latino/Hispanic Studies, which have attracted some of those countries' brightest minds. European countries such as France, the United Kingdom, and Germany host some of the oldest African Studies programs and research centers, though they appear to be losing their competitive edge vis-à-vis the United States toward the closing of the first quarter of the twenty-first century.

Increasingly, France has become a less viable destination for African students, denoting a trend toward Africans feeling unwelcome in that country. On November 19, 2018, the prime minister of France Edouard Philippe made a policy announcement about increased tuition rates for foreign students from non–European Union countries at French universities that was scheduled to go into effect in September 2019. These tuition hikes for foreign students represent a ten to sixteen times increase from 2018 levels (foreign doctoral students in 2020 paid 3,770€ per year, an increase from 380€ previously; and *Licence* and master's degree students in 2020 paid 2,770€ per year, up from 170€ and 243€, respectively). Following legal action taken by several student organizations in France to challenge the constitutionality of the measure, on October 11, 2019, the Conseil Constitutionnel, nullified the government decision on the tuition hike. The principle of higher education as a public good was reaffirmed by the Conseil Constitutionnel to justify why students could only be charged a minimal tuition fee. The highest appeal court, the Conseil d'État, on July 1, 2020, reversed the decision by the Conseil Constitutionnel and validated the tuition increases for students from non-European Union countries. Although considered from an American perspective the increased tuitions are still relatively affordable, the constitutionally enshrined principles of equality and affordability of education for all in France are the impetus for international students' call for wider public rejection of these differential tuition increases.

For African students who would like to pursue undergraduate or graduate studies at French universities, these tuition hikes have made the uphill climb even steeper—when the 1994 devaluation of the CFA franc had already made that possibility seem out of reach for students of modest means. In 2017, there were about 350,000 foreign students in France, including around 150,000 students from Africa; the largest contingents came from Algeria, Morocco, Senegal, Côte d'Ivoire, and Cameroon. In coming years there will likely be a drop in African student enrollments as France sets its sights on attracting high-paying students from Asia and oil-rich countries of the Middle East.[17] As France has closed its borders to economic migrants from Africa, African students will also face an increasingly difficult situation if the recent tuition hikes are maintained, or implemented with little or no financial aid.

For many African students in France this tuition hike could not have come at a worse time, specifically during the COVID-19 health and economic crisis. In the larger context, this reveals an urgent need for African countries to invest substantially in higher education and research on the continent, or for students to start considering other destinations before further restrictive measures are introduced. Generally, foreign students select their destination based on criteria such as affordability of tuition and cost of living, the prestige of the educational institution, and job opportunities upon graduation. On the first and third criteria, African students face increasing challenges remaining in France. So then, the cultural and linguistic affinities with the former colonial power may not be attractive enough in relation to the lure of North American countries such as Canada and the United States.

Changes in US Immigration Law

Former President Lyndon B. Johnson signed into law the 1965 Hart-Celler Immigration Act, which ended the quota system of immigrant selection based on national origin. The quota system was heavily skewed toward white people from European countries. In addressing the class ramifications of the Hart-Celler Act of 1965, Vivek Bald remarks that it may have allowed more South Asian immigrants into the United States, but the diversification has not always benefited working-class immigrants. The Hart-Celler Act opened the door to tens of thousands of skilled professionals from the subcontinent in 1965: "While it seemingly put an end to the exclusion era, the 1965 act essentially maintained the exclusion of working-class immigrants."[18] When examining African migration to the United States, in addition to nationality, race, and ethnicity, the factor of class should be considered. The class divide was not as pronounced concerning African immigrants as it was for South Asian immigrants at the time. Because citizens from the newly independent African countries did not have a significant and visible immigrant presence in the United States at the time of the passing of the Hart-Celler Act, US government officials may not have feared job displacement or major cultural transformations internally, which would have led to a more class-based approach to African immigration, one distinguishing skilled professionals from laborers.

Yet class is not completely absent from post-independence African migration to the United States. The educated professionals who had sufficient resources, cultural capital, and the institutional knowledge to navigate the immigration system would initially make the most of the 1965 act. Members of the middle class, professionals such as teachers, lawyers, and medical doctors—mostly members of the educated elite—moved overseas to escape poverty. The United States was a perfect destination for these *émigrés* with professional credentials and experience. For those immigrants coming from anglophone Africa, their command of the English language and historical and cultural ties with the Anglo-Saxon world made it relatively easy for most of these professionals to integrate fairly rapidly into American society. Diversification by class would later become more prominent with major waves of refugee resettlement and the economically driven African immigration of the late 1980s and early 1990s. The Ethiopian revolution, for instance, started in 1974 under Mengistu Haile Mariam, prompted a major Ethiopian refugee resettlement in the United States at a time when the American resettlement programs were handling mostly Southeast Asian refugees. Later, in the 1990s, Somali refugees were resettled in the United States in the wake of civil war, with a large concentration of Somali communities found today in the Midwest and large US cities. Thus the first major waves of Black African immigrants to the United States were Ethiopians fleeing Mengistu Haile Mariam's dictatorial regime and Senegalese redirecting their migration patterns from Europe to America in the 1980s.

The 1965 Immigration Act ended quotas that previously benefited Caucasians by admitting into the US a diverse pool of immigrants from around the world, encompassing different national, racial, ethnic, and socioeconomic groups. The regularization of the status of undocumented migrants in the 1980s under the Reagan administration brought relief and presence to Africans already in the country. Marilyn Halter and Violet Showers Johnson observe that the 1986 Immigration and Control Act made it possible for undocumented migrants to gain legitimacy; under its provisions amnesty was granted to approximately 35,000 Africans. The measure introduced the lottery system that became part of the 1990 Immigration Act, which sought to increase immigration from underrepresented nations. The green-card lottery is one of the four legal pathways for thousands of Africans who immigrate to the United States every year, the other three being family reunification, employment visas, and refugee and asylum status. Thus the 1990 Immigration Act was another significant pull factor: between 1995 and 2010, 300,000 African immigrants were awarded a Diversity Immigrant Visa (the "immigration lottery") and moved to the United States.[19] In addition to legal regulatory measures, other key factors shaping immigration patterns from Africa to the United States in this period have been family relationships, community connections, and resettlement programs for refugees. Equally important is the role played by the "American dream." The relative weight of all these factors can be fully understood only when considered in the larger context of international immigration patterns.

Pull Factors in the US:
Popular Culture, Economic Opportunity, Mutual Aid

Various pull factors for immigration include available employment, affordable housing, a market for business activities, and established immigrant communities based on identity and cultural affiliation. But the decision of many Africans to come to the United States may also have been formed on the basis of American "soft" power: popular culture, primarily music and movies, and the idea of the American dream. The far-reaching influence of this soft power on francophone West Africa, where most African-born Harlemites come from, has expanded mainly due to screen media. The advent of satellite and cable television in the mid-1990s on the African continent contributed to the disruption of the longstanding relationship between France and its former colonies. Previously, France maintained a dominant role in the audiovisual landscape of French-speaking countries in Africa, the Middle East, and Southeast Asia through several mechanisms, such as cooperation agreements. Canal France International (CFI), a public cooperation agency and media operator, was established by the French government in 1989 to produce and distribute media content for French-speaking national television broadcasts. But thanks to satellite and cable television, US audiovisual content now flows into West African homes beyond the European content. This is particularly significant because these images—which carry an impression of the American dream—are seen by far more viewers than are Hollywood movies, which are screened mostly in urban centers. Uneducated viewers in rural areas who face crises such as drought and unemployment dream of a future for themselves and their families and look for a transatlantic voyage based on what they see on television. Hence the United States has become an appealing potential destination, a new land of dreams, particularly for these francophone West Africans amid Europe's relative economic decline.

In the present-day, due to global interconnectedness through the heavy use of social media, where the circulation of images, videos, and stories is prevalent, the United States has never been so close to young Africans with smartphones—and yet still so far away. The distance between the virtual world and reality is shortened by the transatlantic journey undertaken by the strong-willed and resourceful ones who wish to fulfill their dreams. But even to these immigrants, the road to their dreamland can be treacherous, particularly under hard-line immigration policies, such as Trump's executive order banning entry to the United States from six Muslim countries, and the deportation of undocumented immigrants from African and Hispanic countries under both the Obama and Trump administrations.

American soft power is also manifested through rap music, which young African artists embraced in the early 1990s by fusing it with local influences. The Ivorian rap groups Abidjan City Breaker (ACB) and RAS, the Senegalese hip-hop group Positive Black Soul (PBS), and the Malian hip-hop group Sofa are considered pioneers in francophone West Africa. ACB was founded in 1985, RAS and PBS were formed in 1989, and Sofa was created in 1992. Today there is an explosion of hip-hop music across West Africa, with stars such as Didier Awadi, Serge Bambara (known as "Smockey"), Louis Salif Kikieta ("Smarty"), Iba One, Iba Montana, and Natacha Flora Sonloue ("Nash"). In addition, the rise to continental prominence of Nigerian urban music (aka "Naija" music)[20] from the 2000s onward has further strengthened the attraction of American popular culture for the youth of Africa. The well-choreographed and affluent lifestyles depicted in music videos bear strong similarities with those of iconic American hip-hop and R&B music stars, creating a compelling lure to young West Africans to come to this country.

Most Africans in Harlem today work in the neighborhood and downtown Manhattan in the services sector, as cab drivers, dishwashers, and deliverymen in food establishments. Others sell electronics and African clothes and items in stores and the streets. African street vendors on 125th Street in Harlem constitute a large community of traders who have been successfully navigating the space and politics of the informal business world in New York City. The anthropologist Paul Stoller addresses the integration of African street vendors in the economic landscape of the city in his book *Money Has No Smell: The Africanization of New York City* (2002). Other economic sectors in which Africans are particularly active in Harlem include entertainment, like the Shrine and Silvana music venues, bars, money-transfer services, and hairdressing salons.

African women immigrants showcase the compounding effects of gender, race, and class on migrants to the United States. In New York City, many African women operate or work in hairdressing salons. An increasing number of newly arrived Africans are also finding work in the health care sector as home-care aides, especially females. It is an open secret in the African immigrant communities that it is much harder for women immigrants to find work than their male counterparts. The reasons can range from employers unwilling to hire women for jobs involving physical labor (such as construction and bike delivery of goods) to the initial language and cultural barriers facing any new immigrant. Other reasons include lack of adequate training, failure to transfer recognition of professional credentials from their homeland to New York, or lack of credentials, residual elements of tradition, and subtle gender-based discriminatory practices in the labor market. Often these women end up taking the readily available employment opportunities for their survival, whether as home-care aides, babysitters, preparatory cooks in restaurant kitchens, or cashiers in stores. Often these are jobs paid at an hourly rate with no benefits, lacking long-term job security and protection. The high cost of living requires a regular second source of income for the family. Loss of or reduction in income has serious damaging effects.

The COVID-19 pandemic and the ensuing economic crisis, for example, have revealed the financial vulnerability of working-class African immigrant enclaves in Harlem and the Bronx.[21] The loss of income resulting from the stay-at-home order, which shut down businesses except for essential workers, led to food insecurity and a situation of financial precariousness. Lines for food pantries wrapped around city blocks in Central Harlem, offering a visual and spatial cartography of the disproportionate economic damage to Black and brown communities around the country. The urban poor were the people most affected by the COVID-19 related health and economic crises. The COVID-19 pandemic has had a disproportionate impact on communities of color in New York, and even more so on immigrant women in minority groups who have borne the brunt of the crisis, not only losing their income but also their means of self-empowerment. This may be regarded as a temporary setback, given the resilience that African immigrant women have developed through informal networks of assistance. They have traditionally created and relied on mechanisms of solidarity. In this respect, African women immigrants have shown agency in setting up mutual aid societies and social organizations to fund projects and initiatives through an informal system of microloans to contributing members. The tontine savings system, an informal mechanism among peers, is extremely popular with members of New York's African communities because it helps address financial exclusion that could be based on undocumented immigration status and/or income threshold ineligibility for small bank loans.

Figure 9. Rashidah Ismaili at home during a community event. Photo by Daoud AbuBakr.

This tradition of mutual-aid societies in African immigrant communities in Harlem dates as far back as the 1950s, as is revealed in my oral interviews with longtime residents of the neighborhood. One of the interviewees, Rashidah Ismaili, who is profiled in the appendix in this book, vividly remembers her interactions with the African Brothers society, which was started by African-born seamen.

Rashidah Ismaili arrived in New York City in 1957 from her native Dahomey (present-day Benin) and was struggling financially when a friend of hers suggested that she visit the office of the African Brothers in uptown Harlem who might be able to help her. The African Brothers was a social organization of the 1950s and 1960s for African-born males, located near the Apollo Theater on 125th Street and Frederick Douglass Boulevard. The African Brothers met weekly and made contributions to a fund that helped members and nonmembers alike. They also organized dance parties to raise funds to help their community. The financial aid to Africans was offered with no expectation or obligation to reimburse the money given. This financial assistance went to help pay for rent, education, and funerals. For instance, the Brothers would arrange for the repatriation of bodies to Africa by completing the necessary paperwork and paying the shipping cost. Rashidah Ismaili said she received financial assistance from the Brothers to pay for her school tuition: $500 in January 1960 and another $500 in the fall. At a time in the early 1960s when Africans in Harlem had few resources available to them, the African Brothers provided a safety net and a social network for Africans, forming a self-supporting community built around compassion and lifting up each other.

In addition to small-business owners and workers in service-industry jobs, the community includes students who have come directly from the continent and second-generation immigrants attending colleges in New York. Africans' vibrant economic activities in the neighborhood are evident. There is no detailed data on or thorough study of Africans' contribution to local economics, nor whether they practice any form of group economics, that is, the circulation of wealth within the community: for instance, how many times every dollar bounces in the hands of African immigrants before going out of the community (a higher frequency of this amount is a clear indicator of strong wealth creation, circulation, and retention within a given community). Diasporic communities with a higher frequency of exchanges among themselves tend to create an economic base on which members can build wealth. On the whole, considering the various obstacles facing immigrants, those Africans who successfully migrate to the United States may be regarded as a self-selected group of individuals whose resourcefulness, resilience, family support, and fearlessness have made their journey a reality.

Little Senegal

As an example of the diasporic community-building of West African immigrants in Harlem, the Senegalese community offers a case study of a group that has thrived in the neighborhood. As a reminder, the Senegalese immigrant enclave in Harlem, Little Senegal—or *la 116ème* as it is known among the Senegalese—is located on 116th Street between Malcolm X Boulevard and Frederick Douglass Boulevard. Across Malcolm X Boulevard on 116th, there is the bountiful African market (which moved to its current location from 125th Street), and the Afrocentric multipurpose space MIST Harlem, which used to be known as "Madiba Harlem" (Madiba is an affectionate name for Nelson Mandela).

Both sides of the 116th Street portion of Little Senegal are occupied mostly by Senegalese-run retail businesses from electronics to clothing

Figure 10. Malcolm Shabazz Harlem Market—locally known as the African Market—is located on Malcolm X Boulevard and 116th Street. Photo taken in 2019. Courtesy of Boukary Sawadogo and David A. Sawadogo.

stores, food venues and establishments, and service shops such as notary services, copying, and translation. The location of these businesses in a residential area has allowed them to draw on, maintain, and expand a customer base from African immigrants, African Americans, and people outside the immediate boundaries of Harlem. These Senegalese immigrants come from all walks of life, professional and nonprofessional, who moved to New York in the late 1980s and 1990s in search of better life opportunities. In the early 1980s the Senegalese community, predominantly consisting of single men, lived in a large building on 50th Street and Broadway/ 8th Avenue, from which location they would gradually move northward to the Bronx and Harlem, on 116th Street. The first Senegalese restaurants opened to cater to this clientele of single men living without their wives and working in the fast-paced environment of New York City, which did not allow time to regularly cook at home. The Senegalese Consulate and the headquarters of the *Association des Sénégalais d'Amérique* (Association of Senegalese in America) are both located in Little Senegal, underlining this as a major hub for the Senegalese community in New York.

The formation of the Senegalese immigrant enclave is the encounter of two settlement patterns that I refer to as the North and South currents, the former located in the Bronx and the latter in lower Manhattan. The first Senegalese immigrants did not settle massively in Harlem straight away but were living in the Bronx, where housing was affordable, and in lower Manhattan close to their workplaces. Living mostly between 42nd and 86th streets in the 1980s and 1990s, Senegalese cab drivers would go up to Harlem during theirs break to eat, pray, and socialize among fellow countrymen. Soon, downtown-based Senegalese restaurants noticed the growing movement and relocated to the area. The growing community started attracting the Bronx-based Senegalese because it was a place where they could get jobs and rent apartments through referrals and networking, which was particularly critical for undocumented immigrants with often-limited command of English. In addition to the growing community that 116th Street offered to Senegalese, the decision to move into the neighborhood was based on not only the perceived affinity with African Americans, but also the desire for a safer and more livable neighborhood, supported by New York City council member Bill Perkins who represented portions of Harlem. For many years African *émigrés* have lived in areas with substandard and dilapidated housing conditions—boarded, abandoned, and rat-infested homes in the pre-gentrified Harlem era. The rental units often had no water, refrigerator, or stove, the basic amenities that should legally come with each rentable unit. Ignorance of regulations governing lease contracts was a disadvantage often suffered by the *émigrés*.

For the scholar Ousmane Oumar Kane, in his monograph *The Homeland Is the Arena: Religion, Transnationalism, and the Integration of Senegalese Immigrants in America* (2011), the settlement of the Senegalese community in Harlem resulted from the convergence of two factors. First, the Immigration Reform and Control Act of 1986 "provided amnesty to millions of illegal aliens, including West Africans who arrived in the early 1980s"; and second, the efforts of the administration of Mayor David Dinkins to rehabilitate Harlem in the late 1980s was another factor, as a number of abandoned or partially burned buildings were renovated and rented at low rates.[22] These factors underline the significance of legal and urban policy reforms in the formation of immigrant communities in American inner cities. It will also probably require some policy intervention from the City of New York for longtime residents of Harlem, including African immigrants, to resist the tidal waves of gentrification in order to continue living in their neighborhood. The Senegalese were not the first to establish a visible African presence on 116th Street, however; according to accounts from many longtime Harlem residents, the Somalis were the first Africans to have opened stores in Harlem at the corner of 116th after the end of the Second World War. These Somalis jumped ship and stayed in New York, as did other sailors in the nineteenth and twentieth centuries before them, such as East Indians and free Cape Verdians in Rhode Island.[23]

Burkina Land

In mid-September 2019, I took my students in the English graduate course "Global Harlem" to the Schomburg Center for Research in Black Culture to see the historical exhibition *A Ballad for Harlem*. The exhibition provided a survey of the history of Harlem from its creation to its rise as the Black Mecca. On display were artifacts such as photographs, maps, and memorabilia. At the far end of the room, visitors were invited to get onto a wooden soapbox to read a text of their choice, reenacting in their own way oratory skills that some of Harlem's historical leaders used when talking to people in the streets.[24] The artifact that drew my attention was a piece labeled "A Night-Club Map of Harlem," constructed by E. Simms Campbell. The map captured Harlem's past appearance from 110th Street to 135th Street, stretching from the Harlem River to Seventh Avenue. The map shows then-popular night scenes in Harlem of the 1930s, including the Radium Club, Savoy Ballroom, Gladys' Clam House, Club Hot-Cha, Smalls Paradise, and Cotton Club. The latter is probably one of the few establishments on the map that still exists today. Transformation of the neighborhood since the 1970s as a result of economic crisis, drug-related violence, and gentrification would yield a completely different map of to-day's Harlem night scene from Campbell's. At the end of the visit, I could not shake off the nagging thought of what a sketch, however incomplete, of the African scene in today's Harlem would look like. It would not only pro-vide expression for the African presence but also give something to think about retrospectively and prospectively concerning the neighborhood.

African immigrants own or run businesses in Harlem ranging from restaurants, barbershops, and hair-braiding salons to money-transfer ser-vices, clothing retail, entertainment venues (bars, nightclubs, live music venues), travel agencies, notary services, and electronics stores. African street vendors, located particularly on 125th Street, are also a strong pres-ence. The traffic to these businesses consists of a diverse clientele of locals and visitors. For some African Americans these stalls selling African items (jewelry, clothes, or statues) offer a vehicle to connect with African roots. In his book *Money Has No Smell: The Africanization of New York City*, Paul Stoller noted during his field research in the 1990s the ability of African immigrants to successfully navigate the city spaces, re-creating communal life and becoming an economic presence in one of the most competitive cities in the world. Almost a quarter of a century after Stoller's research, the African economic presence in New York City has evolved from the predominantly informal sector of street peddlers to include today's duly established businesses. Most of these businesses are in the service industry, as is New York City's economy for that matter.

In addition to street vendors, hair-braiding salons serve a dual function as both business and cultural vehicles that bring Africans and African Americans together in conversations about shared affinities and Afrocentricity. Hair-braiding salons are not only locations of business activity but also spaces of cultural negotiation and exchange. Black women take a lot of pride in their haircare, whether they are in the diaspora or on the continent, and that is one of the reasons why the market of Black haircare products is worth billions of dollars annually. As cultural art, braiding connects African Americans to African people and culture; meanwhile, salons become hubs of exchange between Africans and African Americans. On nearly every or every other block in Harlem, there is at least one African hair-braiding salon. Most of the salons are equipped with television sets for entertainment. Nollywood movies playing on overhead TV screens affixed to walls become the entry portal to African visual culture. Many African Americans have been introduced to African screen media productions in hair salons. In certain cases, music videos of African stars steer conversations toward the latest fashion and music trends on the continent and to the global influence of music by African American artists. Similarly rich cultural encounters with African Americans are occurring in other spaces as well, such as in African restaurants.

African businesses along Adam Clayton Powell Jr. Boulevard are a testament to the growing economic influence of African immigrants in Harlem since the mid-2000s. People may already be familiar with the geographical concentration of African businesses on 116th Street in Little Senegal, Lenox Avenue, 125th Street, and the African market on 116th Street. The opening of African businesses on the boulevard over the last decade showcases the expansion of African communities in Harlem beyond the often-referenced Senegalese, Malian, and Guineans to include Burkinabe as one of the fast-growing groups. Located between 133rd and 134th streets on Adam Clayton Powell Jr. Boulevard is what I refer to as "Burkina Land." This block has more businesses owned and run by Burkinabe immigrants than any other place in the city; these include Yentema Art Salon and money-transfer services, Shrine Live Music Venue, Yatenga French Bistro, and Ouaga-Harlem Sports Bar. The last three businesses are owned by Kader Ouedraogo, a self-made businessman who came to New York from Burkina Faso's capital of Ouagadougou, where he was selling masks and handicrafts to tourists. The Shrine, which took inspiration from Fela Kuti's popular music venue called Africa Shrine in Lagos, is a live music venue

Figure 11. Shrine Live Music Venue and Yatenga French Bistro. 2019. Courtesy of Boukary Sawadogo and David A. Sawadogo.

for various musical genres. The Shrine is a monument in New York's live music scene.

Since 2015 when I have personally known Burkina Land, it has grown into a space for the daily gathering of Burkinabe to foster a sense of community around these businesses; the interplay of business and community bears special significance in Burkina Land. The place has become a must-stop for real-estate companies and banks from Burkina Faso prospecting the market that is constituted by immigrants. Likewise, for Burkinabe government officials and cultural icons on visits to New York, this is the uptown stop that everyone is making.

The immigration of Burkinabe to New York is a pattern that has intensified since the mid-2000s, unlike the other African communities which have decades of historical presence in New York. Burkinabe started coming to New York City in droves in the mid-2000s following the end of the civil war in neighboring Côte d'Ivoire (2002–2004) that divided the county into the government-controlled South and the rebel-held North. Since the 1960s, then–Upper Volta (Burkina Faso) has been a source of laborers for the cocoa plantations in Côte d'Ivoire, which is the world's largest cocoa producer. Caught in the crossfire of the warring parties, the estimated 4 million Burkinabe felt unwelcome. Those who had the means, connections, or bureaucratic know-how were able to leave the country for Western countries. As a result of the civil war, Côte d'Ivoire became increasingly less appealing as a destination for young people in Burkina Faso, who would then seek to cross the Atlantic to fulfill their dreams. The Burkinabe migrants in Harlem and the Bronx today are mostly educated young people in their twenties, which stands in contrast to the limited number of illiterate, single-men Burkinabe traders who first settled in the 1990s. A similar trend was noticed earlier in the 1980s as the traders of the Murid community helped lay the foundation for the Senegalese community in Harlem.

New York seems an obvious destination for these young Burkinabe immigrants. The city is historically a magnet for new immigrants as one of the most traveled ports of entry into the country. It offers relative accessibility to employment because of already established connections and the cosmopolitanism of a global city. The perceived affinity with the historically Black neighborhood and the ease of moving into a French-speaking community of West Africans make Harlem an appealing area for the Burkinabe. These specific pull factors may not necessarily apply to every African community, whether defined by ethnicity or nationality. They may not account for a given community's particular geographic concentration and historical trajectory. Other factors may be at play in a community, for instance, in the case of Little Egypt in Queens, the large Nigerian community in Houston, Texas, the Ivorians in Atlanta, Georgia, or the Cameroonians outside of Washington, DC, in Maryland. Although the oil industry connections between Texas and Nigeria may be one of the reasons for the growth of the Nigerian community in Houston, there are no such direct industry ties between Maryland and Cameroon to explain the large presence of Cameroonians in that state. So the formation and thriving of each immigrant enclave might need to be addressed in its own specificity while also recognizing certain commonalities in the larger migration patterns.

The Burkinabe economic presence along Adam Clayton Powell Jr. Boulevard is an example that underlines the transformation of the neighborhood and also shows a change in the profile of the African immigrants working and living in Harlem. Specifically on this street, the African presence coexists with the rich history of the neighborhood. For instance, Shrine Live Music Venue occupies the space that used to be an office of the Black Panther Party in the 1960s, and Ouaga-Harlem Sports Bar is the former site of Club Hot-Cha in Harlem where the jazz singers and composers Billie Holiday, Fats Waller, and Duke Ellington performed in the 1930s and 1940s.[25] Other historical landmarks on the street that no longer exist are the African National Memorial Bookstore and Hotel Theresa,

Figure 12. Former New York City Mayor David Dinkins and former Congressman Charles B. Rangel. 2018. Photo by Maimouna Sow.

which came to represent the site in Harlem Third World's freedom and Black liberation movement. Lewis H. Michaux's African National Memorial Bookstore, which was located on Adam Clayton Powell Jr. Boulevard and 125th Street, was at the center of Black intellectual life and the political movement in the 1950s and 1960s for racial consciousness, Black pride, and social justice in Harlem. The bookstore was a meeting space for writers such as W. E. B. Du Bois, Langston Hughes, and members of the Harlem Writers Guild. Great figures such as Louis Armstrong and Malcolm X also visited the bookstore.

Since its first edition on September 21, 1959, themed "Africa's gift to America," the African American Day Parade continues the decade-old tradition of bringing the community together to celebrate its achievements and richness. Held every third Sunday in September, the African American Day Parade in Harlem follows its route on Adam Clayton Powell Jr. Boulevard from 110th to 135th or 145th Street. The African American Day Parade is a display of pride and celebration by the community of its diverse constituencies and is attended by Black leaders and city officials. The African Square used to be to the rallying place where Malcolm X regularly addressed crowds. Nearby were Hotel Theresa and the African National

Memorial Bookstore, two historical centers in Third World liberation and the civil rights movements.

Economic Power of African Immigrant Communities

Overall, African immigrants are making economic contributions to their neighborhoods, cities, states, and the country, yet voices from the African immigrant communities are not consistently heard on their economic power, nor do they underline their socioeconomic contributions to American society as a way to change the immigrant narrative from that of illegality and profiteering. The anti-immigration rhetoric and measures—often based on immigrants as a liability—are not supported by economic data but rather seem to be driven by the fear and rejection of otherness. As mentioned in the introduction to this book, a report by the New American Economy in 2018 indicated that African immigrants earned $55.1 billion in 2015, contributing almost $15 billion in federal, state, and local taxes. The remaining $40.3 billion in spending power was injected into the economy. Yet this contribution to the US economy by African immigrants has not yet resulted in significant and concrete political relevance in the country. Are African immigrants afraid to speak up for fear of deportation and other potential repercussions? Do they consider their US stay as temporary and therefore not warranting political involvement or engagement? Perhaps the fear of the risk of racial prejudice and discrimination in addition to their immigrant status act as self-censorship mechanisms.

Also at stake here could be what I refer to as the "visitor mentality," which keeps many African immigrants from empowerment, whether it is a question of telling their stories in their own voices or increased participation in the political process for representation and visibility. I refer to the visitor mentality as a long-delayed investment or involvement on the part of immigrants because of their plans to return home one day. In most cases, these plans do not materialize, and years go by without immigrants' investing themselves here, where their families are already becoming rooted. As a result, in most cases, these immigrants have not satisfactorily invested in either their country of residence or their country of origin— they are neither completely here nor there—and this situation could be challenging for the second generation with questions of integration, identity, and accruing intergenerational wealth. In addition, there is equity by accumulation that some African immigrants fail to capitalize on because of the visitor mentality. Often regarded as a temporary setup or situation, the stay is filtered through a mind-set of temporary survival in the United States in order to eventually invest back home after a near-future return. Although lack of homeownership and keeping only a minimum of personal possessions allows for free movement in search of jobs, it does not help contribute to building equity by accumulation.

4

⠿

Social Networks, Community Building, and Gentrification

Garvey brought something very beautiful to us. . . . He made us conscious of the fact that we belong to a big continent, with all of its gold and diamonds and riches. . . . That we were somebody.

—Audley "Queen Mother" Moore

THE AFRICAN COMMUNITY IN HARLEM comprises various social networks that are built on shared membership in voluntary associations, mosques, and churches. Charitable actions and religious services bring immigrants together and help them maintain regular contact, especially in the context of New York City where the constant pressures of daily life can keep apart even the most loyal friends. Baptisms, weddings, and birthday parties are celebrated at places of worship. Festive events that foster a sense of community include private dance parties, birthday parties celebrated at home with friends or in a rented nightclub, and cookout parties in the summer. Communal rejoicings not only knit the community together but also evoke memories of homeland practices under similar circumstances. Voluntary associations are spaces for solidarity, preservation of traditions from their homeland, advocacy, and leadership. They are platforms for organized politics and activism to advocate for and defend members' interests, and they offer certain individuals a base for leadership, which might otherwise be more challenging for them to attain in the larger context of New York City.

Voluntary Associations and Multiethnic Festivals

In West African immigrant communities in Harlem the most active and visible associations are based on national origin. They tend to serve immigrants from one African country or ethnic group; for instance, the Harlem-based Association of Malians in New York, the Association of Senegalese in America, and associations in other NYC boroughs such as the Association of Burkinabe in New York, the Organization for the Advancement of Nigerians, the Gambian Society in New York, the Pulaar Speaking Association, and the African Immigrants' Commission of New York and Connecticut. There are also professional associations whose membership is made up mostly of recent university graduates and young professionals, which inserts the dimension of class in the formation of voluntary associations.

The predominance of nationality-based organizations in the association landscape reveals the complex dynamics of identity formation that West African immigrants face on entering racialized spaces and discourse about identity. In the United States nationality becomes prominent not only in matters of immigration but also as an identity marker around which to build a community. In their home countries they would rarely, if ever, define themselves in terms of nationality or Blackness; ethnicity is, instead, very often the cornerstone around which identity is defined and deployed in everyday life. Indeed, as a response to the question where they are from, the phrase "I am African" is quite revealing, since few African immigrants would have offered this response in answer to the same question on the home continent. Regardless of their membership composition, these organizations build bridges among themselves by co-organizing events and routinely inviting leaders from sister organizations. I have personally witnessed these interrelations from the inside as an organizing committee chair for community events, a guest speaker, and an attending community member.

Celebrations of national independence and International Women's Day are only two examples—among many—that illustrate this blurring of particular nationalities and ethnicities. Since the mid-2010s the annual multiethnic celebration of "Independence Day" (borrowed from the Fourth of July in the United States) organized in New York City by people from countries such as Burkina Faso, Côte d'Ivoire, Mali, Niger, and Senegal has helped weave layers of solidarity among communities and deepen pan-Africanist ties. Held in August, it celebrates the political independence that most of the French-speaking sub-Saharan African countries gained in or around August 1960. Similarly, the annual celebration of International

Women's Day brings together African participants across nationality, gender, and class strata. International Women's Day is noticeably more widely celebrated in their homelands than in the United States; indeed, in certain African countries March 8 is a national holiday. African women's associations and organizations seek to maintain this tradition of honoring women and reflecting on their condition by holding panels on empowerment, entrepreneurship, and community-building. As a guest speaker at an event for International Women's Day in March 2018, for example, I was fortunate to address a group of African immigrant women in the Bronx about making a career in the film industry.

There is also a tradition in the neighborhood of Africans and African Americans coming together for celebrations. As my oral interviews with Senegalese on 116th Street reveal, on the Fourth of July there used to be Senegalese sabar dance performances and wrestling matches at Central Park. On that occasion, tradeswomen from Senegal traveled to sell clothing items on 116th Street and in Central Park, which created another space of exchange and encounter between the two communities. But a principal example of this mutual encounter is the African American Day Parade, a long-standing celebration of Black pride and African heritage, that takes place annually in late September. The parade was founded after the West Indian Day Parade moved to the Crown Heights neighborhood of Brooklyn, home today to the largest concentration of Caribbeans in New York. The celebrations feature elaborate costumes, colorful makeup, and soca music in the streets as New York City's Caribbean community renews every year a carnival tradition that began with the emancipation of slaves on the islands. The parade route proceeds from 110th Street, Central Park North, along Adam Clayton Powell Jr. Boulevard to 135th or 145th Streets. The review stand is often set up in the plaza of Adam Clayton Powell Jr. Boulevard on 125th Street. For several hours these streets host a display of pride, well-rehearsed choreography of marching bands, and spaces to be in communion and community with the neighborhood and beyond. This festival is in continuity with the artistic work of James Reese Europe, the African American composer and bandleader who helped popularize jazz in Europe during World War I, who then brought his expertise in leading marching bands to the streets of Harlem.

I first attended the African American Day Parade in 2018 when it marked its fiftieth anniversary. What struck me as a first-time attendee was how colorful, diverse, and entertaining the parade was. Harlem residents and visitors amassed along the route, cheering passing floats, flatbeds, and marching bands from several states. Music and a euphoric atmosphere

Figure 13. Dancers in African American Day parade. 2009. Photo by Maimouna Sow.

filled the air, as somebody would shout greetings to a person they knew walking the route. The participants honored organizations and celebrated individuals and their accomplishments. Festivities and political messages coexisted, with some participating groups holding banners advocating for the voting rights of prisoners. The way the community came together reminded me of Mardi Gras celebrations in Louisiana, where I lived previously for four years. I was delighted to see Africans in their colorful dress participating in the parade. African heritage and Black pride bound all together beyond any other identity marker.

Celebrations and events help African immigrant communities maintain cultural ties with the home country, which is often significantly more important for first-generation immigrants for whom identity affirmation is more needful and sustaining. Considering that as of this writing there is not yet a designated space in the city for socializing that is readily accessible anytime at reduced or no cost—such as an African cultural or community center—these community-organized events fill a void. In addition to funds contributed by association members, small-business owners in the community, airlines, and diplomatic missions often provide resources in kind or funds to support their activities. Voluntary contributions are made by individuals, such as musicians in the community who perform unpaid at festive events. In certain cases, events may be sponsored by governments from the homelands that not only provide some financial assistance to organizers but also send officials—such as ministers and presidents of institutions—to preside over launching or closing ceremonies. In immigrant-owned or -run barbershops, restaurants, hair salons, and other businesses it is not uncommon to see event flyers showcasing the patronage of a particular government official. For governments, these events represent not only a diplomatic channel to enhance the international image and stature of their country but also to court potential voters in upcoming legislative and presidential elections. Several countries have even passed laws to effectively enable the participation of the diaspora in those elections. Thus, the diaspora has become an influential political force, the support of which is sought after.

This represents a gradual shift in the governmental approach to the diaspora, which has for so long been centered on remittances sent to home countries and local investments by immigrants in building houses or opening joint business ventures. Indeed, hundreds of thousands of families across the continent depend on this form of migratory solidarity as an essential source of revenue for their livelihoods. About \$48 billion[1] in remittance was sent to Africa in 2019 by the new African diaspora, which represents one of the main sources of direct investment in Africa. According to World Bank statistics,[2] remittances sent by immigrants to Mali and Senegal in 2018 represented close to 10 percent of each country's gross domestic product. Such remittances, by the accounts of economists, have surpassed for some time now total amounts of official development assistance (aid and some loans) received by Africa from developed countries every year. In contrast to official development-assistance funding, money transfers by African migrants reach wider and deeper at the grassroot levels in providing relief to families and informal business sectors. Remittances sent by the new African diaspora represented 4 percent of the total gross domestic product of the continent in 2017. This is a two-pronged relationship built around remittances from the diaspora to Africa and the electoral politics or political forces that the diaspora represents.

In view of this growing power and influence, it stands to reason that personal gain sometimes drives the contest for leadership positions within voluntary associations. Since the association's officers often act as intermediaries between visiting government officials or delegations and the diasporic community at large, these positions can be leveraged for self-interest. Getting a direct line of communication to the home country's diplomatic services in New York and Washington, DC—or to government ministers or advisers in that homeland—may offer exceptional networking and access opportunities. The combined effects of high visibility enjoyed by association leaders in the community and the perceived benefits of their function often cause divisions and power struggles within these organizations. In some cases factionalism or self-aggrandizement undermines the unity of action, while in other cases competing voluntary organizations are created by disgruntled or dissenting members. As an active member of several New York City–based Burkinabe and African voluntary associations, I have seen this play out many times in the life cycle of organizations.

Places of Worship and Black Spirituality

In addition to voluntary associations and festivities fostering cultural ties to home and community, places of worship in Harlem also provide spaces of encounter where social networks of African immigrants develop. African immigrants in Harlem seek affiliations with local masjids (mosques) and churches. For West African immigrant Muslims in Harlem, the calls for prayers five times a day at the mosque become a call for making a community where Malians, Guineans, Burkinabe, Senegalese, and Ivorians regularly meet. They need a space of brotherhood and sisterhood in religion that also enables an outreach to African American Muslims in fostering communal relationships. The religious service and gathering space contribute to the intricately woven fabric of community. The formation of such communities is essential to the integration of these immigrants in Harlem, New York City, and the United States. Completely and successfully integrated into a community and American society, these immigrants will now be firmly grounded to reach their potential in pursuit of their dreams. Masjids (mosques) also serve as cultural centers where children regularly attend Koranic teachings on Saturdays and Sundays.

Church affiliations in the neighborhood tend to be based on whether a significant number of people from one's homeland attend a particular church, with the service conducted in French, essential for these mostly francophone West Africans. For example, many French-speaking West Africans attend the Sunday service at the Church of St. Joseph of the Holy Family (on 405 West 125th Street), which offers services in French, with priests sometimes coming from Africa on short stays. It is not uncommon for church members to welcome African priests to lead prayers on special occasions, such as during the time of Lent. Saint Mark the Evangelist Roman Catholic Church in Central Harlem (at 65 West 138th Street) is also regularly attended by West African immigrants. These churches provide spaces and opportunities for socialization, which further develops a sense of community and belonging. Choir rehearsals, birthday parties, and celebrations of personal or professional achievements of members bring them closer as a group. Further down on Manhattan Island, another church attended by Africans alongside a Caribbean community is the Roman Catholic Church of the Holy Name of Jesus (at the corner of Amsterdam Avenue and West 96th Street). For migrants, the church is not only a place of worship and socialization but, most significantly, a sanctuary and advocate whose support and guidance is sought in several matters, including immigration. These are just a few examples of religious institutions attended by communities of French-speaking West Africans in Harlem. In the broader context of Harlem and New York City, it is important to underline other religious institutions with a long history of engagement with Africa such as the Abyssinian Baptist Church, which has historical ties with Africa and African students and immigrants in New York. The Riverside Church was active in the anti-apartheid struggle and is involved in building a post-apartheid society through its South Africa Task Force section (discussed in Chapter 2). As for the African Methodist Episcopal "Mother Zion," it has been in existence since 1796.

Though mosques and churches here are only a sampling gathered in my interviews, there are other religious and spiritual spaces and practices centered on spirituality that link Africa and the diaspora; the place of Ethiopia, for instance, in building these connections is important. Rastafarianism and the historic significance of Christianity and Judaism in Ethiopia have cemented spiritual and religious ties between Ethiopia and Harlem—and African Americans in general. African American writers such as Pauline Hopkins and Langston Hughes repeatedly referred to the image and symbol of Ethiopia in their works in the early twentieth century: biblical Ethiopia, and also Ethiopia as a site of successful Black resistance against colonialization, especially after the Italian defeat at the 1896 Battle of Adwa. Ethiopia, under emperor Menelik, then became a symbol of Black pride and independence. Historically, Haiti was the first Black republic to gain its independence—in 1804—by defeating the occupying French forces. But as the scholar Nadia Nurhussein explains, the Ethiopianist discourse that appeared in the historical fiction by Pauline Hopkins, *Of One Blood: Or, the Hidden Self* (1904), has taken on the contours of "myth-making."[3] The mythologization of Ethiopia in the Black diaspora, in addition to its political dimension (as a space that was never colonized) and its religious dimension (as a historic place of Christianity and Judaism), can also be connected to Rastafarianism as a form of spirituality and a way of life. The coronation of Ethiopian emperor Haile Selassie in 1930 was a catalyst in the development of the Rastafarian movement, particularly in the context of Marcus Garvey's prediction that the rise of a Black king in Africa meant that redemption was near.[4]

The Ethiopian presence is particularly visible in Harlem in 2022 through its longtime residents in the neighborhood and the numerous Ethiopian restaurants. In my efforts to know more about the Harlem-based Ethiopian community from within, I interviewed the longtime resident Wodajo Mogues. He arrived in New York City in 1968 at the age of seventeen on a scholarship to go to a college in Minnesota, but decided to stay in Harlem because he felt affinity with the neighborhood. He still lives in Harlem in 2019. According to his accounts, the Abyssinian Baptist Church in Harlem is central to addressing the history and story of Ethiopians in the neighborhood (Abyssinia is the old name for Ethiopia). Wodajo recounted from personal experience how the Abyssinian Baptist Church provided a meeting space for Ethiopian students and activists in the 1960s and 1970s. The church also developed a long-standing tradition of hosting African leaders on their visits to Harlem, including Haile Selassie and Nelson Mandela. Abyssinian Baptist Church is an African American Protestant church, not an orthodox Ethiopian church. The rumored story of the foundation of the Abyssinian Baptist Church is linked to free Ethiopian seamen and African Americans who left a downtown church in the nineteenth century in protest against segregation. The encounters and exchanges in Harlem went beyond those of good neighbors living next to each other, as large contingents of African Americans from Harlem and Philadelphia volunteered to help fight colonial Italy in Ethiopia. The four-part documentary film *I Remember Harlem* (1981) by Harlem-born and -raised director William Miles, for example, contains archival footage of the solidarity shown by African Americans toward Ethiopians fighting the Italian invasion.[5] Footage featured in Part 2 shows how more than 120,000 people in Harlem marched in mid-July 1935 to protest what they considered Mussolini's fascist invasion of Africa. Registration centers known as "Ethiopian Volunteers" opened up for Black Americans and Caribbeans from different backgrounds and professions throughout Harlem to enlist in a militia force to help support the Ethiopian cause. Against the backdrop of their own struggle for freedom, the solidarity with Ethiopia also reflects Black Americans' political consciousness in rejecting forms of systemic oppression toward Black people at home and abroad.[6]

For African diasporic communities in certain instances and contexts, social networks and kinship are built and reaffirmed through spirituality, ancestors, and death. The African Burial Ground in midtown and the Harlem African Burial Ground provide material examples of the historical presence of African spirituality in New York City.[7] In his book *Black Mecca: The African Muslims of Harlem* (2013), Zain Abdullah documents the presence of African immigrant Muslims in the neighborhood and their interactions with their African American brothers. As part of this African Muslim community in Harlem, there are the Murids and their celebrations of the Senegalese Sufi poet and mystic Cheikh Ahmadou Bamba Day (1853–1927), affectionately known as "Bamba," which kicks off every year at the end of July with a march in the streets of Harlem. Cheikh Ahmadou Bamba is the founder and well-respected figure of Muridism, a Sufi tradition of Islam. Native African religions are also part of the mixed landscape in New York City, as is extensively documented by photographer Chester Higgins Jr. as part of the Black Religion Project,[8] which documents the religious experience of Blacks across continents. Photographs of the 1990s by Higgins document activities of the Yoruba Society of Brooklyn with scenes of Yoruba worship, a shrine to Yoruba Gods, and ceremonies commemorating the deaths of millions of Africans on slave ships during the middle passage.

Mutual Aid and Communication Networks

The scholar Craig Steven Wilder provides an even wider scope of the history of African cultural influence in New York City, specifically addressing how African mutual aid societies supplied the foundation for African Americans in religion and culture. Wilder describes how African voluntary associations emerged in New York City and Philadelphia: "The founding of African voluntary societies preceded the establishment of black churches is a fact. . . . In the aftermath of the Revolution, Africans organized benevolent societies in New York City and Philadelphia in objection to the inferior treatment of their deceased."[9] In other cases, early benevolent African societies in New York City pursued broader goals of racial advancement and moral improvement, as was the case of the nineteenth-century African Society for Mutual Relief. The historian Leslie Alexander writes that the mutual aid group, whose membership consisted of Black elites, entrepreneurs, and abolitionists, filed petitions for more burial grounds for the city's Blacks, held parades and processions in celebration of African culture, and purchased land for the founding of Seneca Village and Mother Zion Church. Alexander notes that the society was also active in the Underground Railroad, using members' properties and the African

Meetinghouse, the society's headquarters, which was located in the Five Points District in Lower Manhattan.[10]

Mutual aid associations in 2021, in calling their members to show compassion or generosity in difficult situations facing other Africans, denote a reconstruction of supportive social networks that African immigrants had known back in their home countries. For instance, Senegalese immigrants brought with them to Harlem the tradition of *daïras*—weekly or monthly contributions to a pool savings that are used for emergencies in the community such as paying for the repatriation of bodies for burial in Senegal and providing bereaved families with some financial assistance.[11] As a member of several Burkinabe voluntary associations in New York City, I often receive social-media messages requesting financial contributions to help defray the burial or funeral costs of a deceased community member or to help send the body back to Africa for burial. For those community members who lack legal immigration status—without a retirement account or life insurance to cover costs of such tragic events—the community as a whole serves as the safety net. Diplomatic and consular services may sometimes provide assistance, but most often voluntary associations and individual community members take the lead in making final arrangements for the deceased. In this way African values of mutuality and communitarian solidarity are renewed and reconfigured in a global city such as New York.

Local organizations providing support services to immigrants and refugees are also a critical component in community-building for African immigrants in Harlem. Nonprofit community organizations serve as the interface between recent immigrants and the local, state, and federal authorities, helping to smooth their transition and integration. Some of the organizations active in Harlem that provide such services are African Services Committee, African Communities Together, African Hope Committee, and Harlem United. The African Services Committee was founded by the Ethiopian refugee Asfaha Hadera in 1981 to help his fellow Ethiopian refugees, and then it gradually came to serve non-Ethiopian African immigrants. These community groups guide and facilitate access to public services and benefits for qualified individuals and offer counseling services. Examples of services provided include (but are not limited to) health care, housing assistance, counseling for survivors of domestic violence, advocacy, and defense of the rights of protected persons. For example, during the 2014–2016 Ebola epidemic in Sierra Leone, Liberia, and Guinea, community-support organizations provided immigration counseling to beneficiaries of the Temporary Protected Status (TPS); other situations that have affected the lives of families of immigrants are the Deferred

Action for Childhood Arrivals (DACA), the travel and refugee ban, and the redefinition of "public charge" for poor applicants of green cards who have received public assistance. A few years ago, the African Communities Together in coalition with other organizations and individuals successfully lobbied for the inclusion of Arabic and French in the list of New York City access languages. The work of advocacy groups helps foster ties of solidarity across community members, neighborhoods, and the city of New York at large. Africa may not be the predominant face of immigration debates in the United States as it is in Europe—with countless African migrants drowning in the Mediterranean Sea—but still the immigrants need voices to advocate for and address their concerns.

Communal links are also built through formal and informal channels of circulating information. Modes and channels determine levels of connectedness and engagement. How does one stay connected to news updates within the community and from the homeland? Free community newspapers are usually distributed in African restaurants and spaces that have relatively high traffic of not only African immigrants but also their African American neighbors. Copies of the newspapers are strategically placed on racks at restaurant entrances, readily visible to incoming and outgoing customers. For instance, titles such as the biweekly *African Abroad–USA* and the monthly *The African Journal* are distributed at Sweet Mama Restaurant on Lenox Avenue and 144th Street, and Accra Restaurant on Adam Clayton Powell Jr. Boulevard and 123rd Street. But it is increasingly common to see these stacks of papers still neatly packed, with only a few copies having been taken, as increasingly community members receive and share news on social-media platforms. This stands in sharp contrast to top-down communication structures in which voluntary associations often play the role of intermediary between nationals and their diplomatic and consular representations.

As most communication among younger generations is facilitated via online platforms by creating Facebook and WhatsApp groups, a communication gap is developing between these young African immigrants and their diplomatic and consular representatives. Most of these highly bureaucratic institutions do not maintain accounts on Facebook, WhatsApp, Instagram, or Twitter as vehicles for communication with their constituencies in New York or the country at large. What may be perceived as lack of interest or engagement on the part of these young immigrants is better accounted for by noting that these diplomatic institutions have not branched out from their traditional channels of communication. Whereas community radio via the internet used to be popular in different African diasporic communities for their music and call-in programs, during the late 2000s and early 2010s they seem to have lost momentum. I was a regular guest as a political commentator in 2013 on a Washington, DC–based radio channel operated by Ivorians on which some Burkinabe friends negotiated a two-hour slot for weekly discussion of news from home. In 2021, with internet connectivity multiplying options, most African immigrants get news by directly accessing the websites of newspapers in their home countries or by subscribing to one of their favorite Youtubers.

Nevertheless, African diplomatic and consular presence in Harlem reflects the growing immigrant communities to whom their countries of origin need to provide consular services. Renewal of passports, certification of copies of various original administrative documents (birth certificates and diplomas), and the need to address social issues within the community are some of the prerogatives of a general consulate. Because the opening of an embassy is a highly political statement of the quality of relations between two countries, it is not necessarily premised on the presence of a large number of its community members in the host country. A consulate, by contrast, is established to provide administrative and social services to a sizable number of foreign nationals residing in a host country. It has a representative function, like an embassy, but more importantly it facilitates relations between nationals and their country of origin. In the fall of 2018, the general consulate of Burkina Faso moved to 125th Street in Central Harlem from midtown, a move that is regarded by many Burkinabe immigrants as the consulate getting closer to the large concentration of Burkinabe in uptown (Upper Manhattan and the Bronx). As for the Senegalese general consulate, it has been located on 116th Street right in the heart of "Little Senegal" for many years as of this writing.

The movement of most African consulates northward from Lower Manhattan may not yet be considered a massive one, but high rental costs in Lower Manhattan and the growing African immigrant communities in Upper Manhattan, the Bronx, and Brooklyn will certainly be significant factors in shaping the map of African general consulates in New York in the coming years.

Housing and Employment Connections

Outside of voluntary associations, religious institutions, and mutual aid organizations, the sense of community and belonging for many African immigrants is first fostered in overcrowded tenements upon arrival. This was true for the first waves of Africans in Harlem in the early 1980s and

Figure 14. Consulate General of Senegal on 116th Street. 2019. Courtesy of Boukary Sawadogo and David A. Sawadogo.

1990s, when the crack epidemic, gang violence, and unkempt neighborhoods pushed Africans to share living spaces with already established connections. In 2021 safety is no longer the reason why these immigrants congregate in tight spaces, but as recent immigrants find themselves priced out of rents in Harlem, and increasingly also the neighboring Bronx, the quest for affordability produces a similar pattern.

Overcrowded tenements inadvertently function as a space for the creation and preservation of solidarity, socialization, and cultural identity, offering African immigrants a buffer zone, a retreat from the anonymous and relentless life in the city, and a cultural continuity with the homeland in New York. The majority of job and housing leads are received through these informal and community ties, often contributing to the formation of an extended community in the workplace by facilitating the recruitment of coworkers from one's group. With the younger generation, as already suggested, housing and job leads and promotion of African-owned businesses are increasingly mediated via Facebook and WhatsApp groups. For instance, the Facebook group *New-York Kissè* (My Life, My Business), initiated by the Burkinabe Aminata Traoré, is a community platform regularly used by Africans in New York City and beyond in search of employment, housing, or simply needing guidance with a particular situation. It is not uncommon to encounter domains of work or markets in New York controlled by immigrant groups of a particular ethnicity or nationality; in certain cases, this may be the outcome of immigrant-owned and -run businesses. This is especially evident in certain employment domains such as cleaning, food delivery, street vendors, bodegas, retail shops, restaurants, and cabdrivers.

The overcrowded tenement is an illustration of the multifaceted dynamics between private and public spheres in community formation. The gradual dissolution of shared spaces usually ensues after immigrants have accrued enough savings to afford their own apartments or feel confident enough in their acquisition of cultural competency to integrate and go beyond community circles. This marks the onset of a less-sustained connection to a particular African community, and the process accelerates with the second-generation immigrant or American-born children who identify as Americans; it will be interesting to find out how subsequent generations of African-born immigrants in Harlem, the Bronx, and Brooklyn self-identify. The second-generation youth often derive their identity or sense of belonging in three ways: The parents bring their identity consciousness into the household; the children make their way to it independently; or the children are shaped by peer relationships and popular culture (addressed further in the next section).

It is not uncommon to hear parents question the work ethic of their US-born children, who are deemed not "hungry" enough for opportunities for upward mobility as they themselves were when they first immigrated. Their children did not have to invest years of their time and financial resources to obtain a green card as a way to regularize their immigration status, nor did they struggle to overcome language and cultural barriers. The parents face misunderstandings and conundrums in their efforts to fathom why their children do not appear eager to climb the ladder of socioeconomic success, the signs of which include higher-education degrees, well-paid employment, and starting a family of one's own. These standards and metrics are similar to the ones the parents grew up with in the homeland. In my discussion of modes of identity transmission with interviewees from Senegal on 116th Street, some parents point to the loss of *djom*, meaning "dignity" in Wolof. This would be apparent in children born here or brought over at a young age who now want to behave like African Americans, or who do not show a good work ethic. They got it all easy, as some interviewees told me. Koranic schooling, usually held on Saturdays and Sundays at many of the centers throughout the Little Senegal enclave and beyond, is regarded as one of the modes of transmission of values and traditions to strengthen a sense of identity and community. What transpires is a challenging effort on the part of immigrants to take advantage of the opportunities for socioeconomic success while remaining themselves in terms of cultural identity, which results in a push-and-pull contest between seeking the security and support of one's familiar ethnic community and striving for integration into the broader society. These questions of identity, assimilation, and knowledge transmission are all part of the changes continually occurring within generations of immigrant communities.

The Impact of Gentrification

Upon my move to Harlem in May 2015 to live in the midst of a large African community, I vividly remember how the then-construction project of Whole Foods on 125th Street and Lenox Avenue stirred heated debates locally as to whether the food retail giant was an accelerating factor of gentrification. More than a dozen years earlier, the opening of an office by former US president Bill Clinton in the heart of Harlem (at 55 West 125th Street) in 2001 brought widespread public attention and discussion of gentrification in Harlem. I have witnessed firsthand unfolding transformations in the neighborhood. Today, new cafes, restaurants, retail stores, and high-rise buildings have come to occupy spaces that used to be vacant lots or tenement apartment buildings, or they have replaced old, dilapidated structures. Harlem's location on Manhattan Island is particularly desirable for young professionals who cannot afford the exorbitant rents in Lower Manhattan, so they move to Harlem, a mere ten-minute train ride to downtown by New York subway lines 2 or 3.

In addition to prime convenient location, other factors that contribute to gentrification include the rezoning of low-income areas for development, tax breaks for developers, and sometimes, indirectly, various forms of incentives to revitalize neighborhoods. The culminating effects of the process of gentrification often leave longtime residents priced out of rents and new amenities. Risks of erasure of physical landmarks, history, and cultural identity are concerns often cited by longtime residents. Whether considered as part of a natural development process of cities or a phenomenon fueled by capitalism, gentrification is not a recent phenomenon, nor is it specific to New York City, of course; longtime low-income residents in most major metropolitan centers around the world face the same prospect of being pushed out of their homes. The word *gentrification* was coined in 1964 by British sociologist Ruth Glass to examine the displacement of working-class people residing in central London by members of the middle class. Gentrification is more about class than race. In the case of Harlem, class and race intersect as a historically Black neighborhood inhabited by the urban working class is predominantly made up of people of color. For the purposes of this book, the focus is on whether African immigrants may be considered the gentrified or the gentrifiers in Harlem. When the West Africans first settled in Harlem en masse in the 1980s and 1990s, they found a crime- and drug-infested neighborhood that was not attracting many outsiders. They moved into previously boarded-up houses, often abandoned in unsanitary condition, and there they established retail businesses and opened some of the largest Black-owned cab companies, thus contributing to greater mobility within Harlem but also facilitating connections to downtown Manhattan.

From personal accounts by Senegalese interviewees on 116th Street, I learned that in the 1990s cabs and delivery trucks often refused to take trips from Lower Manhattan to Harlem for safety reasons; thus, it was predominantly African cabdrivers who maintained the taxi service between Upper and Lower Manhattan. As African immigrants doubled up or tripled up in rooms to afford rent payments, previously abandoned and unkept buildings began acquiring new tenants. Gradually, the demand for residential and commercial spaces grew with more West Africans, such as the Burkinabe settling in the neighborhood in the 2000s. In 2021, the African economic and cultural presence in Harlem is strong and visible, as demonstrated in different moments throughout this book. Africans have contributed to making Harlem an attractive place in which to live and work, transforming the resource-starved neighborhood, helping it recover from neglect after years of drug violence. There is also uneasy reflection on the role played by the recent settlement of middle-class Black people in the process of gentrification. For instance, am I myself a gentrifier—as a Black college professor, originally from Africa, who moved to the neighborhood a number of years ago? Or are there contributing factors to gentrification from within the Harlem community? Are longtime Black residents selling their real estate for higher profit, therefore contributing to gentrification? These are just a few of the questions that delineate the complexity of the phenomenon, once we move beyond the initial reaction to displacement.

African immigrants are themselves the gentrified, as many are being forced out to the Bronx, which is becoming unaffordable in turn. Many Africans are now settling in and around Newark, New Jersey, because of cheap housing and relative proximity to downtown Manhattan by train. What does gentrification mean for the future of African communities in Harlem? Considering the extremely low homeownership rate among African immigrants in Harlem, gentrification would likely impact the size of the residential African community in the neighborhood. As a consequence, it may lead to the formation of a transient community made of successive waves of low-income earners forced to leave after short stays, while others only come to Harlem for work. As for established African businesses with a solid clientele, they will continue to thrive in a niche of ethnic or cross-cultural services and products with a global appeal. Other businesses will struggle to survive after moving to one of the few still relatively affordable parts of Harlem as they gradually lose customers. Some Senegalese stores and restaurants, for example, initially located on 116th Street, have suffered losses in revenues following their relocation from Little Senegal.

Cultural and economic contributions to a place mean being part of the history of that locale. The potential erasure of African landmarks and markers of physical presence by gentrification may lead to invisibility or anonymity, with the consequence that subsequent generations of Africans looking to connect to the neighborhood beyond the word-of-mouth of parents could be questioning their own place in the overall narrative of this space. Hopefully cultural and research institutions in Harlem, such as the Africa Center and the Schomburg Center for Research in Black Culture, will provide spaces to nurture the multiethnic tradition and history of the neighborhood. But most important, Africans themselves need to develop their own initiatives to strengthen community-building and networks for generations to come. It is not the intention of this book to dwell on identity politics but to attempt to understand the invisibility of certain groups of residents, particularly Africans, in the dominant narrative of an emblematic neighborhood such as Harlem.

Building Economic and Political Power

Integration of African immigrants in the political process—in local governance bodies and representation in elected offices—it is still embryonic in 2021. The notable cultural and economic presence of Africans in Harlem has yet to translate to a similarly strong presence in the political sphere, maybe partly out of concerns of possible deportation for getting involved in US internal politics, and partly because of the strategic choice to focus primarily on accumulating wealth. This stance will certainly change with the generation of their US-born children, who will be more likely to be engaged in political conversations on matters such as racial prejudice and discrimination, Blackness, and the inclusion of minorities in decision-making circles. The election to the US Congress of Ilhan Omar of Minnesota (who came to the United States as a Somali refugee) and Joe Neguse of Colorado (the son of Eritrean immigrants) is likely to inspire younger generations to increased political participation and awareness, particularly in the wake of travel and immigration restrictions. At the national level, the rapidly growing number of the US immigrant eligible-voter population is poised to provide a conducive environment for naturalized citizens to become more politically active. The immigrant electorate in the 2020 presidential election was nearly double that of 2000, reaching 23.2 million, which represented one in ten US eligible voters in 2020.[12]

Historically, the emergence of community leaders in Harlem often occurred against the backdrop of structural imbalances in the provision of public services (education, health, housing, and infrastructure) to inner-city dwellers. Certain members of the community would rise to lead a movement against social injustice that public policies contributed to creating in urban spaces, resulting in disenfranchisement and socioeconomic exclusion. In certain cases, spatial exclusion is exemplified by features of ghettos or shantytowns, which often entail spatial confinement for many, inferior quality of services, or disproportionate policing of public and private spaces. Some of these traits are addressed in Gilbert Osofsky's book *Harlem: The Making of a Ghetto*, which provides an insightful historical account of Harlem from the late nineteenth century through the 1930s, chronicling Black migration and segregation in the neighborhood.

Africa-born migrants in 2021 are integrating economically and socially, which needs to continue to deepen. An important means to achieve this is through the culture and practice of homeownership, which needs to be developed organically in the community—as opposed to what I refer to as "visitor mentality," which is characterized by long-delayed investment or involvement in neighborhoods because of an intention to return home one day. In most cases, that return to the home country does not materialize, and years go by without immigrants' investing here, where their families have already started growing. Homeownership is crucial to the creation and accumulation of wealth in the United States, offering families more financial security and certainty; it is a strong marker of upward social mobility. But it is increasingly out of reach for the majority of African immigrants in Harlem. Because of rising rental prices, they are being pushed out to the Bronx, Queens, Brooklyn, or out of New York State altogether into neighboring Newark, New Jersey.

African immigrants face challenges in accessing mortgage loans as well, largely because of insufficient income from employment in low-paying jobs.[13] If they do happen to meet the financial qualifications for a mortgage, they are excluded from the financial system for various other reasons. In many respects, the low rate of homeownership among African *émigrés* in Harlem is parallel to systemic obstacles such as redlining and eminent domain, which African Americans still face in their efforts at homeownership.[14] The mechanism of the obstacle may differ slightly, but the end result is the same: African Americans and Africans struggle to achieve homeownership in a neighborhood that has long been considered the capital of the Black world. Measures to allay this might include financial education, assistance to those wishing to start their own businesses, and supportive consultation concerning the rules and obligations governing apartment rentals and opportunities for first-time homebuyers. Information that may be viewed as simple and self-evident to established New Yorkers may prove invaluable to the immigrant attempting to make his or her way in a new community, especially one as competitive as New York.

In sum, emerging migration trends in Harlem should be monitored to see how they develop from 2020 onward. The future of African immigrant communities in uptown and Harlem is likely to be shaped by the factors just addressed: homeownership as a means to build generational wealth, improved and sustained collaboration between Africans and African Americans, better integration into the socioeconomic and political fabric of New York, and mechanisms to cope with displacement caused by gentrification. Yet the future of the community also rests on its resilience and preparedness for the unpredictable and the unknown, which may upend lives and livelihoods at any moment on a larger scale. This has been the case, for example, with the recent coronavirus pandemic.

5

Relations in Harlem between Africans and African Americans

> Since the 22 million of us were originally Africans, who are now in America, not by choice but only by a cruel accident in our history, we strongly believe that African problems are our problems and our problems are African problems.
> —Malcolm X's speech at the summit of the Organization of African Unity in Cairo, Egypt, 1964.

SINCE AT LEAST THE EARLY twentieth century, Africans and African Americans in Harlem have made deliberate attempts to form collaborations of various kinds. Very often, though, these attempts are cyclical because they arise from shared problems, and once the problems are addressed, collaboration disintegrates quickly—until the next problem arises. Relations between African immigrants and African Americans are made of solidarity and mutual understanding, but also of tensions at times. Harlem is naturally a locus of these issues, as a place where thousands of Black African immigrants live and work beside African Americans. Though there is no denying that there is sometimes friction between African immigrants and African Americans in shared spaces, certain longtime residents of Harlem, including the Ethiopian Wodajo Mogues, prefer to speak of misunderstandings instead of friction or conflicts. Regardless of the term used to characterize the inevitably strained relations between African immigrants and African Americans—whether these are based on clashing subjectivities or a consequence of insufficient communication—it remains a reality to contend with. Since these tensions can be regarded as divisive or emotionally charged topics to address, they are rarely aired outside of private circles, especially in the case of undocumented Africans who may feel vulnerable because of their immigration status. Other Africans dismiss it out of hand due to its divisiveness or the inability of the two communities to extensively address their relations. Discussion of uneasy relations between African immigrants and African Americans in Harlem should be framed in a larger context in which three factors are essential to grasp the situation: the differentiating background context of slavery, the growth of enclaves or subcultures, and socioeconomic factors. The attempt here is to provide insights into factors that contribute to keeping the two communities at some distance from each other and also show how the younger generation is fostering a broader African cultural identity.

Solidarity or Competition?

Three cases provoked public contention concerning the decision to have Black British actors of Nigerian and Ugandan descent play African American characters: There was a backlash when the British actress and singer Cynthia Erivo was cast to play Harriet Tubman in the eponymous movie *Harriet* directed by Kasi Lemmons, which was released in 2019 (she was nominated for best actress at the 92nd Academy Awards). Similarly, some criticized the choice of British actor Daniel Kaluuya to play a young African American male in *Get Out* (2017), directed by Jordan Peele. A few years earlier, the casting of British actor David Oyelowo to play Martin Luther King Jr. in *Selma* (2014), directed by Ava DuVernay, likewise came under criticism. The larger question here concerns Blackness, representativity, and the relationship between Black immigrants and Black Americans. The release of these movies may have brought national attention to the subject, but these questions have long been playing out at the grassroots level where Black immigrants and Black Americans share spaces and interact in social and professional settings.

The film *Little Senegal* (2001), directed by Rachid Bouchareb, set in Harlem around the Senegalese community, has scenes that give insight into some African Americans' stereotypical perceptions of Africans or Africa that lead to friction between the onscreen characters. In one scene, the auto mechanic Hassan is verbally abused by an African American driver for improperly servicing his car: "Get your hand off my car, you big ape. Fucking African" (15:55). In another scene, Karim's African American girlfriend Amaralis is frustrated with him for not knowing answers to questions on American history and the US Constitution for his upcoming immigration interview. Karim shoots back at her: "And what do you know about Africa?" Amaralis replies: "I don't need Africa. You need America and it's your ass on the line" (17:49). From these and other scenes in the film, the viewer assumes that the conflicting relations portrayed between the two communities are reflective of some misunderstandings happening in daily interactions in Harlem. For this neighborhood with a history of Black internationalism, the uneasy relations between African immigrants and African Americans may be indicative of a new Harlem in which Blackness is a unifying factor of solidarity, or they may signal a competition for opportunities. Ida may be right in telling the protagonist Alloune: "Now there's no black or white. Only green [dollars]" (53:14).

Four hundred years of separation as a result of slavery have led African Americans, including the Black diaspora around the world, to establish different historic and cultural referents than Africans. This situation results in different experiences of Blackness, identity, and belonging—hence the talk of "the African American experience." They have endured racism for generations through systemic oppression and disenfranchisement, which is not the case of most Africans until they first arrive in the United States, where race suddenly becomes a significant factor in daily interactions and socioeconomic power dynamics. Meeting after four hundred years of separation, these frictional relationships are based on misconceptions that are driven by stereotypical portrayals in media and internalized racism whereby each group has developed negative images of the other.

How does coming to America affect Africans' experience of race and racism? In this respect, there are two kinds of lived experiences. The first kind of experience is that of Africans for whom the issue of race was not a defining factor in structuring relations in the private and public spaces in their home countries, especially not in the form of institutionalized or systemic racism. It is important to note in those spaces, however, the issues of colorism and subtle Black-on-Black racism that may exist without necessarily rising to the level of systemic racism. The second category concerns Africans who have lived through experiences of racism before coming to the United States: in apartheid South Africa, parts of Southern Africa, and relations between Black Africans and Arabs. Regardless of these differences in their prior lived experiences of racism, their stay in the United States brings to the fore an acute perception of race and racism because they suddenly find themselves regarded as minorities. In this context, assigned or assumed categorizations of race and identity are reshuffled, alliances are readjusted, and solidarity becomes necessary for survival.

Furthermore, slavery remains a contentious issue in creating a dialogue between Africans and African Americans for reasons pertaining to Africans' active role in the transatlantic slave trade or the shame of the slavery experience that may be felt by the diaspora. Anger and resentment from the diaspora are palpable, even as the subject is not substantively addressed on the continent. A conversation on the slave trade would be one constructive way of helping to bridge the gap between Blacks who are separated by four hundred years. Some parallel can be drawn between the need for conversation on slavery between Africa and the diaspora and the need for conversation on the issue of slavery and its ongoing legacy as it shapes African Americans' sense of full citizenship: Debates on reparations should be understood in the context of the need for the United States to address the institution of slavery in its past for healing to happen. Likewise, healing and mutual understanding will better prevail in the relationships between Africa and the diaspora when the issue of the slave trade is not left out of the larger conversation.

Enclaves and Subcultures

A second major factor at play is congregation in ethnic enclaves and subcultures. The economic migration since the 1980s has allowed the formation of sizable African communities that are caught between the inward pull of isolation and the outward advance toward deeper engagement with African Americans. The implementation of the US immigration reforms addressed in Chapter 3 (the Immigration Act of 1965, the regularization of undocumented migrants' status in the 1980s, and the Immigration Act of 1990) led to a rerouting of African migration patterns that, until the early 1980s, were predominantly oriented toward the former colonial powers of France, the United Kingdom, Belgium, and Portugal; there was also an African immigrant presence in other European countries such as Italy, Germany, and Spain. As these countries experienced an economic slowdown in the 1980s and started closing their borders to economic migrants, Africans began to see the United States as a land of opportunity.

The resulting African mass migration into the United States meant that Africans could congregate among themselves, forming enclaves in neighborhoods and cities. As their critical masses increased, subcultures began to develop through the founding of voluntary associations by affiliation on the basis of nationality, churches, and mosques. The tendency for immigrant communities to congregate among themselves in host countries is not unique to Africans, as immigrants may feel that safety, validation of one's identity, and a sense of belonging are hard to obtain beyond their immediate social circles. Moreover, the moral burden or obligation to take care of extended family members who stayed home makes the African immigrant feel that they have no choice but to pursue economic success; anything other than that risks making them a "failure" and discounts their obligations to their family. The pressures for economic success make them less likely to be politically engaged, as do fears of possible deportation if arrested. This leads to limited interactions between Africans and African Americans, even though it is the gains of the very activism of the latter that have allowed the former to pursue opportunities in this country. One of the multifaceted ramifications that stem from having a relatively large population is an ability to leverage numbers for economic empowerment and prosperity. Concretely, it means finding or building partnerships to create businesses or joint ventures. In this respect, Africans in Harlem can look for business partners among themselves or outside the African American community. This situation can indirectly contribute to a lesser mutual understanding and a failure to move beyond the stereotypical images that each group has of the other.

Zain Abdullah argues in *Black Mecca* that the often uneasy relations between African Americans and Africans in Harlem is based on flawed perceptions stemming, for instance, from the portrayals of African Americans as criminals in movies, or the perception by certain African Americans that they are superior to Africans in Harlem. These stereotypical or subjective representations by the one group of "the other" clearly demonstrate that the lines of communication between these two groups are not what they could be. Dividing lines and misunderstandings are still persistent for lack of sustained engagement beyond walking past one another in the street or sitting next to one another on an uptown train. For Abdullah there is a "Black encounter" where "a contingent of Africans and Blacks increasingly talk less about their differences and more about a shared Blackness."[1] I agree with Abdullah's assertion to some degree, but I feel that the engagement of a "contingent" is not enough; something of a larger scale dialogue is required. Historically there have been periods during which the interaction and conversation between Africans and African Americans have been sustained, but they do not generally extend beyond their specific context of exigency, nor have they been appropriated at the grassroots level for longer periods.

The Free South Africa movement in the 1980s, a coalition in the US that sought to end apartheid, stands as an exception where intellectuals and community members came together. Other instances of transatlantic dialogues have not always translated into better engagement at the grassroots level between Africans and African Americans over the long term, maybe because these conversations are considered too intellectual or elitist, or the interactions are undertaken in conditions of exigence. These moments of transatlantic dialogue include, for instance, the encounter of leaders of the Negritude literary movement and the Harlem Renaissance, the encounter of nationalist and socialist governments in Africa (Algeria, Tanzania, Benin, and Ghana) with exiled leaders of Black Panther Party, and the election of Barack Obama to the US presidency, which provoked conversation among Africans and African Americans because of Obama's Kenyan roots on his father's side. From within the community, whenever I ask African immigrants in Harlem about their relationships with African Americans, I invariably get the answer that they have no relationship or little dialogue with them. When pressed to elicit why they feel this way, the surveyed respondents say that they have little in common in terms of cultural and historical referents.

In an effort to unpack the situation to achieve a better understanding from an African American perspective, I conducted interviews. I sat with Clara Villarosa in Harlem on October 4, 2018, at the Senegalese-owned Restaurant Renaissance to talk about the African presence in Harlem through her own experience as a former bookstore owner. Villarosa had owned and managed the only Black store, Hue-man Bookstore, in Denver, Colorado, for sixteen years before moving to Harlem in 2000. She had opened another bookstore by the same name in Harlem in 2003, which was located next to the Magic Johnson movie theater on 124th Street at Frederick Douglass Boulevard. Several Black leaders and celebrities attended the opening ceremony, including Charles Rangel, Stevie Wonder, and Maya Angelou. But she left Hue-man Bookstore in 2004. Villarosa stated that her primary goal was to provide Blacks greater access to books. Villarosa added that the customers of her bookstore were mostly African American males who had a keen interest in knowing more about where they came from historically by reading books on African civilization. Few of the bookstore customers were African immigrants, however, for reasons that are still unclear or difficult to articulate. Maybe this can be explained within the larger context of the interaction between African Americans and African immigrants in Harlem where, as Villarosa asserted, there are barriers, including language barriers, on both sides, with one side meanwhile immersed in a foreign place, and the resultant cultural differences.

For both communities to transcend these barriers, it has to be intentional because it is not likely to happen organically without organized efforts. In this respect, the question is where is the best entry point to make a difference for greater, smoother, and sustained interactions: Is it at schools, churches, or mosques, in the streets, or community organizations? The assumption of this question is not that African Americans and African immigrants are living in insular environments in Harlem, but instead that they should deliberately strive to build bridges between them beyond the daily professional and community interactions that might bring them into contact. There are already spaces in Harlem where African-born and second-generation immigrants are making connections with African Americans, especially in elementary schools and after-school sports programs for soccer and basketball. Large numbers of students, mostly from francophone West African immigrant families, are enrolled in the French American charter school on 116th Street. A little farther south, between 65th and 66th Streets, Martin Luther King Educational Campus has produced many high-school soccer talents, some of whom are of African roots. Places of worship—churches and mosques—are also spaces of congregation for the two communities. For instance, Friday prayer brings together significant numbers of Africans, African Americans, and Arabs at the Islamic Cultural Center of New York located in East Harlem between 96th and 97th Streets.

To a certain extent, the complexity of the relations between Africans and African Americans in Harlem reflects a larger picture of often distorted perceptions because of lack of profound mutual understanding or differences based on each community's contextual history and culture.[2] Their exchanges and interactions appear to lack sustained collaborations. Often the instances of coming together are on-again-off-again, as moments of collaboration disintegrate quickly, creating a vacuum until the next phase of occasional conversation develops. Social media has been a space of storytelling and expression of pride in African roots, but it is also a site of anti-immigration views by groups such as the American Descendants of Slavery (ADOS) movement in 2019 and 2020. Though this is not yet a mainstream movement, it is generating debate in Black America on identity and relations between African Americans and Black immigrants from Africa and the Caribbean.[3] Whether ADOS is regarded as a social-justice movement advocating for better opportunities for African Americans or a Black conservative birtherist or nativist movement claiming Americanness by rejecting African heritage and focusing on slavery as a foundational marker of one's history and identity, it creates tensions with foreign-born Black immigrants.

This rejection of foreign Blacks by American-born Black people has some parallels—though obviously with contextual and historical differences—with other countries such as South Africa, where xenophobic violence targeted at Africans from other areas of the continent has repeatedly occurred over the last decade. The term "Negrophobia" coined by historian and philosopher Achille Mbembe to designate fear and hatred of other Black people captures this phenomenon. Negrophobia can be used as a lens to examine intragroup dynamics of economically and politically disenfranchised groups; it can also be deployed across racial lines. The relations between Africans and African Americans largely remain a sensitive issue and a polarizing subject, with reactions on both sides often being raw. Sustained dialogue has yet to begin between the two communities, as was the case at the height of Black internationalism, the anti-colonial struggle, the civil rights movement, the Black Arts movement, and the anti-apartheid movement. Since then, unresolved questions of identity and history, coupled with the rising influx of immigrants—all in a global context of disenfranchisement of minorities and the working class, may contribute to resentment and accentuate misunderstanding.

Interrelations in Academia, Social Media, and Popular Culture

Academia is another locus where the relations between African immigrants, especially native-born African scholars, and their African American colleagues at North American universities remain understudied. African American writer and sociologist Tressie McMillan Cottom partly addresses the subject in her book *Thick and Other Essays* (2019). In the chapter titled "Black Is Over (or, Special Black)," McMillan Cottom writes about how "black ethnic" (such as Black Africans and West Indians) are regarded and treated as superior to "black-black" on campuses.[4] While McMillan Cottom is writing from her personal experience in academic spaces, there is no generalizing evidence that Black African and Caribbean immigrants are better treated in American society, especially in the lower-paying jobs in which these working-class immigrants often work. Not all Black immigrant groups are privileged or wealthy, hence McMillan Cottom's argument needs to be situated in the context of increased competition between Blacks in the wider society for the same opportunities to achieve upward social mobility, including education and employment.

A further question arises along departmental and disciplinary lines as to how native-born African scholars fit in with African and African American Studies, Africana Studies, and Black Studies, as well the question of whether Africa represents a curriculum priority in these departments. These interrogations are still understudied, and the findings could provide illuminating insight into the relationships between African immigrants and

African Americans in academia. African-born scholars teaching in Black or African Studies programs often face antagonisms for various reasons, ranging from the perception that they are taking jobs away from African Americans to the sentiment that Africans are unduly profiting from gains of the civil rights movement. The interactions of Africans and African Americans in academia reflect the complex dynamics that are at play between the two communities in the larger society; whether it is the interpersonal relations between Black colleagues in and across academic units, the intersectionality of their research and teaching interests, or ethnic Black students being regarded as superior as argued by McMillan Cottom, the core issues still remain to be fully explored. More bridges should be built between Africa and the diaspora while acknowledging differences in experience, history, and culture. In this regard, the widely acclaimed Kenyan writer Ngũgĩ wa Thiong'o[5] addresses the necessity to bridge Africa and the diaspora through what he refers to as the re-membering of Africa, a process that seeks the restoration of African wholeness following a fragmentation caused by slavery and colonization.

Nonetheless, a broader African cultural identity appears to be developing against the backdrop of any perceived or assumed differences between Africa and the diaspora as young people are creatively showing Black pride in many ways across spatial boundaries. The generations of the 1960s and 1970s, who were brought together and defined by global struggles for freedom and third-world politics, tend to be more preoccupied with the economic standing and sociopolitical place of Black people in the world than they are with administrative identity (nationality) and cultural differences. Black consciousness has come to shape the interactions of this generation of Africans and African Americans in Harlem. The annual African American Day Parade, already discussed, provides a window into that tradition of Black consciousness that binds people from different backgrounds and nationalities.

Tech-savvy Millennials and Generation Z (or iGen) who are adept users of social media have breathed new life into Black consciousness through their digital online activism. Hashtag movements exemplify these encounters and exchanges not only between Africans and African Americans in Harlem but also with Black people around the world. This represents a generational shift in how political engagement around issues of identity and belonging have been reconfigured. For young Africans born or raised in Harlem, the contact with their African roots and Black neighbors has never been livelier. With YouTube, Facebook, Instagram, Twitter, and TikTok, there seems to be more interconnectedness between young

Africans and African Americans on social media and online audiovisual media platforms through which African Americans can learn about African music, fashion, dance, and films. Social media is the space where Black consciousness is rising and expanding through advocacy, information-sharing, organizing, community-building and affirmation, and pride. The Black consciousness and pride movements among Millennials manifest themselves, for instance, through terms such as "woke" and "nappy," which gained tremendous attention and circulation through social-media platforms. It is again fashionable for young Black women to proudly wear their naturally kinky hair without attempting to emulate the Caucasian-centric beauty canon, according to which straight hair is one of the defining traits. "Black is beautiful" has once again become a mantra, a philosophy of life. The pride in one's roots, Blackness, and knowing oneself and one's history has become empowering. Also, though they may be disproportionately fewer than the overall Black population, there are more Blacks with African originated names. African audiovisual productions, especially Nollywood films (Nigerian video-films predominantly in English and Yoruba) are readily available online and have become a cultural phenomenon through which Africans and African Americans engage in conversations on culture, identity, and language. In some contexts, speaking English with a conspicuously Nigerian accent has become fashionable.[6] Even beyond university campuses, Nollywood movies have garnered general interest in the African diaspora.

In addition, global stardom has been a vehicle or conduit for the appropriation and transmission of African fashion in the diaspora—especially in the case of music and movie stars. Figures on the global stage such as Beyoncé, Rihanna, Janet Jackson, Tracee Ellis Ross, and Lupita Nyong'o have helped build bridges between the continent and the diaspora in an impactful way. Their appearances at events or in music videos are often the subject of attention and online commentaries in magazine lifestyle and fashion columns, blogs, and social media (Twitter, Instagram, and Facebook). It is no surprise that social-media posts and feeds are filled with comments on Black stars wearing clothes by African designers at high-profile industry events such as the American Music Awards (AMA) or the Oscars. That was the case, for instance, with Tracee Ellis Ross, daughter of Diana Ross, attending the 2019 AMA wearing a print wax dress by the Cameroonian designer Claude Lavie Kameni, who also designed Janet Jackson's dress in her music video *Made for Now*. Beyoncé has likewise worn clothes on several occasions from the Africanista t-shirt collection by Franco-Mauritanian designer Aïssé N'diaye. Seen from historically

Afrocentric and Black-conscious places such as Harlem, these examples of cultural crosspollination are celebrated as fruitful contact zones between Africa and the diaspora.

There are dissenting voices, however, among Black people who question what they perceive to be capitalist-driven motives in appropriating African culture (fashion, music, and dance). Critical debates on whether these are genuine expressions of Black consciousness or opportunistic cultural appropriations will continue to be waged in person, in print, and more frequently among younger generations via online platforms. Young Africans may choose to appropriate African American culture either out of identification with American popular culture (heavily influenced by Black celebrities) or to blend into the mainstream more easily than their parents did, with their conspicuous accented English and traditional attire. Young people are generally more open to engaging with new environments than their parents were. Many of these African youth have not reached the age—around fourteen—when second-language acquisition becomes more challenging, hence their ease in acquiring a native fluency in the new language—the very vehicle of circulation and transmission of the local imaginary—makes their cultural transition smoother.

Crossing Ethnic Lines

Another phenomenon I have witnessed in the community is African immigrants passing as locals by simulating the ways that African Americans dress and speak. This identity performance is probably designed to enable them to move freely across different spaces and access any privileges that come with it. On several occasions I witnessed this performance played out at my barbershop, located on 135th Street and Adam Clayton Powell Jr. Boulevard, where some African immigrants were highly critical of other African immigrants for what is perceived as an identity complex, identity performance, or erasure of identity markers—African immigrants passing as African Americans. It would be revealing to know how African Americans regard such identity performances by African immigrants. However, some African Americans showcase pride in their African ancestry through their discourse, attire, and trips to the continent. My anecdotal accounts here are not meant to serve as a basis for generalization but only to highlight some of the many configurations in the relationships between African immigrants and African Americans. Moving across ethnic and racial lines, especially between minorities, is not peculiar to African immigrants and African Americans, nor is the practice a new one. Vivek Bald mentions, for instance, how some African Americans passed for Hindu in the Jim Crow South in the early twentieth century: "It was possible to move across lines between 'Negro' and 'Hindoo,' from a denigrated to an exotic otherness, from an unacceptable to a nominally acceptable blackness, by simply donning a different costume, speaking in a different way, performing a different identity."[7]

Certain Black immigrants strategically choose crossing ethnic lines because cultural difference can sometimes be used advantageously for upward social mobility. The foreigner privilege—an ethnicity of difference—is used today by many Black immigrants to escape the systemic racial prejudice and discrimination to which African Americans have long been subjected. Some Black immigrants choose to retain their identity markers (clothing, accent, cultural practices) as a means to mark out differences that may afford opportunities not otherwise as readily available to them. Although it is true that foreigner privilege can be leveraged for opportunities, it is also a reality that it does not protect Black Africans, Afro-Caribbeans, or Latinx individuals from racism. And although it is important to recognize differences in the Black experience, the widespread resonance of the Black Lives Matter movement surfaces commonalities in the experiences of Black, Brown, Asian, and other minorities.

In sum, relations between African immigrants and African Americans should be understood within the larger racialized identity politics of diasporic communities, provoking the question whether there should be some alliance or active solidarity between them because of racial prejudice. What forms and expressions should the relations between racial and ethnic minorities in the United States take, not only among themselves but also with whites? Connected with this also is the question of who gets to "claim" Blackness in America today as mass migrations of Africans, Afro-Latinx, and Afro-Caribbeans have created demographic shifts throughout the twentieth and twenty-first centuries. As a result, Blacks in America constitute a diverse group beyond the common reference to African Americans, a diversity within the Africa-originating race to which the rest of America, including white America, is being exposed. US-born children of these Black immigrants and subsequent generations, however, tend to identify as African Americans, thus blurring Black ethnic lines of distinction. This complexifies relationships and categories between Blacks and racial identity tremendously.

6

⫶⫶⫶

Depictions of Africa in Cinema, the Arts, and Literature

Upon seeing a performance of Les Ballets Africains in New York City in 1959, the jazz icon Miles Davis shares his enthusiastic experience: I had gotten into the modal thing by watching the Ballet Africaine [*sic*] from Guinea.... We went to this performance by the Ballet Africaine and it just fucked me up what they was doing, the steps and all them flying leaps and shit. And when I first heard them play the finger piano that night and sing this song with this other guy dancing, man, that was some powerful stuff. It was beautiful. And their rhythm! The rhythm of the dancers was something. I was counting off while I was watching them. They were so acrobatic. They had this one drummer watching them dance, doing their flips and shit, and when they jumped he would play DA DA DA DA POW! in this bad rhythm.

—*Miles: The Autobiography*, by Miles Davis and Quincy Troupe

THIS CHAPTER SEEKS A deeper understanding of the encounters and exchanges between Africa and Harlem by employing cinema, the arts, and literature to glean insights into larger trends. The Black Renaissance underway—with its ongoing conversation with Africa—is not happening predominantly in literature as it did during the original Harlem Renaissance movement. Instead, today's ever-growing African presence and influence on the cultural scene in Harlem encompasses stage productions, film, music, photography, and other arts side-by-side with literature. The diversity of these cultural productions should be understood in the context of what Harvard professor Henry Louis Gates Jr. refers to as the fourth Black Renaissance, which started in the 1980s and continues as of this writing. For Gates, the three previous Black Renaissance movements were the New Negro Movement (1890s–1910s), the Harlem Renaissance (1920s), and the Black Arts Movement (1965–1970s). The fourth Black Renaissance is wider in scope, as he notes, "From television to op-ed pages, from the academy to hip-hop, never before have so many black artists and intellectuals achieved so much success in so very many fields."[1]

With the influx of African immigrants since the late 1980s came massive contributions, both economically and culturally, to the rebirth and attraction of Harlem after decades of neglect and drug-related violence in the 1970s and 1980s. So in contrast to the previous Black Renaissance movements centered in New York, the fourth renaissance is centrifugal and happening at a time when there is a larger number of African immigrants who are physically present in the city. Migration is vitally shaping the visual rendering of cultural ties to home and, more important, how the visual media is produced, distributed, and consumed in places like Harlem. In many ways local exhibitions and productions of films are broadening the creative parameters of African cinema and arts, while also remaking the imaginary of Africa in immigrant enclaves.

Several factors contribute to the pivotal role Harlem plays in the distribution of African cultural productions. First, the relocation of the Maysles Documentary Center from Midtown Manhattan to Harlem in 2008 has facilitated the theatrical circulation of African screen media productions in Harlem because the venue, with its name recognition, provides an alternative distribution circuit for independent filmmakers and artists. Second, the concentration of African-immigrant communities in Harlem and the nearby Bronx provides an audience for African film and photography exhibitions, drawing on a more diverse group than would be the case in, say, Lower Manhattan. Third, higher education institutions have developed initiatives for increasing exposure to Black cinema, such as the Blackness in French and Francophone Film series by the Institute of African Studies at Columbia University, which was inaugurated in 2018. In addition, cultural events such as Congo in Harlem, the New York African Film Festival, and the Uptown Flicks series help anchor the immigrant experience. As we shall see in this chapter, literary works, stage performances, and the fine arts further establish the multiple African visual cultures, artistic, and literary connections to or within Harlem.

African Harlem in Screen Media

There exist many twenty-first-century feature-length films that represent the Black experience: the Oscar-winning *Twelve Years a Slave* (2013),

Hidden Figures (2016), *Queen of Katwe* (2016), *Moonlight* (2016), *Get Out* (2017), *Black Panther* (2018), and *BlacKkKlansman* (2018), though more needs to be done to push for increased representation of the Black experience on screen, as well as to have minorities in the decision-making circles of the film and media industry. The boycott of the Oscars in 2016 for being "so white" brought mainstream attention to the urgent need for representation of minorities on screen and in executive suites. The Black Renaissance is attracting tremendous attention with television productions such as Henry Louis Gates Jr.'s television series on the African diaspora and African history, *Africa's Great Civilizations* and *Finding Your Roots,* and the TV series *Insecure* by Issa Rae, who was born to Senegalese parents in Los Angeles but identifies mostly as an African American. The work of television producer and screenwriter Shonda Rhimes and of South African native Trevor Noah, the host of the satirical *The Daily Show with Trevor Noah,* also have significant presence on the media landscape.

An increased interest in African screen media production results from the confluence of two phenomena: the Black Renaissance that is unfolding, just mentioned, and the reconfigurations of African cinema under the influence of migration. West Africans in Harlem, with their cultural and economic transformation of the neighborhood, have sparked the production of visual media portraying immigrants' attempts to bridge the divide between their home countries and their new space in New York City in such films as *Little Senegal, Restless City*, and *Mother of George*—the first two are set in Harlem, the third in Brooklyn. In the 2001 film *Little Senegal,* directed by Franco-Algerian filmmaker Rachid Bouchareb, the Senegalese immigrant community in Harlem is presented through the spiritual journey and identity quest of the protagonist, the slave-museum tour guide Alloune Guire, who has immigrated from Goree Island, Senegal, to New York City in search of living descendants of his enslaved ancestors, brought to the country centuries ago; he seeks to uncover the missing lineage. The movie title and setting draw on the Senegalese immigrant enclave located on 116th Street in West Harlem. Encounters between Africans and African Americans are explored in this film in a multilayered approach through situations of work and intimacy, such as the experience of Alloune's nephew Hassan working in an African American–owned auto shop and the romantic relationship between the characters Karim and Amaralis. *Restless City* (2011), directed by Andrew Dosunmu, is set in Harlem's Morningside Heights area. A twenty-one-year-old aspiring Senegalese musician, Djibril, is looking to realize his American dream but gets caught in the underworld of drugs and prostitution through his African American love interest, Trini.

These two narrative films, both set in the 2000s, focus primarily on the experiences of francophone West African immigrants who started moving to Harlem *en masse* beginning in the 1980s. Being timely and topical, they spark conversations about the relationships between African immigrants and African Americans in the neighborhood. The 1940s and 1960s were historic periods of sustained dialogue between Africans and African Americans as they fought systemic forms of oppression: colonialism, racism, and segregation. Neither *Little Senegal* nor *Restless City* makes any explicit reference to this backdrop against which the immigrant survival stories are unfolding. Instead, the films present a shift away from arts, the politics of pan-Africanism, and militant discourse on the liberation of Black people from oppression to focus on the personal and professional realms playing out in daily street interactions in Harlem. Upon its completion in 2001, in anticipation of its official theatrical release, *Little Senegal* was screened with free admission at the Apollo Theater, where one thousand African Americans and African immigrants came together to watch a film that talks to and about them and their neighborhood.[2] The special preview was intended to foster conversation and mutual understanding between Black neighbors.

In terms of cinematography, the African presence in *Little Senegal and Restless City* is conveyed visually by shots of storefronts, particularly African hair-braiding salons, and the African Square sign at the intersection of 115th Street and 7th Avenue. Visual evidence of African immigrants' engagement with Harlem is rendered mostly though their going about their daily routines. Dosunmu's *Restless City* offers particularly compelling audiovisual storytelling in sequences that are seemingly juxtaposed with no smooth transitions between them. As a result, the image construction of the story could be likened to a collage, in which film and photography are enmeshed in a symbiotic relationship. This imagery helps render the constructed nature of the reality of West Africans in Harlem. These immigrants chose to settle in Harlem not only because of its glorious past but primarily because a predominantly Black neighborhood potentially offers a better cultural fit, and Harlem, as a metaphor for struggle, hustle, and pride in Blackness, functions as a location as well as a character in the films. Films such as *Little Senegal* and *Restless City* give voice and visibility to the African presence in Harlem while also providing African immigrants with more relatable audiovisual stories.[3] The earlier migration of activists, writers, and artists from anglophone African countries to Harlem in the 1960s and 1970s is not even referenced, probably to better situate the fictionalized accounts of the immigrants' stories in Harlem in the larger context of 1980s economic migration. The music score, with dissonant jazz accompanying most of the outdoor scenes, contributes to the portrayal of the hectic life in New York City, which these immigrants and African Americans share.

Indeed, for many African immigrants, their first contact with African American culture prior to arriving in Harlem is an exposure to jazz music, and jazz has significantly shaped the image of Harlem globally. In African films such as Ousmane Sembène's 1988 film *Camp de Thiaroye*, jazz is portrayed as the bridging factor in the relations between Africans and African Americans, as is showcased in the interactions between the main characters, chief sergeant Diatta and a Black American soldier. Set in Dakar, Senegal, in 1944, the movie is about the plight of African veterans of the Second World War—known as *tirailleurs*—who are temporarily stationed outside the city while waiting for their demobilization. Their first encounter occurs in this situation of limbo: Diatta is arrested by a military police patrol under the Black GI's command for hanging out in the white quarters of the city. Tensions run high between *tirailleurs* and the French and American soldiers when Diatta is beaten up and injured. As the plot unfolds, reconciliation between the two Blacks is facilitated by listening to and discussing jazz, which brings them closer physically and symbolically.

In the larger context of African American popular culture, many sports fans still remember the boxer Muhammad Ali's defeat of the world heavyweight champion George Foreman during the eighth round on October 30, 1974, in Kinshasa, the capital city of the Democratic Republic of Congo (at the time Zaire). Popularly known as "The Rumble in the Jungle," this fight cemented Ali's rise to fame and celebrity as one of the world's greatest heavyweight boxing champions of all time. The documentary about the fight, *When We Were Kings* (2002), shows the Congolese crowds in the streets and around the ring supporting Ali, chanting, "Ali, boma ye," meaning "Ali, kill him." Ali was able to win over the public of Kinshasa, which had initially supported his opponent, Foreman, who was thought of as more "African" because of his dark complexion. In the end the fair-complexioned Ali was claimed by Kinshasa as one of their own, their hero, despite the issues of colorism that then existed in the Congo and beyond. A fictionalized account of this championship fight is offered in the novel *J'irai danser sur la tombe de Senghor* (2014) by the Canadian writer Blaise Ndala, originally from the Congo. By hosting the boxing fight in times of economic prosperity, the nation's president Mobutu Sese Seko not only garnered international attention for Zaire but also a way to entertain the country as he prepared to tighten his grip on power; the following years would demonstrate the dictatorial turn of his regime.

Thus, images of the immigrant diaspora, the encounter of the local and the global, global south-to-north migration patterns, and the multi-country work and residence of several African filmmakers are all reshaping the production, aesthetics, distribution, and reception of African visual media. These productions certainly breathe new creative life into African narratives of home. In imagined homeplaces and "abroad," identities and affiliations constantly shift, and so will African screen media in years to come. But it bears noting that, as of 2021, a certain lack of encounters and exchanges of images and symbols is evident in the parallel movement of African cinema and African American cinema, such as African Americans playing Africans in big-budget productions, such as in *Sanders of the River* (1935), *Coming to America* (1988), and *Invictus* (2009). This trend is also seen in African directors making movies that are set in Harlem, such as *Little Senegal* and *Restless City*. There are very limited joint creative ventures between these two cinematic practices or productions that feature encounters between Africans and African Americans. Here again, only a few examples are the exceptions: the 1977 miniseries *Roots*, *Daughters of the Dust* (1991), *Sankofa* (1993), and most recently *Black Panther* (2018).

Black Film Festivals

In addition to serving as a character and backdrop in African visual productions, Harlem is increasingly becoming the center of African film and photography exhibitions in New York City. Traditionally, the distribution of African visual media has taken place in venues around Lower Manhattan or Midtown such as at the Film Society of Lincoln Center, the Museum of Modern Art, the Brooklyn Academy of Music, and some independent theaters such as Film Forum and Quad Cinema. Even more significant, though, are the individual and grassroots efforts to get more visibility for visual productions from Africa by promoting events locally that have international resonance. The Uptown Flicks series, which features French and African co-productions, has been promoted since fall 2017 by Adeline Monzier, the US representative of UniFrance, an official French organization with the mission of promoting and distributing French films worldwide. Both types of productions find the perfect audience in the francophone West African immigrant communities in Harlem. Screenings of the series take place in the Maysles Documentary Center and at locales such as the live-music venue Silvana, a Burkinabe-owned and -operated business near the A, B, and C subway stops on 116th Street. Other recent grassroots initiatives in the exhibition of African films at the Maysles Documentary Center include the Festival of Francophone Shorts by Lucie Chabrol-Nyssens and the New York African Animation Convention that I myself, a Harlem-based film scholar, launched in 2020.

As for the New York African Film Festival and the African Diaspora International Film Festival, both regularly organize African film screenings in Harlem, specifically at Maysles Documentary Center and on the campus of Columbia University. In addition, the Schomburg Center for Research in Black Culture and the Apollo Theater also feature African cinema in some of their programs. The distribution of African screen productions in Harlem should be considered in the larger context of the circulation of African cinema in the United States, where distribution falls into three categories: festivals, the academic circuit, and online streaming platforms.[4] The festival and academic circuits appear be the most common vehicles for screenings and engagement with the Harlem community. The large presence of French-speaking West African immigrant communities and the status of Harlem as a historically Black neighborhood are significant pull factors for distributors—both festival organizers and individual initiatives alike. In sub-Saharan Africa, Harlem is generally perceived as the iconic cultural and political center in the struggle for liberation by Blacks in America and around the world.

Recent grassroots initiatives in the exhibition of African films at the Maysles Documentary Center targeting the local African immigrant community not only affirm the existence of the community but also function as a conduit for pre- and post-screening exchanges between African immigrants and African Americans. The transnational space of work and residence of contemporary African filmmakers has meant that immigration and diaspora have become a focus of an increasing number of films. Also, distribution of African films in the diaspora is the subject of a growing corpus of scholarship.[5] Such critical interventions on African cinema are discussed in works such as Daniela Ricci, *African Diasporic Cinema: Aesthetics of Reconstruction* (2020), Boukary Sawadogo, *West African Screen Media: Comedy, TV Series, and Transnationalization* (2019), Noah Tsika, *Nollywood Stars: Media and Migration in West Africa and the Diaspora* (2015), and Lindiwe Dovey, *Curating Africa in the Age of Film Festivals* (2015).

The medium of animation holds great promise in enabling African Americans to reconnect African roots through historical figures and oral storytelling traditions. In addition, animation is a modern artform that is

HARLEM AFRICAN ANIMATION FESTIVAL

14 - 22 NOVEMBER 2020

Online and Free Edition

SATURDAY, NOVEMBER 14, 2020 AT 2:00 PM (EASTERN TIME)
PANEL: MOUSTAPHA ALASSANE, A PIONEER IN AFRICAN ANIMATION

4:00PM LIVE STREAMING OF FILMS: SAMBA LE GRAND, MALIKA ET LA SORCIÈRE, ET KOKOA.

SUNDAY, NOVEMBRE 15, 2020 AT 10:30 AM (EASTERN TIME)
LIVE STREAMING OF FILMS: BROOM ON DECK ET THE TOAD VISITS HIS IN-LAWS.

10:50 AM PANEL: ANIMATORS SPEAKING

6:00 PM LIVE STREAMING OF THE FEATURE: SOUNDIATA KÉÏTA, LE RÉVEIL DU LION

NOVEMBER 16 - 22, 2020:
ACCESS THE FESTIVAL SELECTION ANYTIME AT YOUR CONVENIENCE. .

CULTURAL SERVICES
FRENCH EMBASSY
IN THE UNITED STATES

the
City College
of New York

La
Cinémathèque
Afrique

INSTITUT
FRANÇAIS

HARLEM AFRICAN ANIMATION FESTIVAL   HARLEM AFRICAN ANIMATION FESTIVAL

Figure 15. Poster of the Harlem African Animation Festival. 2020. Courtesy of Boukary Sawadogo.

quickly developing and changing the way Africa is represented on screens to all ages and ethnicities and races. Many animated films are bringing contemporary Africa into focus, with topics ranging from demand for more democratic governance to changing urban spaces to narratives of individual and collective advancement. The technology and polysemic nature of the animated image are contributing to shaping how Africa is represented beyond recurring stereotypical images of poverty, war, famine, and disease. For both the historical African diaspora and the African immigrant communities, the change in the representation of Africa in our consciousness also indirectly changes perception on them.[6]

The Congo in Harlem film festival was founded in 2009 with the backing of cinematographer Nelson Walker and his partner, film editor Lynn True. This event, which features films, panel discussions, performances, and more, takes place the third week in October every year. The selection of Harlem as the event location happened organically when Harlem residents Walker and True reached out to the Maysles Documentary Center when it opened in 2008. As Walker recounts, it was post-screening discussions of True's feature documentary *Lumo* (2007), about survivors of sexual violence in the Democratic Republic of Congo, that demonstrated the need for more information on the Congo from Congolese perspectives. Congo in Harlem thus came into being thanks to a collaboration between Walker and True, the Friends of the Congo organization, and the Maysles Documentary Center to allow Congolese artists and activists to promote their works abroad and to provide local support in their home country. Congo in Harlem is a series of events and activities. In addition to screenings, it puts Congolese filmmakers in contact with US distributors, holds grant-writing workshops, and organizes photography exhibitions of Congolese artists. The tenth year, in 2018, featured a film lineup of *Félicité* (2017), *I'm New Here* (2017), *Che in Congo: A Dream of Liberation* (2017), *E'Ville* (2018), *Maki'la* (2018), *Kinshasa Makambo* (2018), and the group photo exhibition *Persona non Grata: In a Floating World of Radiant Sorrows and Perfumed Warfare.*

In terms of density of geographical distribution, the Congolese community in New York City is relatively fragmented as compared to the French-speaking West African immigrants in Harlem and parts of the Bronx. Yet it is important to emphasize Harlem's long-standing connection to the Congo (formerly known as Zaïre) through the Patrice Lumumba Coalition, a Harlem-based group founded in 1975 by the pan-Africanist activist Elombe Brath (1936–2014). The coalition bears the name of the first prime minister of the Congo Patrice Lumumba (1925–1961), who is

Figure 16. Poster of Congo in Harlem. 2018. Courtesy of Nelson Walker.

regarded as a prominent pan-Africanist and a political leader who fought against oppression under Belgian colonial rule. The coalition has contributed to bringing tremendous local attention to and support for liberation struggles in Africa, such as the Angolan liberation movements in the 1970s and the fight to end apartheid in South Africa in the 1980s.

"Black on Black" Literature

The notion of the "New Negro" popularized by American writer and philosopher Alain LeRoy Locke in his book *The New Negro: An Interpretation* (1925) called for dignity for Blacks and the rejection of racial discrimination and segregation. The concept inspired founding members of the Negritude literary movement, African and Caribbean students in Paris at the time, to give voice and existence to the humanity and self-governance of their own people by denouncing French colonialism. The cultural vibrancy of Paris enabled the meeting of the Negritude poets with African American writers and entertainers such as Alain Locke, Countee Cullen, Langston Hughes, Josephine Baker, and Paul Robeson. This was an unprecedented historical convergence around Black pride and consciousness. While African Americans were seeking to frame a new image of the Negro—one dissociated from the historical identity of the plantation slave—in order to claim their full humanity and citizenship, concurrently the nascent Black intelligentsia from the French colonies in Africa and the Caribbean were demanding political independence. The independence movement would later gain further momentum in the aftermath of the historic Bandung Conference that met in Indonesia in 1955, which brought together leaders from newly independent nations of Africa and Asia.

In his critically acclaimed book *The African Image* (1974), the South African writer and educator Ezekiel Mphahlele examined the African representation in selected literary works of the 1950s and 1960s by Chinua Achebe, Ngũgĩ wa Thiong'o, Ousmane Sembène, Ferdinand Oyono, Mongo Beti, and Kofi Awoonor. Images and representations of Africans in these works are analyzed in the context of white power under colonial rule and apartheid. These works of Black writers on the Black condition represented a shift in how images and symbols of the continent were conveyed to Africans and the rest of the world. This is "Black-on-Black" writing, in contrast to "white-on-Black" writing, in which white authors such as Joseph Conrad, E. M. Forster, and William Faulkner write about cultural groups outside their own.[7] Without implying that white-on-Black writing should face opposition, this section seeks to examine the significance of images and symbols of Africa by African writers in works that are set partly in Harlem.

Many immigrants come to Harlem with the feeling of familiarity with the neighborhood after having been exposed to the history and culture of the place well before leaving home; "Blaxploitation" movies, literary figures, jazz music icons, and civil rights movement leaders have collapsed the cultural distance between Africa and Harlem.[8] Manthia Diawara's semi-autobiographical book *We Won't Budge: An African Exile in the World* (2003) offers in-depth insights into the cultural attraction that Harlem carries for many young Guineans and Malians who, like him, grew up in the 1960s and 1970s. Diawara explains how he and his friends embraced African American culture through music and literature. Increasingly, as part of this transatlantic influence and continuity, African writers in the diaspora are fostering a conversation between Africa and the United States through fiction and nonfiction works that showcase stories and narratives from African perspectives. These stories often collapse spaces and historic time frames by engaging local communities of African writers in the United States and their countries of origin in Africa. These literary works are often referred to as Afrodiasporic literature. The steady increase of African immigrant population in the United States—doubling every decade since the

1980s—has contributed to establishing an African presence in the country, specifically in its metropolitan areas.

This is the larger context in which two contemporary award-winning novels, *Behold the Dreamers* and *Homegoing*, by female African writers who reside in the United States should be understood. Cameroonian writer Imbolo Mbue's critically acclaimed debut novel *Behold the Dreamers* (2016) is set in Harlem and the Bronx against the backdrop of the 2008 financial crisis. The couple Jende and Neni Jonga and their young son, Liomi, have moved to New York City from their native Cameroon. As newly arrived immigrants, Jende and Neni face various challenges settling into their new socioeconomic environment such as finding jobs with a living wage, maintaining legal-immigrant status, and realizing their dreams of social mobility. When Jende finds a job as a chauffeur for Clark Edwards, an executive of the investment bank Lehman Brothers, the hope arises in the family that its fortunes may now change for the better. As the Jonga and Edwards families are brought closer through work and personal relationships, Jende and Neni face disenchanting questions about their own dreams and chances of success in America. The soul-searching and unfolding dramas of both families are examined through the ramifications of the world financial crisis—triggered in part by the collapse of Lehman Brothers—on individuals rather than corporations. The Lehman Brothers failure is not presented at the macroeconomic level, nor are the systemic shocks and aftershocks of the 2008 economic crisis; rather, the focus homes in on the fate of a Cameroonian immigrant family's struggles to realize their American dream.

Three questions can serve as entry points into the novel in view of the multilayered meanings of "dreamers," the (dis)similarities with works of fiction by African authors living in the United States, and the images and symbols of Africa in Harlem. Let us explore these questions in turn.

(1) *Who are the dreamers?* The Jonga family has moved to New York City for the American dream of a fair chance at prosperity, and the end of the novel is inconclusive about whether they are on a solid footing to realize that dream. The Edwards family is also, to a certain extent, a family of migrants seeking the American dream. Working as an executive at Lehman Brothers represents the culmination of Clark's professional trajectory because he "migrated" to Wall Street, New York, from California and Virginia to pursue his dream of prosperity and career fulfillment. The character of Cindy, Clark Edwards's wife, is particularly revealing in the way that the emptiness of capitalism affects individuals in different ways. She felt she was nothing growing up poor, and still feels some emptiness in her life even

after becoming part of the upper middle class. She struggles constantly with how to reconcile her humble background with the higher social class she married into. Are she and, by way of extrapolation, other poor and low-income Americans "dreamers" for constantly striving to move up the social ladder? Or are they dreamers because they pursue an ideal, but the achieved ideal does not turn out to be what they had envisioned, rendering their dreams nothing but illusion or fantasy?

(2) *How does one best consider this novel within the context of literature produced by young African diasporic writers living in the United States?* The financial world of Lehman Brothers is an environment far away from that of the Jonga family, yet very close insofar as the ripple effects of the bank's collapse are felt down in the streets of all the boroughs of New York and beyond. A similar structure is evident in the novel of Franco-Congolese writer Alain Mabanckou, *Les cicognes sont immortelles* (Storks are immortal, 2018): the far-reaching consequences of the military coup that deposed the Congolese president are unexpectedly threatening the lives of a poor family in Pointe-Noire, which is far from the capital city, Brazzaville. These are stories of big events dramatically affecting the lives of people who know little or nothing about them, and had no part in shaping the events in the first place. *Behold the Dreamers* also shares stylistic similarities with the National Book Award– and Pulitzer Prize–winning *The Grapes of Wrath* (1939) by American novelist John Steinbeck, which concerns the realistic portrayal of characters in times of socioeconomic distress. The dynamics and interactions between the "have nots" and the "haves" are examined in depth in both works: farm laborers in California and the immigrant Jende family, both struggling for survival, as contrasted with farm owners and the upper-middle-class Edwards family.

(3) *What images and symbols of Africa in Harlem can be drawn from Behold the Dreamers?* There are relatively few literary works that bring African and African American characters and stories into a sustained dialogue; those few include Chimamanda Ngozi Adichie's critically acclaimed novel *Americanah* (2013) and Nnedi Okorafor's fantasy novel *Akata Witch* (2018). In general, instead, there seems to be a parallel between the two in which Africans' and African Americans' images are fragmented rather than portrayed together in the same frame, image, scene, and story line. But *Behold the Dreamers* provides literary representation and images of Africans in Harlem that is innovative in and of itself.

The debut novel *Homegoing* (2016) by Yaa Gyasi connects West Africa and Harlem of the 1960s through the character of Sonny, who is involved in the Harlem jazz scene. The novel's title draws on the idea that after the death of a slave, his or her soul goes back to Africa. Gyasi was born in Ghana and raised in the United States, where she now lives. Tracing the genealogy of two half-sisters, Effia and Esi, torn apart in eighteenth-century Africa, *Homegoing* spans two hundred years of history, moving from Ghana to the American South to California to Harlem. The novel opens lines of dialogue between Africans and African Americans around the themes of slavery, colonialism, and representation of Black masculinity, love, and family. This conversation between Africa and its diaspora in the novel is by itself a step forward in addressing the topic of slavery, which can often be a source of tension between Africans and African Americans, given that criticisms are often leveled at Africans for their active role in capturing and selling their own people into slavery. This criticism needs to be nuanced because African captors have also made African victims. As for conversations in Africa on the transatlantic slave trade, it still lacks attention in public debates and in-depth treatment in school curricula, probably because the slave trade did not have the same historical, cultural, and identity implications for Black people on each shore of the Atlantic. Considering the current multifaceted encounters between Africa and the diaspora, relations are being reconsidered and developed. Those encounters—in person and/or online—are further facilitated by contemporary migration to and from Africa, video and online communication platforms, and present-day image-driven culture, which connect distant lands. Literature, as is the case with the novel *Homegoing* and many works, also (re)creates and fosters links through its creative possibilities, evocative power, and symbolic representation of Africa.

Fine-Art Photography

The arts in the 1960s and 1970s, especially photography, painting, and sculpture, showed evidence of sustained exchanges between Africa and Harlem. Two examples of this are the Harlem-based Black photographers' collective Kamoinge, created in 1963, and the YUC collective of Black painters and sculptors whose works are primarily Afrocentric. The name *Kamoinge* comes from the ethnic language of Kikuyu, from Kenya, and means "a group of people acting together." African American photographer Shawn W. Walker, one of Kamoinge's founding members, was born in Harlem and lives and works there. His Africa-related images taken in Harlem are important to the conversation of the African and African American experience in Harlem. As a photographer who was regularly invited to take pictures at private and official functions during the Black Power and Black

Arts Movements, Walker possesses photographs and stories that document numerous African artists' and activists' visits and stays in Harlem in the 1960s and 1970s. The black-and-white photographs hanging in his apartment, and his more experimental recent color pictures, give a sense of the breadth and chronology of the work by the artist. Another dimension of Walker's work focuses on the costumes and rituals of New York City's ethnic minorities and immigrant communities. Since 2000, Walker has photographed members of different ethnic communities dressed in their traditional garments during celebrations—such as the African American Day Parade and ethnic community events for Puerto Ricans, Koreans, and Indians—all in New York City. Another notable member of the Kamoinge collective is the widely acclaimed African American photographer Ming Smith. She is particularly known as a portrait photographer of Black life, with photos taken in Harlem, but also in Senegal ("Dakar Roadside with Figures," 1972) and Egypt ("Womb" and "Masque," 1990).

Photographic images by another Harlemite photographer, Ozier Muhammad, grandson of Elijah Muhammad, a founder of the Nation of Islam, cover Africa extensively. As a photojournalist, he traveled to Tanzania in 1974 for the sixth Pan-African Congress, then to Mali and Burkina Faso in 1984 to cover the drought and famine affecting these countries, and more recently to South Africa for the funeral of Nelson Mandela in 2013. As a photojournalist, Muhammad won the Pulitzer Prize in 1985 for his reporting on the drought in Africa. The subjects in his photographs are shown demonstrating dignity and resilience. In addition, the photographic work by the Harlem-based African Jazz-Art Society and Studios (AJASS) in the 1960s and 1970s portrays the intersection of African artistic expressions and Harlem; original members include Elombe Brath, Kwame Brathwaite, Frank Adu, Chris Hall, Bob Gumbs, and Ernest Baxter. The images showcase "Black is beautiful," challenging the Eurocentric beauty canon and celebrating African features in African American subjects.

The history of the connection of Harlem and Africa in photography, however, reaches back to the early twentieth century with the African American photographer James Van Der Zee, who owned a studio in Harlem during the height of the Harlem Renaissance in the 1920s and for the next four decades. He made portraits of ordinary residents of the neighborhood as well as its celebrities, such as the 1924 photo of Marcus Garvey with George O. Marke and Prince Kojo Tovalou-Houénou taken in Harlem. The latter had traveled to New York City to attend Marcus Garvey's Universal Negro Improvement Association (UNIA) conference, where he gave a speech critical of French colonialism in West Africa. Kojo

Tovalou-Houénou was a prince of Dahomey (present-day Benin), educated in France, who later became very active in the intellectual circles of Paris in the 1920s. His presence at the UNIA conference underlined Harlem as a site of solidarity and cooperation for Black people worldwide struggling for liberation from subjugation and oppression.

Performance Arts

Live performances of African theater, dance, and music in New York—and throughout the United States—provide key historical junctures in the trajectory of the transnationalization of modern African performance. These performances shed light on artistic and symbolic ties between Africans and African Americans—ties that are certainly best captured and represented in popular culture today by the award-winning Broadway musical *The Lion King*. New Yorkers, international visitors, and people around the US are familiar with the touring musical. Decades before the popular success of *The Lion King*, in the late 1950s and mid-1960s, Les Ballets Africains was the first global touring African performance company to have made an impact in the United States. Keïta Fodéba founded Les Ballets Africains de Keïta Fodéba in France in the late 1940s, and the group's performance at the Théâtre de l'Étoile in 1952 marked its rise to international fame. The troupe is made up of members from three West African countries: Guinea, Senegal, and Mali (named Sudan before 1960). From 1953 onward the group toured several countries in Africa, Europe, and Central and South America before coming to the United States for its first tour in 1959, which debuted in New York City.

Les Ballets Africains's first Broadway productions took place in February and March of 1959. The troupe was reconfigured as the National Ballet of the Republic of Guinea in 1960 after the country gained its independence in 1958, and returned to Broadway in 1960, 1966, and 1968. To put the Ballets Africains performances in New York City in larger historical context, it should be noted that already in the early twentieth century ties to Africa were evident in the stage performances of African American comedians Bert Williams and George Walker, playing leading roles in the musical *In Dahomey* (1903–1904), which opened in February 1903 in the old New York Theatre. This was the first full-length musical performed in a major Broadway theater that was written by and starring African Americans.

As for the long history of African dance on Broadway, it includes the Sierra Leonean–born choreographer and dancer Assadata Dafora, a pioneer of African modern stage performance in New York City. In the historical period from Dafora's arrival in New York City in 1929 until his death in 1965, African Americans were examining their relations to Africa as Africa was engaged in political liberation struggles from colonialism. This shows how New York City in mid-twentieth-century America was a site of globalism in dance—as is argued by Rebekah Kowal[9]—but also a space where solidarity and mutual understanding between Africans and African Americans were forged. Another early transnational figure of African dance who performed in New York City was the Senegalese-born dancer and model François Féral Benga (1906–1957). Born to a wealthy family in Dakar, he arrived in France in 1923, where he pursued a career in dance, performing with entertainers such as Josephine Baker. He then rose to prominence in his own right as a dancer in the music-hall scene, actor in films such as *The Blood of a Poet* (1930) by French director Jean Cocteau, owner and operator of a cabaret, and as a muse of modern visual artists such as the African American sculptor Richmond Barthé. On the presence of Féral Benga in the modern visual culture of the period, James Smalls notes: "His body and its visualization by others helped foster the political and creative expressions and complications of black modernist consciousness and agency within the vigorous energies and contradictions of modernism and primitivism."[10]

The Guinean Ladji Camara, a member of Les Ballets Africains, made a popular contribution to the presence and influence of African dance and drumming in New York, adding to earlier work accomplished by Assadata Dafora and Féral Benga. "Papa" Ladji Camara stayed in New York City after touring with the Ballets and performed with renowned African American artists including Nina Simone, Charles Moore, Chief Bey, Yusef Lateef, and Alvin Ailey. In 1971, Camara opened an African drumming and dance studio in the Bronx and taught drumming classes in schools and museums. He also made individual contributions outside the Ballets troupe to bring African dance to different areas of New York City and beyond. His legacy is as a great djembe drummer for Les Ballets Africains, but most important is his influential role in popularizing African drumming in New York City.

The itinerary of Camara to some extent reflects the historical trajectory of the development of arts in postcolonial Africa, and also how governments have gradually disengaged from supporting the performing arts, which has led many artists to migrate to the global North. After most African countries gained independence in the 1960s, governments funded and supported arts as an extension of diplomatic channels or as part of broader national cultural agenda. State support and funding would cease in certain countries, such as Guinea, because of military regime change. More generally, significant cuts to state funding for culture resulted from austerity measures imposed on African governments by the World Bank and the International Monetary Fund in the 1990s. In this context of reduced support and the absence of ambitious cultural programs as in the 1960s, several artists migrated overseas for better professional and life opportunities. Nonetheless, it should be noted that international mobility of African artists—troupes traveling and performing in Western and non-Western major cities—is not a recent phenomenon. Indeed, the long-standing tradition of global circulation of African dancers and artists between Africa and the United States continues today, with contemporary African-born dancers performing in New York City and across the country at different venues.

African-inspired creative live performances continue in Harlem today at the Apollo Theater, the National Black Theater, and the Studio Museum in Harlem, as well as on Broadway, as was the case with the musical *Fela!* (2008), based on the story of the late Nigerian Afrobeat singer Fela Anikulapo-Kuti. Founded in 1913, the Apollo Theater is not only a landmark cultural institution in Harlem but is recognized worldwide as the venue that introduces the next generation of Black musicians, comedians, and entertainers. Performing at the Apollo is a mark of achievement. Iconic Black musicians and entertainers such as Aretha Franklin, Josephine Baker, Ray Charles, Lionel Richie, Stevie Wonder, Prince, and Michael Jackson all performed there. Although the Apollo has a long and documented tradition with Black diaspora musicians, its connections to African artists based on the continent remain relatively unexplored and often little publicized beyond the Apollo's home website. But historical records show that a number of African musicians have played at the Apollo, individually or as part of the Africa Now! festival. African musicians who have performed individually at the Apollo include the South African musician and activist Miriam Makeba, who first performed there in 1967. Other South African musicians followed, particularly the male choral group Ladysmith Black Mambazo in 1986 and 2014, and Hugh Masekela in 2004. The Nigerian Afrobeat star Fela Kuti, just mentioned, played a three-and-a-half-hour concert at the Apollo in mid-July 1991.

These performances contribute to reinforcing cultural ties between Africa and the Black Atlantic. Certain African musicians at the Apollo give voice on the international scene to issues of the moment facing the continent, such as then anti-apartheid struggle (Makeba and Masekela) and corruption and African unity (Fela Kuti). The music star of the Democratic

Republic of Congo, Fally Ipupa, held a concert at the Apollo on July 13, 2019. In addition, the Apollo's annual Africa Now! music festival features contemporary African musicians whose works fuse local and global influences; the festival's lineup includes established and emerging African artists. Founded in 2012, many individuals and groups from the continent have played at the festival: the acclaimed Afrobeat drummer Tony Allen (Nigeria), the DJ Black Coffee (South Africa), the Afrobeat star Burna Boy (Nigeria), the singer and songwriter Somi (born in the United States to parents from Rwanda and Uganda), Songhoy Blues (Mali), Daby Touré (Mauritania), and Mbongwana Star (Democratic Republic of Congo). The Africa Now! festival fosters a conversation between Africa and its diaspora that embodies and reflects Black global culture in flux. In addition to the music scene at the Apollo, there are other live-music venues owned and operated by African immigrants in Harlem (see Chapter 7).

The Influence of African Art

Active scholars, writers, and art collectors in the Harlem Renaissance debated the question of African art in the movement and what it represented for African Americans who were claiming their Blackness during the New Negro Movement of the 1920s. African arts could be used creatively in telling stories of the African American experience and as a pedagogical instrument to educate people about Africa. Alain Locke, one of the foundational figures of the Harlem Renaissance, advocated that African art represents a source of aesthetic inspiration for African American visual artists. Imitating African art at the turn of the twentieth century meant being "modern"; for example, African primitive art was a source of inspiration for Pablo Picasso's hugely controversial painting *Les Demoiselles d'Avignon* (1907), a perfect example of the role that African art played in the creation of modernism, abstract art, and cubism. Léopold Sédar Senghor, a founding member of the Negritude literary movement, underscored the contribution of African cultures to modern art in his seminal essay "Ce que l'homme noir apporte" (What the Black man contributes) in 1939, building on the pioneering study of African art *Primitive Negro Sculpture* (1926) by art collectors Paul Guillaume and Thomas Munro. Using a comparative approach, Senghor contrasts the Greco-Roman aesthetics of reproduction and idealization of reality with the aesthetics of emotion in African sculpture, which attempts to capture what is behind reality.

The exhibition *Primitive Negro Art, Chiefly from the Belgian Congo* at the Brooklyn Museum in 1923 and the exhibition of African Negro art at the Museum of Modern Art in 1935 provided some of the earliest exposure of New York City to African Art. In his writing about the exhibition, Alain Locke argues that African art has become classic given its rich aesthetic elements. African art, Locke further notes, complexifies our understanding of art and its underlying creative process: "The modern artist, as a sophisticate," he writes, "was always working with the idea of authorship and a technically formal idea of expressing an aesthetic. The native African sculptor, forgetful of self and fully projected into the idea, was always working in a complete fusion with the art object."[11] As the movements of modernism and cubism changed the cultural imagination in the West regarding the significance and role of African art globally, to some extent it followed that being modern meant being African.

Alain Locke recommended that African American visual artists take inspiration from African art because he thought it could contribute to transforming the image of the Negro. This recommendation is consistent with the tenets of the New Negro Movement, inspired by Locke, to replace the early American image of the plantation Negro with a positive and modern image of the liberated Black. But Locke's interest in African art extended beyond the scholarly realm. Not only was he a collector of African art, but in 1927 he actively pursued, in collaboration with art critics and philanthropists Charlotte Osgood Mason, Walter Pach, and Amy Spingarn, a project to create the Harlem Museum of African Art. His attempt to create the museum was inspired by the traveling Blondiau Theater-Arts Collection of primitive art from West Africa and the Belgian Congo, with exhibits in Paris, Cairo, and New York City, but unfortunately Locke's plans for a Harlem Museum of African Art were not fully realized owing to an inability to secure the necessary funds.[12] The African objects that had been collected in anticipation of the opening of the museum went to different places, one of them being the Harlem branch of the New York Public Library, which would later become the Schomburg Center for Research in Black Culture.

Though Locke's museum never came to fruition, the project attests to the presence of African art on the New York artistic scene at the beginning of the twentieth century; it also demonstrates the central importance of Harlem in building a permanent institutional home for African art in the city. Indeed, the unrealized Harlem Museum of African Art provides a thread of historic evidence tracing back to the 1910s, showing that New York City has been the gateway of African art into the United States. The journey of African objects from the continent to New York follows a triangular route—one that is to some extent similar to the transatlantic slave trade decades earlier. African objects were brought to Europe predominantly from French and Belgian colonies in West and Central Africa. These objects entered the art market in Europe through collectors, explorers, missionaries, and the colonial administrators returning from Africa with works obtained by force or dubious means. Generally, many of the artifacts also found a home in European ethnographic museums and collections, such as the Trocadero Museum of Ethnography in Paris (later moved to Musée de l'Homme, then to Musée du quai Branly, where they are housed today). This plunder is the result of colonial violence, which paved the way for a forced migration of objects of African cultural heritage. African artifacts were then acquired from Europe by New York collectors and museums. Exhibitions of African art in the 1910s and 1920s invariably juxtaposed African art and modern art, until the Brooklyn Museum's display in 1923 presented African art on its own.[13] Through gallery exhibitions and traveling series, African art moved from New York to various parts of the country. Today, entry points for African art into the United States extend beyond New York.

The ongoing debate about African art restitution has yet to enter the public discourse in the United States as it did in Europe following French president Emmanuel Macron's pledge to return museums' extensive colonial-era African artifacts, and upon the release of the commissioned report in November 2018, which was published in 2019 as a book, *Restituer le patrimoine africain* (Restitution of African cultural heritage), coauthored by Senegalese scholar Felwine Sarr and Berlin-based art historian Bénédicte Savoy from France.[14] The US government may not recognize historical colonial ties with Africa as some European countries do, or it could be that the silence on the subject is simply consistent with its long-established stance of disengagement in setting and implementing such cultural policies. Museums and collectors in New York City have not yet taken a forceful public stance on the debate over African art restitution,[15] at least not to the extent of what has occurred in Europe—as to whether items in their larger collections will be returned to Africa or allowed to circulate on the continent through traveling or loan programs to enable contemporary Africans to (re)connect with objects created by their ancestors as part of efforts to give young Africans a fuller sense of being and belonging beyond a truncated or fragmented history. This is a work of both memory reconstruction and relational history. Through restitution, new meanings and relationships will be established between museums, objects, and the public, and between Africa and the global North. Africans' (re)appropriation and building of a cultural identity are essential for self-confidence and growth as a way to better engage the larger world after years of alienation as a consequence of the colonial past. Access to this cultural heritage can help facilitate this transformative process, contributing to the knowledge of our shared humanity.

Other New York City institutions regularly hosting Africa-related events include the Africa Center and the Schomburg Center for Research in Black Culture in Harlem, and the annual Brooklyn Academy of Music (BAM) DanceAfrica Festival. These institutional spaces afford awareness, learning, and exchanges where Africa is discussed in terms of its creativity and contributions to knowledge beyond stereotypical media-grabbing headlines that perpetuate a negative image of the continent. The continued programming around Africa at such institutions is itself an affirmation of a contemporary and sizable African immigrant community in New York as its audience, contributors, and critical thinkers. Though admittedly, on the basis of my personal observations in attending Africa-related events at various institutions throughout the city, Africans at these events appear to be educated elites coming from relatively higher socioeconomic backgrounds. Financially struggling families and undocumented workers tend to be absent from such public programming, whether it is because museum-going is not part of their socialization or because there exists a felt difference in socioeconomic markers between the location of the institution and their residential neighborhood, a lack of expanded networks, or limited mastery of the English language. So despite well-intentioned plans, access and relation to programming at the city's cultural institutions could be disenfranchising at times. The important first step, however, is that African stories be told and represented in these spaces for a broader public—a step to foster self-empowerment for Africans, scholarly research, and public education.

An example of such a public event was the recent show *Sahel: Art and Empires on the Shores of the Sahara* on exhibit at the Metropolitan Museum of Art, January 30–October 26, 2020. Drawing on material culture, the show underlined major historical and cultural crossroads during precolonial times in a region that encompasses the present-day countries of Senegal, Mauritania, Guinea, Mali, and Niger. The show brought institutional presence and attention to Africa, and (re)introduced the region to the world by connecting past and present. Contemporary African presence in New York was notable on the opening evening and in later programmatic events, such as a panel on African women filmmakers and storytelling hosted by the founder of the New York African Film Festival, Mahen Bonetti, originally from Sierra Leone; and a conversation with Manthia Diawara on change and continuity in the region.

As we have seen, African contributions to the current Black Renaissance are diverse, building on historical exchanges of ideas between Africa and previous Harlem-centered renaissance movements, and most significantly this time capitalizing on the strong African immigrant presence in the neighborhood. Unlike previous times—when African writers, filmmakers, musicians, and intellectuals were either absent from or only occasional visitors to New York City—many reside and work here. Although the audience for African artistic productions in Harlem is predominantly African and African American, these producers and creators enjoy attention from multiethnic audiences in Manhattan and the outer boroughs in cultural and educational institutions such as museums, galleries, and universities. So then, the participation of African artistic creativity in the current Black Renaissance should be looked at from the inside, not only in terms of the usual framework of outside contributions.

7

⠿

A Few Notable Africans in Harlem in 2022

Harlem is a location and space for African migrants; emancipated enslaved Africans recoiling and fleeing a violent and oppressive "South" (location of sufferance) and an "exodus" to a safe(r) haven of the "North" and in particular, Harlem. This migration and establishment of a Home is replete with the establishment of a "Village" formation and offers succour and instruction to the émigrés from West Africa, as to how to negotiate the new place. This is the farming of "Africans in Harlem" where Africans from Africa find a Home in Harlem over one hundred years later. The two Africans join in community and support, understanding the tenuous situation of both place and circumstances.

—Rashidah Ismaili, poet

HARLEM HAS BEEN A second home to many African writers, intellectuals, artists, and political activists over the decades, whether they were fleeing persecution in their native lands, searching for a community that sustains dissenting voices, or looking to enrich their creativity.[1] Some of these prominent African-born figures resided in Harlem only at one point in their careers, while others still live or work in the neighborhood. Although these African-born Harlemites may not have the name recognition of their African American counterparts—such as James Baldwin, Malcolm X, or Maya Angelou—they are nonetheless worthy of attention. Prominent African entertainers, artists, and activists whose personal and professional journey led them to Harlem, whether for a long or short stay, include Léopold Sédar Senghor, Zenzile Miriam Makeba, Hugh Masekela,

Kewulay Kamara, Alexander "Skunder" Boghossian, and Rashidah Ismaili AbuBakr. The Appendix to this book offers their biographical details.

As I have already noted (in Chapter 1), the early historical formation of Black Harlem was shaped by the contributions of great artistic, intellectual, and business figures—from Philip Payton and Madam C. J. Walker, to writers and artists of the Harlem Renaissance, to civil rights leaders—and the presence of such figures contributed to community building and visibility. Similarly, the process of the formation of Harlem cosmopolitanism in the early twentieth century featured leaders from other communities such as Marcus Garvey and Amy Ashwood Garvey, the Jamaican cofounders of the Universal Negro Improvement Association. In the 1960s and 1970s, liberation-movement leaders, political activists, artists, and writers from anglophone Africa found in Harlem a home away from home. From the late 1980s onward, the connections between Africa and Harlem have shifted from militant and political dimensions to an economic migration of mostly francophone West African immigrants. They have transformed Harlem culturally and economically with their visible presence.

In view of these historical examples and precedents, one cannot help but wonder whether the African immigrant presence in Harlem since the 1980s is continuing and extending this same pattern or if it displays features of a different mechanism of construction of a diasporic community. A larger question we might pose, moreover, is to what extent these individual luminaries simply reflect or themselves actively constitute the process of formation of a minority community. This could allow greater insight into the process that has led to the creation of African-immigrant enclaves in the United States and elsewhere. For instance, what explains the geographic concentrations of Africans in certain areas of New York City—or throughout the country—such as Ethiopians in the Washington, DC, area, Cameroonians in neighboring Maryland, Ivorians in Atlanta, Nigerians in Houston, Somalis in Minneapolis, and Burkinabe in Newark, New Jersey? To many African immigrants, the spatial mapping of poverty in inner cities stands in contrast with what they were used to seeing in their homelands, where the poor are confined to the outlying areas of the ever-expanding city limits, rather than around city centers. In the United States one has to be relatively rich to afford to live away from city centers. This is one of the many reasons why African immigrants tend to settle in large metropolitan areas in the US.

Leaders within communities of Africans who moved to Harlem decades ago, or who now reside in the neighborhood, can be defined along generational lines or within the context of the two basic migration patterns that characterize Africans' settlement in Harlem. The first African figures in Harlem were intellectual and artistic figures ranging from Nnamdi Azikiwe and Kwame Nkrumah to the exiled activists and artists of the 1960s and 1970s (see Appendix). This generation gave voice and presence to Africa in Harlem, thus contributing to receptive spaces for the economic migrants from the late 1980s onward to find a home in Harlem in their footsteps. This reminds us to consider the catalyzing role that is played by central figures in racial or ethnic diasporic community formation. Such key figures may act as a pull factor spurring the organic process of the early formation of a diasporic community and ensuring its later development. Today the leadership in immigrant African communities in Harlem is less dominated by intellectual and artistic figures and more by young entrepreneurs, leaders of voluntary associations, and not-for-profit organizations providing support services to immigrants. These new African leadership figures in the community reflect Harlem's history of activism, while also illustrating the larger pattern of how immigrant enclaves come to inscribe migrants' stories and cosmogonies in their residential areas and workspaces, in their neighborhoods and cities.

Harlem: The New Paris?

The African presence in New York today speaks to the inherent diversity of metropolitan areas, underscoring how the circulation of people and ideas can bring about social, economic, and political changes that have far-reaching ramifications. The cultural and literary scenes in Paris played a similar role in the first half of the twentieth century, when the search for creativity and freedom by African Americans and Afro-Caribbeans brought them to France, provoking an encounter with the future generation of African leaders. Paris became a place of relative freedom for African American writers, where their American-ness and Blackness were recognized as distinguishing qualities, in ways they were not recognized at home. Still today Black American-ness is recognized there in a way that has not been afforded to African *émigrés* and Afro-French or Afro-Europeans.

These encounters are especially exemplified in the Paris-based publishing house Présence Africaine, which has historically been at the crossroads of circulating ideas by Blacks from North America, the French West Indies, and Africa. First founded as a review in 1947 by the Senegalese intellectual Alioune Diop and his wife Christiane, Présence Africaine added a publishing house in 1949 for wider circulation of works by African and diasporic writers, and then a bookstore followed in 1962. The creation of Présence Africaine at the end of World War II was historically significant, as Black people were still denied their full humanity, including any serious recognition or consideration of their intellectual and literary productions. The catalog of Présence Africaine includes works by Negritude writers (Léopold Sédar Senghor, Aimé Césaire, and Léon-Gontran Damas), writings on Black identity, and writings on anticolonial struggles by major literary figures such as Ousmane Sembène, Albert Camus, André Gide, Michel Leiris, and Édouard Glissant. In late October 2019, the august publishing house celebrated its seventieth anniversary; in attendance were the president of Senegal Macky Sall and several African intellectuals and writers such as Wole Soyinka and Ngũgĩ wa Thiong'o. Its tradition of circulating ideas and works by Black writers continues today with a younger generation of authors. In the footsteps of some of the great African American writers such as Chester Himes, Richard Wright, and James Baldwin, the Harlemite Ta-Nehisi Coates elected to publish a French translation of his recent book *We Were Eight Years in Power: An American Tragedy* (2017) with Présence Africaine.[2]

That the intellectual connection between African American writers and Africans immigrating by way of Paris continues is illustrated by the case of Ta-Nehisi Coates, who lived in Paris for one year (2015–2016). Coates is an African American journalist and writer whose works are centered mostly on contemporary American politics in the United States; he is currently one of the prominent voices on race in politics and culture. In a short chapter titled "Like a French Person," added to the 2018 revision of *We Were Eight Years in Power*, Coates relates his experience learning French at Middlebury College in a six-week summer program in 2014. Learning the French language allowed Coates access to a worldview different from the Anglo-Saxon perspective of his native English. Beyond any linguistic and cultural differences, Coates's intellectual evolution, as he journeyed from Black nationalism to humanism, corroborates how a shared humanity enables us to relate to different cultural conditions and experiences. "Like a French Person" is a clear message articulating the keen relevance of the condition of African Americans depicted in his book to that of Blacks in France and from French former colonies. Coates moves from a Black-nationalist discourse to a humanist one by situating the experience of African Americans within the larger context of oppression and power dynamics.

The premise of Coates's book resonates beyond the particular context of Blacks in America to various other social groups marginalized by those with power and influence. Coates's year in France was spent among various minority groups—such as Arabs, Blacks, and Romas—who live in the *ban-lieues,* housing projects that are comparable to those in US inner cities for African Americans. Francophone Black African immigrants constantly face different forms of discrimination in their efforts to integrate into French society. Coates's humanism is also applicable to advocacy for the rights of minorities such as LGBTQI+, and Indigenous people fighting to hold onto their lands and ways of life. His writings address the human condition, much in the same vein as the work of James Baldwin.

Coates's work offers ethnic and racial minorities in France, including African immigrants, ways to rethink and strategize about their own situation and lived experiences. Black and Arab identities may not be considered as separate and distinct ethnic categories in France because these populations are racialized in parallel ways—which in itself contradicts the official discourse around race. Constructions of French identity and nationality exclude the idea of race, which is based on the "colorblind" ideal of France's Enlightenment-inspired universalism. It is as if multiculturalism were incompatible with the very ideal of a republic. The national narrative should be more diverse and inclusive than it has been up until now because France's sense of its own universalism leaves little room to include race and ethnicity as parameters: In short, there are no Arabs, Blacks, or hyphenated identities, only French citizens. The mention of race is absent from the French constitution, and the collection and dissemination of racial and ethnic statistics is prohibited by Law No. 78–17 of January 6, 1978. Article 8.1 of the law stipulates, "The collection and processing of personal data that reveals, directly or indirectly, the racial and ethnic origins, the political, philosophical, religious opinions or trade union affiliation of persons, or which concern their health or sexual life, is prohibited."[3] The law thus makes it extremely difficult to collect data and document practices as either a means to effectively contribute to public debates on discrimination or as an instrument of public policy.

In this context, how should racial issues be addressed in France? What resources are available to the Afro-French to bring their experiences into the public discourse and to defend their interests? These are some of the challenges faced by racial and ethnic minorities in France, and possibly in other European countries as well. This idea of equality in French citizenship—and by extension its projection of universalism—seems more aspirational than reflective of minorities' quotidian life experiences and socio-institutional realities and practices in the country. In response, a new generation of Black French scholars and activists—mostly children of immigrants from French former colonies—is fighting for policy change and for race and ethnicity to enter the public discourse. Some of those voices include the scholar Maboula Soumahoro, the journalist and activist Rokhaya Diallo, the historian Pap Ndiaye, and activist Assa Traoré.[4] Coates, as a Black writer addressing discrimination and racism from the perspective of lived experiences, reminds the African reader of the critical race theorist Frantz Fanon, whose anticolonial experience in the Algerian War shaped his writings, including *Black Skin, White Masks* (1952) and *The Wretched of the Earth* (1963). Like Fanon's works, the writings of Coates have found resonance beyond the sociohistorical context of the overt subject matter and its immediate intended audience. Racism and power structures of domination are laid bare by both writers' acute sense of observation and analysis of history and social interactions.

Harlem-Based Academics: Diouf, Diagne, Diawara

Since the mid-1990s and early 2000s three notable professors' academic activities have provided an intellectual presence in Harlem that gives shape and resonance to the increasing presence of African immigrant communities: Mamadou Diouf, Souleymane Bachir Diagne, and Manthia Diawara. Trained in the French tradition of higher education, these three major figures of the African intelligentsia could be considered public intellectuals working at the intersection of scholarship and public life. France features prominently in the migratory trajectory of these intellectuals, as was the case with many francophone African students in the 1960s and 1970s, whereas today young African students and economic migrants alike travel directly to the United States from their home countries, as France has become a less attractive final destination or transit point for the "universalist" reasons suggested above.

Indeed, there is some resistance to the development of ethnic and postcolonial studies in French universities. An online article by Amandine Hirou, published on the website of the French weekly news magazine *L'Express* on December 24, 2019, raises alarm over the impending danger of postcolonial studies invading French universities and research centers (CNRS and CNAM). The vitriolic article, "Les obsédés de la race noyautent le CNRS" (The race-obsessed takeover of CNRS), argues that the presence of postcolonial studies is a threat to the universalist values of the French republic, which could not be any further from the truth. In response to the article, Alain Mabanckou and Dominic Thomas, scholars at the University of California Los Angeles, published an article in *L'Express* on January 16, 2020, "Pourquoi a-t-on si peur des études postcoloniales en France?" (Why such fear of postcolonial studies in France?). They not only interrogate the fear that postcolonial studies raise in France but also underline how French theorists and scholars who have been trained in France, then recruited by American universities, have historically contributed to the development of postcolonial studies in the United States. Attempts at discrediting postcolonial studies are symptomatic of France's unwillingness to critically address its colonial past, and also its reluctance to open conversation between the ethnic and racial banlieue-dwellers, who came from former colonies or territories, and the majority white population. It is quite telling of the situation how there are attempts to close off research and higher-learning spaces to the development of certain disciplines. Though the United States may not have fully addressed its own past of slavery and colonialism, it has allowed public discourse on and academic investigations into the continuing legacies of this systemic oppression.

Let us consider these French-educated, Harlem-based African scholars in turn. Mamadou Diouf (b. 1952) is a scholar of African history trained in France, who taught at Cheikh Anta Diop University and also worked for the Council for the Development of Social Science Research in Africa, both located in Dakar, Senegal. Before joining the faculty at Columbia University, where he is the Leitner Family Professor of African Studies, Diouf taught at the University of Michigan from 1999 to 2007. He was the director of the Institute of African Studies at Columbia University from 2008 to 2017, before his compatriot Diagne took over in 2018. As its website description notes, the Institute of African Studies is an Africa-centered forum and resource center that fosters the study of Africa through lecture series, seminars, programs, and workshops. Columbia University's close proximity to Harlem, with Little Senegal just blocks away, positions it perfectly for such studies. Diouf, along with the Cameroonian historian Achille Mbembe, and the Senegalese economist and writer Felwine Sarr at Duke University, are currently the leading voices on the necessity to critically read the continent's history, culture, relation to the world, and knowledge production from an African perspective.

Souleymane Bachir Diagne (b. 1955) is arguably one of the best African philosophers today within or outside Africa; his work on universalism through the lens of language translation is particularly relevant in the present-day context of the rise of ethno-nationalist and extremist forces in the world. His scholarly productions[5] on philosophy in Islam are equally celebrated. Diagne is also the director of Columbia University's Institute of African Studies, which organizes Africa-related events (film series, talks by invited scholars, and seminars). Souleymane Bachir Diagne has a similar academic trajectory to that of Mamadou Diouf, moving from France, to Senegal, to the United States. He joined Columbia University from Northwestern University.

Manthia Diawara[6] (b. 1953) is a cultural theorist and filmmaker at New York University. Originally from Mali, he came from France to the United States to study in the late 1970s. He has previously taught at the University of California at Santa Barbara and the University of Pennsylvania. His scholarship in the field of African cinema—especially his analysis of forms, aesthetics, and politics in African cinematic productions—has opened more lines of inquiry for academics and has helped popularize African cinema studies. The Institute of African American Affairs (IAAA) at New York University has been a particular bridge between Africa and its diaspora under the leadership of professor Manthia Diawara. The IAAA has developed several initiatives to bring Africans, African Americans, and Caribbeans/West Indians into conversation through cultural productions and events. Under Diawara's twenty-six-year directorship (1992–2018), IAAA became the center of Black culture in New York City, with a residency program for scholars and artists that has featured some of the brightest minds of the Black cultural-intellectual world: Wole Soyinka, Angela Davis, Walter E. Mosley, Salif Keita, Danny Glover, Jayne Cortez, Hugh Masekela, Spike Lee, Randy Weston, and Rokia Traoré. Public events sponsored by scholars and artists in residence can be likened to those of an intellectual or literary salon, where bright minds and the general public discuss contemporary issues relating to Africa and its diaspora. The magazine *Black Renaissance Noire*, a publication of IAAA, showcases Black poetry, essays, photography, art, and fiction. The institute's Return to the Source film series has brought Black filmmakers from Africa, Europe, and the Caribbean to New York to screen and discuss their works.[7]

Rashidah Ismaili AbuBakr (b. 1940) is an educator and poet residing in Harlem where she has lived since the 1980s after moving from Lower Manhattan. She has taught at several American universities and is the author of many publications.[8] She runs the literary Salon d'Afrique from her Harlem apartment, with African and the diasporic invited guests. In addition, she regularly hosts celebrations such as Kwanzaa that bring together Africans and African Americans. Her hosting of Kwanzaa has been featured in the *New York Times*. Rashidah Ismaili AbuBakr is a central figure in the African community's social life, and she is also highly regarded as someone who is very knowledgeable about the history of the African presence in Harlem. Born in Dahomey (present-day Benin) to an Ashanti mother and a Nigerian father, AbuBakr migrated to New York City in 1957.

The United States has been a relatively fertile ground where African intellectuals and artists can thrive compared with other Western countries. For Diawara, Diagne, Diouf, and Mbembe, working from the United States has offered them a platform and context where their ideas are allowed to emerge in the public discourse and be well received internationally. The reason for this is that the historical presence of Blackness and African Americans in the public and political spheres in the United States is the strongest and most visible of that of any other developed country in the world. African Americans have had to fight relentlessly against systemic racism and discrimination in order to allow their voices to be heard in the public sphere. One can hardly think of Africa in the New York City academic scene today without noting Diouf, Diagne, and Diawara, especially with respect to their ability to carry the discourse on Africa from university campuses to local communities. Under their leadership, African scholarship has been opened to public awareness and discussion in forums that might not otherwise have occurred. These educators are facilitators, producers, and disseminators of knowledge about Africa to the African diaspora as well as to the general public. Mbembe has asserted that African diasporic voices are the artistic and intellectual avant-garde of Africa.[9] They not only bring visibility and attention to Africa in the current climate of information overload, they also—most significantly—propose new visions by which to rethink the continent. According to Mbembe, the development of Africana and African American studies at American universities and colleges—as contrasted with France, for instance—is a result of the visible presence of African Americans in the public discourse.

Burkinabe Entrepreneur: Kader Ouedraogo

Through much of the twentieth century, relations between Africans and African Americans were particularly centered on the intellectual and artistic encounters and exchanges around the liberation movement. As these exchanges and encounters continue today in different configurations, the economic presence and influence of Africans are increasingly visible in neighborhoods and communities. This is embodied in young African entrepreneurs who have been shaping economic and cultural transformations since the start of the new millennium. Harlem is a neighborhood where such a cultural-economic presence is part of the changing landscape. No better way to convey African economic migrants moving in and positively transforming the neighborhood than to profile a successful African entrepreneur in show business.

Figure 17. Front of Shrine Live Music Venue. 2019. Courtesy of Boukary Sawadogo and David A. Sawadogo.

Kader Ouedraogo is undoubtedly the most successful Burkinabe self-made businessman in Harlem. He is in show business. He owns and operates four entertainment venues in Harlem, including the Shrine Live Music Venue, Yatenga-French Bistro, and Ouaga-Harlem Sports Bar, all located on Adam Clayton Powell Jr. Boulevard between 133rd and 134th Streets. Silvana, the café-bar and live music venue, is located on 116th Street and Frederick Douglass Boulevard. Nothing could have predicted that this native of the northern city of Ouahigouya, in Burkina Faso, would wind up thousands of miles away in Harlem. The story of Kader Ouedraogo may reflect the larger narrative of the American dream, yet it remains singular in how the self-described hustler moves across spaces and cultures. The sixth-grade dropout turned shoeshine boy left his hometown for the capital city of Ouagadougou in search of better economic opportunities. Hustling in the big city, for Ouedraogo, came in the form of making and selling musical instruments (balafon and djembe), working as a crew member of mobile cinema, and as a movie actor and show business promoter. As a member of the local rap group of Wu-Tang Clan, Kader Ouedraogo organized live-music concerts and *matinées* in the French Cultural Center, Centre National des Arts du Spectacle et de L'Audiovisuel (CENASA), and in then-popular nightclubs Jimmy's and New Jack in Ouagadougou. This was in the 1990s and very early 2000s, as youth started creating and promoting their rap music in West African countries like Senegal, Guinea,

Burkina Faso, and Côte d'Ivoire. In general, youth were active on the scene of rap music out of passion, not seeking to build the business side of it. When the Burkinabe government made it illegal for tobacco companies to sponsor music and sporting events, it became challenging to make a living as a concert show business or cultural promoter. Ouedraogo took this as a cue that it was time to discover something else, and the opportunity to relocate to the United States came through an American photographer whom Ouedraogo had known in Ouagadougou in the circles of contemporary dance. Ouedraogo first arrived in New York in 2002 and after two years of traveling back and forth between the United States and Burkina Faso he decided to settle in the city in 2004.

His hustler's attitude to life was helpful living in New York City. He vividly remembers the contrast: "I was hustling in Ouagadougou but never making enough money, but this was quite the opposite in New York. I was so happy when I got my first weekly pay of $300 as a dishwasher. I never made that much money in a single week back home." Ouedraogo then moved on to another job as a doorman at Piano, a bar-restaurant and live-music venue on the Lower East Side. This was a dream job because he was able to reconnect with show business; the experience of working at Piano was a great inspiration to him, as Ouedraogo himself underscores, and he continues to maintain a relationship with Piano. Between the night shifts at Piano and his days off, Ouedraogo was selling pirated CDs in front of the Apollo Theater in Harlem. Because of the cold weather and police crackdowns, he says, he had to cease this activity. He then created the Burkinabe Moving Company to work during the daytime, supplementing his evening job at Piano. As one of his managers at Piano moved out of his apartment in Harlem, Ouedraogo was able to occupy that apartment on 113th Street between 7th and 8th Avenues. Soon Harlem was not only his residential neighborhood but also the center of his professional activities in entertainment. He launched the Mafrica World Music Festival in 2006, which continues to be held annually on the first Sunday of June at Marcus Garvey Park. The following year he opened Shrine Live Music Venue with the money he had saved over the years. From jazz, rock, blues, Latino, and reggae to African music, Shrine offers a wide range of programming every night. Shrine is well known in New York City's live-music scene. Ouedraogo expanded his business from Shrine to include three more ventures, named above.

Kader Ouedraogo might be regarded to some extent as the Burkinabe Clarence Avant of Harlem. Clarence Avant, known as "the Black godfather" (Netflix released a documentary on his life by that title in 2019) was

Figure 18. Performance stage in the Shrine. 2021. Courtesy of Boukary Sawadogo and Mira Steinzor.

an extremely influential and well-connected figure in the entertainment business of music and movies. Based in Los Angeles for several decades, from the 1960s onward, Avant was a powerful agent, producer, negotiator, a behind-the-scenes mover and shaker also very involved in the African American community. The success of Kader Ouedraogo extends the traditional association of hustling with New York City and African Americans to include Black immigrants. This is quite powerful in terms of image and narrative, specifically African immigrants as economic and cultural influencers in the Black mecca of Harlem. Three influential figures have shaped Ouedraogo in his core principles of self-reliance and grit. The first is Fela Kuti, his musical idol and source of spiritual inspiration; a large poster of Fela greets patrons upon entering the premises, and he named his son Fela Kuti Ouedraogo for his deep appreciation of the Nigerian Afro-beat star. As for the other two, the ideas of self-reliance advocated by Thomas Sankara and Malcolm X provide the ferment behind his entrepreneurial endeavors.

8

⸬

Searching for Africa
in the Diaspora

What does a contemporary African—like me—feel when he sees an African American? First all, I feel my humanity finally accepted by the world. Whenever I see a black person from the diaspora, I see Toni Cade Bambara, I see Kamau Brathwaite, I see James Baldwin, I see Bob Marley, I see James Brown, I see C. L. R. James, I see Muhammad Ali, I see Paule Marshall, I see Malcolm X, I see Edwidge Danticat, I see Walter Mosley, I see Maryse Condé, I see myself.
—Manthia Diawara, *In Search of Africa* (1998)

BECAUSE THE RECURRENT pattern has been for the Black diaspora in the Americas to go to Africa in search of their roots, it may sound counterintuitive at first, or even controversial, to assert that the search to locate cultural identities of Africa could effectively be undertaken in the diaspora rather than on the continent—or to propose that Black consciousness in the diaspora can help sub-Saharan Africa (re)discover its own Black pride. To be sure this poses challenges, given that Africa and its diaspora, separated by the four centuries of slavery, have not approached and problematized identity in similar ways. The erasure of memory and history that descendants of slaves have endured made their sense of identity as Black people much more acute than it is for people in Africa. Blackness in Africa has not historically been a subject of public discourse or of systemic policies, except for apartheid segregation in South Africa and, to a lesser degree, issues of colorism and caste systems that still exist in certain countries. This stands in contrast to systemic racial subjugation and white supremacy being central issues at the birth of the United States and throughout its historical development, as extensively treated in the writings of W. E. B. Du Bois, James Baldwin, and Ta-Nehisi Coates. In the Black Atlantic world, a number of Black pride and consciousness movements have been created, including the pan-Africanism movement born in the diaspora that had its first conference in London at the end of the nineteenth century, the Black Power movement and the Black Panther Party in the US during the 1960s, the British Black Arts movement in the 1980s, and very recently the Black Lives Matter movement. The Black diaspora has founded these movements to resist systemic discrimination by affirming Blackness as a collective and differentiated experience worldwide.

Searching for Africa in the Diaspora

Increasingly, Africa has been looking into the diaspora as into a mirror that is able to reflect back what it is. The encounter with the diaspora allows Africans a form of self-discovery. Individual trajectories of Africans who developed consciousness of Blackness during their stay in the United States provide some evidence of their own self-discovery as a Black man or woman. In this respect, the musical and ideological development of the Nigerian Afrobeat music icon Fela Anikulapo Kuti is telling. Fela's discovery of the potential militant dimensions of his Blackness or Africanness during his 1969 performance tour of Los Angeles was to profoundly change his style of music and his ideological leanings. Contextually, this happened for Fela at the height of the civil rights movement and also in physical proximity to the birthplace of the Black Panther Party in Oakland, California. His encounter with Sandra Iszadore, as described by Benson Idonije and Teju Olaniyan, opened a new world for Fela.[1] The two first met at an event of a local chapter of the National Association for the Advancement of Colored People (NAACP) in Los Angeles. She would later introduce him to books on African history and urge him to play African music. Through her influence, Fela shifted from highlife jazz to Afrobeat, which is a fusion of traditional African rhythm, highlife, rock, jazz, and funk. For Fela, music is a weapon for social-political change and is not meant for mere entertainment. His live music venue Africa Shrine in Lagos was the place where people could come to listen and partake in his songs denouncing corruption and military regimes. Fela, "the Black President," as he was also known, saw it as his mission to raise consciousness and educate his people. As indicative of the development of Fela's own conscious awareness as African are the changes of the band's names over time from Fela Ransome-Kuti Quintet, to Koola Lobitos, to Africa 70, to Egypt 80. In Africa and the diaspora, images of Fela remain ingrained in the public conscience like those of global Black stars Bob Marley and Michael Jackson. Iconic images of Fela are abundant in the press, on T-shirts, and in street graffiti: Fela is celebrated as the rebel, stage performer full of stamina, musical genius, and man of the people. The on-stage images often show his bare torso, African face paint, clenched fists raised in the air, or hands firmly holding a saxophone.

Unlike Fela, the author of this book is not a celebrity, so the self-discovery of his Blackness in the diaspora is like that of the anonymous hundreds of thousands of African immigrants in the United States. Their Blackness was revealed to themselves, sometimes in shocking ways, only upon coming to the United States from their home countries, where racialized discourse is often absent from the public sphere. Most recently arrived immigrants in the United States would agree that they are compelled to self-identify in ways that they might not otherwise have done in their country of birth. In certain instances, one's country of origin becomes less significant as an identity marker as racial and ethnic affiliations supersede it in one's everyday experience. This situation forces the immigrant to self-identify in terms of national origin, race, and ethnicity—such as Black, Asian, African, Hindu, or Songhai. Conversely, it may also be argued that the immigrant is forced into racial and ethnic categories because of the social environment into which they came. Whether it is considered as self-affiliations or assigned identities, the awareness of racial and ethnic identity becomes more acute than it was before the time of arrival. My own personal journey in the United States has taken me to different parts of the country, from states with a majority white population, Southern states where Jim Crow laws once enforced racial segregation, the cosmopolitan urban center of New York City, and the historically Black mecca of Harlem. This experience has provoked me to constantly readjust and define my own Blackness—a formative journey and experience that has probably all along the way planted the seeds of this book. The journey across the Atlantic that led me to Harlem may be my own personal awakening moment within the larger cultural-historical question of the relation immigrants have to their adoptive neighborhood, their ties as newcomers to a community in which they become fully integrated and accepted members. Local stories and histories reflect and constitute the multiple journeys of community members, some of those members coming from afar.

The Search for Africa Portrayed in Film

The search for Africa in the diaspora is the subject of several films by African directors. These screen media productions often take the viewer on the journey of protagonists leaving Africa to trace descendants of former slaves in the Americas. Often, the quest takes the form of a spiritual journey of self-discovery for the protagonist, and an encounter with Africa for the diaspora. The most illuminating examples of such films for my purposes here are *Black Goddess or A Deusa Negra* (1978) by the Nigerian director Ola Balogun, *Little Senegal* (2001) by the Franco-Algerian director Rachid Bouchareb (treated in Chapter 6), and *Bigger Than Africa* (2018) by the Nigerian filmmaker Toyin Ibrahim Adekeye.[2] These three films examine how West African culture has survived the slave trade and the plantations to date in Brazil, Cuba, Haiti, the United States, and the Caribbean. The narrative appears to suggest—though to a lesser degree in *Little Senegal*—that African culture, religions, and spirituality are best preserved in the diaspora. Maybe Africans should look to the diaspora to learn more about their own history and culture. Clearly this is not a quest for purity or a bid to return to an imagined or dreamed Africa that may have never actually existed. Rather, the key point is that in the diaspora the hybridization of cultures or encounters of several cultures has given birth to multiple identities. In this respect the PBS series *Black in Latin America* (2011), directed by the Harvard University professor Henry Louis Gates Jr., underlines the creation of rich cultures under the influence of people of African descent in countries such as Mexico, Peru, Brazil, Cuba, Haiti, and the Dominican Republic.

In a similar vein, Balogun's film, *Black Goddess,* tells the story of the Nigerian Babatunde, who, in response to his father's deathbed request, travels to Brazil to locate and bring back the descendants of his great-grandfather; although the latter returned to Nigeria after the abolition of slavery in Brazil, his offspring remained in the New World. Babatunde's spiritual journey leads him to Rio de Janeiro and Bahia in search of the contemporary descendants of his family. The Yemoja sculpture of Yoruba divinity left to the family by the great-grandfather serves as the guide to the protagonist's journey as well as a narrative device of the film. And as we saw in Chapter 6, Bouchareb's *Little Senegal* is about a museum worker who leaves Goree Island in Senegal to locate living descendants of his family who were sold as slaves centuries ago. The symbolic and spiritual quest of identity brought the protagonist Alioune into contact with the African

American community in Harlem. In both films the family's history and memory, spiritual journey, and cultural transmission and connectedness are explored in the diaspora by African characters moving through spatial and temporal boundaries.

Beyond the intrinsic interest in African ancestry that compels such a look into the past, most significantly this encounter between Africa and the diaspora has a prospective dimension to it—offering an opportunity to (re)imagine the future of the continent around culture. Already, transformations in contemporary West African culture demonstrate a variety of influences, including the culture of the diaspora, which Manthia Diawara, an African film and literature scholar at New York University, underlines in his semi-memoir *In Search of Africa* (1998). Diawara shares his reflections on African culture as the continent struggles to define itself in the postcolonial era. In the twenty-first century, internationalization—circulation of information and images in borderless spaces—has redefined the pathways of cultural production and distribution, and Africa exhibits that cultural fusion today through a very digitally connected youthful population that is in constant dialogue with the rest of the world.

The State of the African Diaspora

The institutional mapping of the regions that make up the African Union (AU) also demonstrates how the African continent views its diaspora. The continental organization of the African Union divides Africa into five regions: the four geographical regions of North, South, East, and West Africa, plus a fifth virtual region that covers the diaspora, all people of African ancestry. The addition of this fifth region underlines how the continent projects itself beyond its physical boundaries to include African-descended populations around the world. In doing this, the African Union is renewing the pan-Africanist vision of its founders when they first created the Organization of African Unity, founded in 1963. The current African Union, which is modeled on the European Union, was founded in 2002 to replace the Organization of African Unity. While the AU strives to build unity and solidarity between the continent and Africa, it is also working to achieve economic integration through the African Continental Free Trade Agreement, which went into effect on May 30, 2019. One of the objectives of the trade agreement is to help reverse the global northward movement of African migrants and raw materials in favor of more intra-African exchanges.

At the African Union's thirty-first summit in Mauritania in July 2018 the decision was made to officially launch the State of the African Diaspora, thus enacting an intention that is already articulated in the constitution of the African Union. The idea is to build Africa and the diaspora by strengthening their mutual ties. The State of the African diaspora is expected to gather the 350,000,000 people of African descent and African migrants around the world into a borderless state. The idea of a borderless state is a conceptual challenge to the traditional nation-state, whose classical definition and status as an actor in international relations are built on a territory with physical borders. Most of the institutions of the State of the African diaspora are still under construction; as of the writing of this book, Louis-Georges Tin was nominated the prime minister to lead a gender-parity government of ten men and ten women selected from the different world regions. Georges-Louis Tin is a French academic, activist, and a spokesperson for the Representative Council of Black Associations (CRAN) in France. One parliament in each region of the world is also expected to be created under the leadership of the prime minister. Full details are yet to emerge about sustainable funding mechanisms for the State of the African Diaspora; such issues as funding and shared sovereignty with countries will need to be sorted out for this pan-Africanist vision to be fully realized.

Among African immigrant communities there is a growing belief that meaningful and lasting changes in the development of the continent will come from its diaspora. This has historically been the case with the creation of the pan-Africanism movement in the nineteenth century and the decolonization movement in the mid-twentieth century, whose early leaders were inspired by their encounters with African American writers, artists, and activists. This belief in the capacity of the diaspora—second- or third-generation immigrants—to foster socioeconomic and political changes in Africa rests on the diaspora as a positive disruptive force in changing the status quo, traditions, and outmoded old formulas. As young people of the diaspora are less constrained by traditions and more susceptible to break codes than are their parents' generation, born and raised on the continent, innovation and risk-taking will push the boundaries of the possible. Being between two or more cultures, countries, or continents need not be regarded as a liability but far rather as an asset in bringing much-needed sociopolitical and economic reforms to Africa. This is a site of the creative energies of the in-between for the immigrant. In writing this book, for example, I find myself in a position of duality working to explain relationships between African immigrants and African Americans in Harlem, or garnering insights as an "insider" that African community members in Harlem might not readily expose to an outsider.

As Paul Stoller argues in *The Power of the Between: An Anthropological Odyssey* (2009), this is a liminal space where the migrant seems not to belong—neither in the adopted place of residence nor in the place of origin. This is not a space of dispersed energies, however, but one in which power is accessed and synergies are created. The liminal is "a space of enormous growth, a space of power and creativity."[3] For instance, the creation of the Presidential Council for Africa (*Conseil présidentiel pour l'Afrique*) by French President Emmanuel Macron in 2017 is meant to use the African diaspora in France as the go-between to facilitate and deepen ties between France and Africa. The Presidential Council for Africa, a consultative body consisting of selected members of the African diaspora, was actively involved in the preparation and organization of Africa2020 Season[4] in France. Critics of the Presidential Council on Africa regard it as just another neocolonial instrument for the defense of France's strategic and economic interests, but regardless of the motives of the French government, the mere creation of the council substantiates the potential role of the diaspora as a rising changemaker in Africa. Unlike their parents, who came to the United States often with the single goal of making enough money to, say, build a big house in the home country or manifest socioeconomic success, these later generations show more willingness to get involved in Africa for causes beyond their self-interested goals. This is the case, for instance, for the R&B music icon Akon, who works to bring electricity to African countries through his Lighting Africa project. Similarly, his compatriot Thione Niang, who served in several leadership roles of the Young Democrats of America, is now very active on the continent as a social entrepreneur to empower youth for change. It can be argued that some of these talented leaders of the diaspora could have presidential destinies in Africa, and maybe even as the next Black president of the United States. They are highly educated political leaders with a willingness to get involved in the community—in the US and in Africa—in service of the public good.

Lastly, it should be pointed out that African immigrant diasporas have started returning to the continent to invest, settle, and live there. The number of these returnees, repats, newcomers—or *bengiss*, as they are referred to in certain African countries—is today comparatively low compared with those seeking to emigrate to the West against all perils. The migration of Africa's young able bodies and bright minds to the West will continue for maybe another generation, after which we will start noticing African immigrants returning to the continent en masse. This will be similar to the kind of return-migration patterns observable today in the case of Chinese and

Indian professionals and intellectuals, now moving back to their countries after generations of immigrants coming to North America. The phenomenon is commonly known as "reverse brain drain"—which is tantamount to some "brain gain" for those countries in question. This return-to-Africa movement is steadily growing. Though no official statistics are available to measure its magnitude, this trend has been emerging since the 2010s as African immigrants resettle in their home countries. This trend is based on individual choices, but it is also driven by government-sponsored programs to bring their countries' talent and professional expertise back to strategic economic sectors. For several years now, African countries such as Rwanda and Côte d'Ivoire have incentivized the return of its bright minds and highly trained professionals residing in the West. In addition, programs of paid voluntary return to Africa developed by countries such as France in the past—though mostly unsuccessful—have somewhat contributed to West African migrants returning home.

Another trend worth noting concerns African American settlement in Africa. Though there are limited published data to show the scope and evolution of the movement over time, it has certainly gained increased visibility through individual stories shared on social media and YouTube, and by highly publicized visits to the continent by African American cultural and sports icons. Several factors have made the move to Africa an appealing option to consider, including the desire for a communal life where Blackness is not a liability, and to connect with the motherland and contribute one's skills to its development where they might be the most impactful. The Year of Return, initiated by Ghana in 2019, has seen thousands of African Americans visit the continent. These trips, the Ghanaian authorities hope, will yield sustained business opportunities and settlements in the country.[5] Ghana has a constitutional mechanism, "the right of abode," which facilitates the settlement of African Americans in the country. In some cases, individual decisions on the part of African Americans to settle on the continent is made after a trip to an African country or from tracing their ancestry through DNA tests. English-speaking countries such as Ghana, Liberia, Kenya, Tanzania, and Nigeria are among the preferred destinations for reasons pertaining to language and historical ties to the United States, while French-speaking countries have yet to attract a comparable volume of visitors.

African Americans moving to their adopted countries may face several challenges: integration into local communities, renunciation of American citizenship and its privileges in terms of protection and ease in international travel, and the possibility of having to return to the United States after a failed attempt to move permanently abroad.[6] These challenges are equally applicable to those who move away from their place of birth and childhood, of course. The size and frequency of the settlement of African Americans in Africa in the coming years may provide insight into the depth of the interactions between Africa and the diaspora—mutual understanding, solidarity, and economic cooperation through collaboration and investment.

Thinking Decoloniality with Diagne and Glissant

The search for Africa should not be bound up with essentialism—harboring a fixed identity or idea—but rather it should hold out the expectation of an evolving continent. We should look for several Africa(s) within and outside its geographical boundaries to better grasp a continent in motion. Africa is in the process of unfolding, revealing a multiplicity to itself and others. This Africa cannot be encapsulated in one single monolithic unit. In the book *In Search of Africa(s): Universalism and Decolonial Thought* (2020), the Senegalese philosopher Souleymane Bachir Diagne and the French anthropologist Jean-Loup Amselle engage in conversations on the universal, pan-Africanism, and cultural and linguistic specificities of Africa. Steeped in decolonial thought, the argument centers on how connecting different people and cultures would ease the fragmentation of the world. The key question here is not concerned with returning to the homeland for recognition, or giving back to the country of origin, experiencing a profound awakening in the diaspora, or forming tight-knit and supportive communities locally. Rather, the ultimate question may be directed to creating a more human, open society that operates beyond differences in race, tribe, national origin, and neighborhood—a vision of society that is only possible in theoretical constructions divorced from reality as we live it. This is an encounter of universalism and humanity as a collective endeavor for which all would commit to work. Such an outcome requires several paradigm shifts, one of which Souleymane Bachir Diagne proposes as the construction of a horizontal universalism. This stands in opposition to a Western-centered vertical universalism, with which the rest of the world is obliged to align.

Here Diagne builds on the work of the French phenomenological philosopher Maurice Merleau-Ponty in his book *Signs* (1964), about how languages can be a vehicle of horizontal or lateral universalism. For Merleau-Ponty the universal is grounded in the understanding that no region of the world is superior or destined to rule the others, but is rather a space where we must all strive toward understanding, embracing difference without hierarchization. In his short essay "From Mauss to Claude Lévi-Strauss," he discusses kinship structures and systems of exchange in the works of French sociologist Marcel Mauss and anthropologist Claude Lévi-Strauss, underlining how a new universal can be birthed—different from the then-prevailing Eurocentric order of the nineteenth and twentieth centuries—by being able to speak other languages. "This provides a second way to the universal: no longer the overarching universal of a strictly objective method, but a sort of lateral universal which we acquire through ethno-logical experience and its incessant testing of the self through the other person and the other person through the self."[7] Merleau-Ponty's treatment of globalization and the universal intersects with the work of French Carib-bean theorist and writer Édouard Glissant, particularly in his well-known book *Poetics of Relation* (1997) on relational belonging, where "relation" is defined as what connects us beyond filiation. One of the laws of this relation is "opacity," meaning to accept what we don't understand about ourselves and others. This can lead to acceptance of difference.

However, it is important to note some conceptual differences between Souleymane Bachir Diagne's proposed construction of horizontal univer-salism with creolization as advocated by Édouard Glissant and his fellow Martinican writer Patrick Chamoiseau. Creolization of the world refers to a transcultural process which is driven by relational exchanges, resulting in an inclusive world. Glissant and Chamoiseau are critical of universalism because of its colonial taint, the historical association with the Western canon (of hierarchies), and the dominance of the systemic neoliberal thought today which is often equated with universal. The operative struc-ture of creolization is based on relation whereas translation is the vehicle to universalism that Diagne proposes. In the ecosystem of relation, humans are considered alongside all the living, so there is no vertical humanism as is also the case with rejection of vertical universalism. There may be con-ceptual differences between Diagne, Glissant, and Chamoiseau but they all pursue the same objective of achieving inclusion and equity across our differences. In matters of exchanges and encounters, a recurring question is often asked about how to accept the other without losing oneself. To this question, creolization theorists such as Édouard Glissant and Patrick Chamoiseau argue that we should accept the opacity in others, which means that conformity should not be a requirement for acceptance. The focus on relation is best rendered in the humanist philosophical concept of Ubuntu, in the Zulu and Xhosa languages (South Africa), which means building community through our shared humanity. As a result, this can lead to acceptance of difference and unified action against transnational challenges, which is of contemporary relevance in the context of anti-immigration rhetoric, ethnonationalism, environmental changes, and racial and social injustice.

For Diagne the universal is brought about through translation, and indeed the concept of translation—between languages, world regions, disciplines and knowledge, and civilizations—is central to his work in general. In the end, the question is how differences and antagonisms may be transcended into a collective humanity. It is also important to note how technological development in media and communication is significantly shaping the universal in its different configurations. Whether it is spreading African culture or deepening connections between Africa and the diaspora or transforming the local into the global to mobilize attention and engagement for political change on the continent, the digital space wields tremendous power despite its limitations.

Thinking between Africa and Its Diaspora

New York City has continually sustained connections to Africa through its Black mecca, Harlem. The history of Black New York, the intellectual and artistic exchanges between Africa and its diaspora, and the latest immigration waves of Africans to the city are all a testament to New York's being a nexus for collaboration and flows of creativity among Black people. As we have seen, this encounter sowed the seeds for African decolonization and liberation movements. From continuing encounters, alliances are formed, creative experiments are conducted, and plans are devised and put in motion for the sociopolitical advancement of Blacks. New York and Harlem have become fertile ground for the African diaspora's self-renewal, a place where Africans can envision their place in the world. The story of African immigrants in Harlem reflects the larger history of immigration to America, where diasporic community building transforms neighborhoods and cities across the country. What I would like the readership of this book to take away is the continued transformation of the socioeconomic fabric of American society through immigration, which has been one of the creative catalysts of the country's development throughout its history. Nowhere is this truer than in New York City, where grit, resilience, and risk-taking can lead to opportunities for social mobility for recent immigrants and economic development for the entire country. Today, the economic, academic, and cultural encounters between Africa and its diaspora in New York hold the potential of ushering in positive transformations for the continent.

Hopefully this potential will be recognized and creatively acted upon as the twenty-first century progresses.

Though I am not asserting that New York City is the foremost center of the Black world today, I am underlining the long-standing history of a place that brings together and fosters the creative energies of Africa and the Black Atlantic. To be sure, around the time of the Harlem Renaissance there existed other urban Black centers of Black culture and economy in different parts of the country from the late nineteenth century through part of the twentieth century. These include the historic African American neighborhood of Sweet Auburn in Atlanta, Georgia; the Bronzeville neighborhood in Chicago, also known as the city's Black Metropolis, which was formed around the 1930s during the Great Migration by sharecroppers from the South; South Central Los Angeles in the 1970s and 1980s; and the Black community on Martha's Vineyard off the coast of Boston facing gentrification in the 1980s.[8] In addition, there was a thriving Black community of thirty-five blocks—known as Black Wall Street—in Tulsa's Greenwood district, Oklahoma. "It is said that in Greenwood, a dollar bill changed hands a dozen times before it ever leaves the district."[9] Black Wall Street was razed to the ground by a white mob on May 31 and June 1, 1921, and 300 African Americans were killed in the racially motivated massacre. A white woman who falsely accused a young Black shoe shiner of sexual assault sparked the destruction of the Black community.

Since the mid-2000s, Atlanta has surpassed New York as the thriving center of Black visual and expressive arts, as movies, TV shows, music, and literature are produced in Atlanta more than in any other major city. The growth and visibility of cultural productions by Black people are undeniably increasing, and Atlanta is culturally and economically at the heart of urban Black America. Demographic shifts are also occurring as a result of more African Americans, African immigrants, and other minority groups such as Hispanics and Asians moving to Atlanta and its metropolitan areas. The literal and figurative meaning of "going up north"—upward social mobility—during the Great Migration may soon change to "go down south" to Atlanta.[10] I am not here advocating for a massive Black migration to the South but merely underlining a growing trend of Black cultural vibrancy in Atlanta, Georgia. However, there are some African American voices who call for a reverse-migration to the South. For instance, the journalist and author Charles M. Blow, in his book *The Devil You Know: A Black Power Manifesto* (2021), makes a Black power proposition for Black Northerners to reverse-migrate to the South to turn it into a Black power center by transforming its conservative electoral politics. But even as such new centers of Black culture emerge in the country, Harlem retains its special place in the history of world politics and culture for the African diaspora.

Yet undeniably the position of Harlem in the creative world of Black culture in the United States is shifting with the increasing gap between the idea of Harlem—expressed through various creative mediums—and the socioeconomic reality of its residents, who are hurting because of gentrification and rising living costs in New York City. This gap between literary-artistic representations of Harlem and the economic condition of its longtime residents has long been the case, even during the Harlem Renaissance movement. To protect its true legacy, we should not fail to recognize that what is enduring about the neighborhood is not its world-wide name recognition or its brightest luminaries per se so much as the entire social fabric created by the residents' pride in their neighborhood, and the interest and enthusiasm that this pride of place still inspires creators and visitors.

The Decline of Black Internationalism

The relations between African immigrants and African Americans in Harlem can enable larger conversations between Africa and the Black Atlantic world. It is worth noting that this can be a sensitive issue to address, with the likely pitfalls of divisiveness due to issues of identity, citizenship, and differences in lived experience. Charges of cultural nationalism, moreover, are not far away. Although Africans are in constant interaction with African Americans through various settings in New York and around the United States, the two communities seem not to be developing a profound knowledge and understanding of each other—not only in the United States but also in continental Africa. As an age cohort that grew up in the 1990s in Africa, I am part of a generation that was exposed to African American culture through music, cinema, sports, and literature. But this exposure was only afforded to city dwellers and remained inaccessible to the majority rural population in most countries. Even among the urban youth, consumption of African American popular culture has not always served to open up the conversation on Blackness, racial injustice, and the relations between Africa and the diaspora. Substantial reflection may have occurred at times in specific educational settings, but with limited impact in the larger society. So then, despite the pervasiveness of Black popular culture—avidly consumed in Africa as it is elsewhere in the world—deep reflection on the Black diaspora is lacking on the continent.

Likewise, substantial critical engagement with Africa by African

Americans visiting the continent seems to be lacking. Visits appear to be limited to historical sites of the transatlantic slave trade and tracing ancestry in Africa based on results from DNA testing, which is ever growing in popularity. Stereotypical media images of Africa portraying the continent as home to misery, civil wars, diseases, or lacking in modern amenities are obstacles to Africa becoming more than just a travel destination but a place with which to identify. Even the designation "African American" is often rejected on the basis of a disconnected linkage to the continent as a result of centuries of slavery and self-identification as American. In some cases, the use of "Black" as an identifier is preferred to African American. The Black internationalism movement has been in relative decline since the late 1980s. I have argued elsewhere that a parallel movement best captures the lack of a deep, meaningful conversation between Africa and the Black diaspora over several decades, specifically in the film industry.[11] A call for deliberate and organic action is certainly needed, with a view toward the formation of strategic coalitions. Differences in historical trajectories and cultural references between Blacks should cement the shared identity-in-difference rather than widening the gap.

As a reminder, the migration of Africans to Harlem fits within the larger context of US immigration reforms since the 1960s: Two immigration laws allowed the formation of African immigrant communities in the United States. First, the end of the quota system on the basis of national origin by the 1965 Hart-Celler Immigration Act coincided historically with most African countries gaining their political independence in the 1960s, paving the way for these citizens of newly sovereign countries to migrate with relative ease. Second, the Immigration Reform and Control Act signed by President Reagan in 1986 granted legal status to millions of people. Since the enactment of the Immigration Act of 1990, tens of thousands of Africans have been granted resident visas every year through the visa lottery system. Since the turn of the twenty-first century, however, a period of retrenchment has set in. Immigration has become such a polarized political issue that a bipartisan compromise in the US Congress increasingly appears distant. Debates on immigration reform are often embroiled with related questions of enforcement, need for a labor force to retain global competitiveness, and fear of profound change of the social fabric. The stalemate on immigration reform was exemplified by President George W. Bush's failure in 2007 to move his own Republican party to advance reform legislation in Congress.

Even stopgap measures such as the Deferred Action for Childhood Arrivals (DACA) under the Obama administration faced constant hurdles in securing renewal during his successor's term. The renewal of work permits and driver's licenses for the "Dreamers"—as the beneficiaries came to be known—remains a major concern. Measures to curb both illegal and legal immigration by Western countries have had a real deterring impact on immigrant candidates around the world, including Africans. The various barriers to both legal pathways into the United States and illegal entry have led to what is often referred to as the "invisible wall."[12] The (im)migrant may be regarded as the new Black of today, suffering institutional discrimination and rejection that is reminiscent of the degrading treatment Black people endured under Jim Crow–era segregation. Racism is a gripping reality in everyday life. When you are Black and (im)migrant, the suffering and burden are twice as heavy to bear. It is an even harder reality when intersectional gender and class factors are also considered.

Throughout the world nowadays, the (im)migrant has come to represent the figure of difference and otherness whose rejection has taken the forms of scapegoating discourse and policies that target groups along racial, ethnic, religious, and national lines. This is the rise of ethnonationalism. Interestingly, this rejection of difference and negation of pluralism is unfolding in increasingly globalized contexts where physical barriers or borders may prove ineffective to contain or regulate migrations and tidal exchanges. African immigrants in Harlem, much like the many ethnic and minority communities in Western countries generally, face an increasingly difficult sociopolitical environment in which to assert their presence. Efforts at affirmation may be stifled or self-censored, precariousness and fear drive voicelessness, and scapegoating underpins anti-immigration rhetoric and measures. Meanwhile, the rising presence of ethnonationalism in several countries further highlights the situation. African immigrant communities in Harlem face challenges stemming from the decline of the momentum of Black internationalism, its lack of visibility today, and the intersecting challenges of gentrification, anti-immigrant sentiment, and ethnonationalism.

Thinking the World from Africa

Black internationalism was at the peak of its influence throughout most of the twentieth century, uniting Black people in their struggle for freedom and against racism and white supremacy. W. E. B. Du Bois referred to this struggle as the global color case. Black causes brought about transatlantic collaborations and intellectual and cultural exchanges in freedom struggles: full-fledged citizenry and civil rights for African Americans, colonial liberation movements in Africa and the Caribbean, and the anti-apartheid fight. Africans were visibly present and active in these struggles. Harlem has played a significant role as a center of Black politics and culture in these freedom struggles and also fostered mutual understanding beyond differences and geographical boundaries. That time of intense international Black activism receded with the end of the Cold War. While "local" and "global" are increasingly interrelated and interwoven, Black internationalism has lost momentum in relative comparison to its heyday. Local(ized) Black causes mostly draw local or national responses—such as the Black Lives Matter movement in the United States against police brutality—though activism over social media may help induce indignation and protest at the global level. This is not to argue for a nostalgic return to the Black internationalism of the past, but rather to underline the ushering in of a new era of activism whose forms and mechanisms of deployment around Black issues are still unfolding. It is the age of influencers—thought leaders, music, cinema, and sports icons have more influence on the population than of political leaders; Beyoncé is one example of melding global stardom with an explicit affirmation of Blackness.

In the absence of a strong Black internationalist movement, how can the voice and presence of Africans in Harlem be helpfully constructive in the broader context of the Black world? On the one hand, African communities have developed a cultural and economic influence in the neighborhood since the 1980s, which should provide a platform to continue to build bridges between communities. On the other hand, transatlantic flows of people—African Americans and second-generation immigrants visiting or settling in Africa—need grassroots-level exchange projects and African government initiatives (like Ghana's Year of Return) to enable connections to be sustained and further deepened. These unmediated and unfiltered in-person physical interactions between Africans and African Americans will help them dispel misconceptions about each other in order to forge better economic and cultural exchanges across the Atlantic.

The new African diaspora also needs to be understood in the context of the Africanization of the world. By projected estimates, Africa's population will account for a quarter of the world's population in 2050, which is just a generation away. This will constitute the largest portion of the world's young population of any nation. The massive northward migratory patterns of Africa's young and able bodies will reverse by the middle of this century. Instead of regarding the youth as a potential liability, we should recognize how their agency will contribute to making Africa the creative laboratory of the world in the coming decades. As a result, there will be an Africanization of the world—Africa as a center of innovation and forward-thinking in (re)imagining solutions to challenges facing the world. Africans will bring innovative transformations to the economy, address environmental questions and sustainable management of resources, and foster artistic creativity and scientific breakthroughs. Africanization of the world should not be viewed solely from the standpoint of Africa's contributions to the future of humanity, but also as a way to (re)conceptualize knowledge production as such. The power of discourse and representation is particularly important in communities that have historically experienced systemic violence or oppression as they attempt to appropriate their own narrative. In this regard, deconstruction of ideas and representations is necessary in the process, as the Congolese scholar and writer Valentin Yves Mudimbe demonstrates in his book *The Invention of Africa* (1988) how the continent was discursively constructed from European texts. This is thinking about the world from Africa as advocated by the Cameroonian historian Achille Mbembe,[13] Senegalese economist and writer Felwine Sarr,[14] and Senegalese historian Mamadou Diouf; and in the footsteps of widely acclaimed thinkers such as Ngũgĩ wa Thiong'o[15] and Wole Soyinka[16] in (re)thinking Africa from African perspectives. Indeed, these are all indications that it may be time to think about the world from Africa and its diaspora. And Harlem will remain a bellwether of these cross-Atlantic transformations.

⋮⋮⋮

Africans in Harlem, Past and Present

THIS LIST OF AFRICANS in Harlem is not exhaustive but is offered to serve as a beginner's guide. Further research is needed to discover the diverse personal and professional journeys of these and other African-born residents in or passing through Harlem.

Azikiwe, Nnamdi (1904–1996)

Nnamdi Azikiwe was part of the generation of African-born students who came to America in the 1920s and 1930s to pursue higher education, very often at Black colleges, and religious or Quaker-affiliated universities. Azikiwe attended Howard University and Lincoln University. The paths of Nnamdi Azikiwe, the first president of Nigeria (1963–1966), and Kwame Nkrumah, the first prime minister (1957–1960) and first president of Ghana (1960–1966), crossed in Harlem (New York) and Lincoln University (Philadelphia). Azikiwe authored the following books: *Ideology for Nigeria: Capitalism, Socialism, or Welfarism?* (1980), *My Odyssey: An Autobiography* (1970), and *Renascent Africa* (1937).

Benga, François "Féral" (1906–1957)

Upon moving to Paris from Dakar in the early 1920s, the career of the Senegalese dancer Féral Benga started in music hall cabarets. He shared the stage with Josephine Baker in the *La folie du jour* show. His expanded artistic repertoire included acting in cinema and posing as a model for visual artists. Benga moved to New York City in the 1930s where he posed for Harlem Renaissance artists such as the painter James Amos Porter and the sculptor Richmond Barthé.

Boghossian, Alexander "Skunder" (1937–2003)

Alexander "Skunder" Boghossian was an Ethiopian painter who lived in Harlem during part of his exile from his country after a military regime came into power. Before moving to the United States in 1970, Boghossian studied and taught art in Europe before returning to his home country of Ethiopia for a short stay. His works can be found in the Museum of Modern Art and the Schomburg Center for Research in Black Culture.

Bonetti, Mahen (1956–)

Mahen Bonnetti, a Sierra Leonean native, is a film programmer, curator, and founder of the New York African Film Festival which was launched in 1993. The New York African Film Festival runs educational programs and film screenings across different parts of New York City, including Harlem, mid-town, Bronx, Brooklyn, and Governors Island. Mahen Bonetti comes from a political family with deep connections with America, where her grandfather moved in the late 1800s followed by her father in the 1930s for college.

Camara, Ladji (1923–2004)

Ladji Camara is a Guinean drummer who launched his international career in the 1950s and 1960s with Les Ballets Africains, a troupe that acted as a cultural and diplomatic arm to then newly independent Guinea under Sékou Touré. In New York City where he lived for decades, he was regarded not as a talented drummer but most importantly as an educator (Ladji Camara African Dance Studio) and a person who immensely contributed to popularizing African drumming.

Dafora, Assadata (1890–1965; birth name Austin Dafora Horton)

Born to a wealthy family in Freetown, Sierra Leone, Assadata Dafora received formal music training in Europe prior to moving to New York in

1929. The success of his Broadway musical *Kykunkor* (The witch woman) in the 1930s was instrumental in introducing African drumming music to New York and the United States. This pioneering work in African dance and performance would later be furthered by Les Ballets Africains and Ladji Camara, both from Guinea. As a renowned and talented dancer, Dafora regularly performed at community events in Harlem.

De Bankolé, Isaach (1957–)

Born in Côte d'Ivoire, West Africa, Isaach de Bankolé's long acting career extends from France to big-budget Hollywood productions: *Chocolat* (1988), *Otomo* (1999), *Casino Royale* (2006), *The Limits of Control* (2009), *Night on Earth* (1991), and *Black Panther* (2018). De Bankolé is one of the few African actors who has been successful in Hollywood. He resides in Harlem.

Diagne, Souleymane Bachir (1955–)

Regarded as one of Africa's greatest philosophers, Senegalese Souleymane Bachir Diagne is a professor of philosophy at Columbia University. Initially trained in the history of logic and mathematics, Diagne's work focuses on African philosophy, identity, and translation, and philosophy in the Islamic world. His work includes *Identity and Beyond: Rethinking Africanity* (2001), *African Art as Philosophy: Senghor, Bergson and the Idea of Negritude* (2011), *The Ink of Scholars: Reflections on Philosophy in Africa* (2013), and *Open to Reason: Muslim Philosophers in Conversation with the Western Tradition* (2018).

Diawara, Manthia (1953–)

Manthia Diawara is a professor and filmmaker at New York University, with a large body of work—both in print and visual—in African cinema, Black diaspora, and culture. A selected list of his books and documentary films includes *An Opera of the World* (2017), *African Film: New Forms of Aesthetics and Politics* (2010), *Edouard Glissant: One World in Relation* (2008), *We Won't Budge: An African Exile in the World* (2003), *In Search of Africa* (1998), *Rouch in Reverse* (1995), *Black American Cinema* (1993), and *African Cinema: Politics and Culture* (1992).

Diouf, Mamadou (1952–)

Senegalese historian Mamadou Diouf is a professor of African Studies and History at Columbia University. He has also served as the director of the Institute of African Studies at Columbia and has published extensively on the subjects of African history and social transformations in Africa. Some of his publications are *Les sciences sociales au Sénégal: Mise à l'épreuve et nouvelles perspectives* (2016), *Tolerance, Democracy, and Sufis in Senegal* (2013), and *Rhythms of the Afro-Atlantic World* (2010).

Ismaili, Rashidah (1940–)

Born in Dahomey (present-day Benin) to an Ashanti mother and a Nigerian father, Rashidah Ismaili migrated to New York City in 1957. She moved to Harlem in the 1980s from the West Village in Lower Manhattan. She was active during the 1970s in the Black arts movement and many pan-African student associations in New York. In Harlem, Ismaili is active in the African and African American communities and has deservedly earned the reputation of being the "collective memory" of the African presence in the neighborhood. AbuBakr is a writer and educator, and also runs the literary "Salon d'Afrique" from her apartment.

Kamara, Kewulay (1953–)

Kewulay Kamara is a poet, storyteller, and performer originally from Sierra Leone. His stories draw on the oral traditions of the *Jali* (griot) from his native country. His documentary *In Search of Finah Misa Kule* (2016) is built around the issue of preserving and handing down oral storytelling traditions.

Kane, Ousmane Oumar (1955–)

Ousmane Oumar Kane has been a professor of contemporary Islamic religion and society at Harvard University since 2012. Prior to joining Harvard, Kane was on the Columbia University faculty in international and public affairs between 2002 and 2012. His most recent publications include *Islamic Scholarship in Africa: New Directions and Global Contexts* (2021), *Beyond Timbuktu: An Intellectual History of Muslim West Africa* (2016), and *The Homeland Is the Arena: Religion, Transnationalism and the Integration of Senegalese Migrants in America* (2011).

Makeba, Zenzile Miriam (1932–2008)

Zenzile Miriam Makeba was an entertainer and anti-apartheid activist. She kept an apartment in the African community that developed into Central Park West Village (around 100th Street) in the 1960s, which was also known as "Little Africa." Some of her most popular songs were "The Retreat Song" (1960), "Malaika" (1965), "The Click Song" (1965), and "Pata Pata" (1989).

Mamdani, Mahmood (1946–)

The Ugandan scholar Mahmood Mamdani is the Herbert Lehman Professor of Government at Columbia University, specializing in African history and politics. His selected publications include *Neither Settler nor Native: The Making and Unmaking of Permanent Minorities* (2020), *Citizen and Subject: Contemporary Africa and the Legacy of Late Colonialism* (2018), and *When Victims Become Killers: Colonialism, Nativism, and the Genocide in Rwanda* (2001).

Mandela, Nelson (1918–2013)

Nelson Mandela, the widely celebrated leader of the anti-apartheid struggle in South Africa and global icon for the fight for justice, visited Harlem on June 21, 1990, giving a speech at the Riverside Church, followed by a rally held in his honor at Yankee Stadium on June 22, 1990, in the Bronx. This New York City visit occurred only a few months after Mandela had been released from prison on February 11, 1990, after serving twenty-seven years. He was jointly awarded the Nobel Peace Prize in 1993. Mandela was sworn in as South Africa's first democratically elected president on May 10, 1994.

Masekela, Hugh (1939–2018)

Hugh Masekela was a South African activist, trumpeter, composer, and singer, who is regarded as the father of South African jazz. His music advocates for political change and to fight apartheid oppression, as exhibited in his songs "Soweto Blues" (1977) and "Bring Him Back Home" (1987). He was married to singer and activist Miriam Makeba from 1964 to 1966. His younger sister, Barbara Masekela, a poet, educator, and activist, has also lived in Harlem.

Ndlovu, Duma (1954–)

Critically acclaimed South African playwright and director, Duma Ndlovu was nominated several times for Tony and Grammy awards. Ndlovu has played a significant role in popularizing South African theater in the United States. In recognition of his great contribution to the arts former US Congressman Charles Rangel, who represented Harlem, declared May 9, 2016, to be Duma Ndlovu and Mbongeni Ngema Day. Mbongeni Ngema is a South African playwright and theatrical director.

Ngũgĩ wa Thiong'o (1938–)

Ngũgĩ wa Thiong'o is a Kenyan writer and academic at the University of California at Irvine. He has authored many fiction and nonfiction books that showcase African cultural richness and contemporary issues, decolonizing knowledge production and dissemination, and advocating for "re-membering" Africa and its diaspora. A selected list of his publications includes *The Perfect Nine: The Epic of Gĩkũyũ and Mũmbi* (2018), *Birth of a Dream Weaver: A Writer's Awakening* (2016), *Re-membering Africa* (2009), *Wizard of the Crow: A Novel* (2006), *Decolonizing the Mind* (1986), *A Grain of Wheat* (1967), *The River Between* (1965), and *Weep Not, Child* (1964).

Nkomo, Aubrey Xolile (1936–2017)

Aubrey Xolile Nkomo joined the African National Congress in 1950 and remained active in anti-apartheid political activities and mobilization. Nkomo held different professional positions in his multifaceted career. He worked for the United Nations, was appointed South African ambassador to Argentina in March 1997, and was a professor of political science at various US universities, including the Massachusetts Institute of Technology. Nkomo was a resident of Harlem.

Nkrumah, Kwame (1909–1972)

Kwame Nkrumah was a pan-Africanist political leader who served as Ghana's first president from 1960 to 1966, and whose connection with Harlem is rarely brought to public attention. During his stay in the United States, Nkrumah made short visits to Harlem that nurtured his pan-Africanist ideals. In Harlem, he sold fish on street corners to support himself while taking advantage of the neighborhood's politically active scene to further promote pan-Africanist ideas, talking about the need for Black people to unite. As a leader of independent Ghana, Nkrumah returned to Harlem in October 1960 to address a rally of several thousand African Americans.

Senghor, Léopold Sédar (1906–2001)

A Senegalese poet, cultural theorist, and founding member of negritude literary movement, Léopold Sédar Senghor was also a politician, founder of the Senegalese Democratic Bloc party, and former president of Senegal. He was the first African member of the Académie française (1983–2001). A selected list of his publications includes *Le dialogue des cultures* (1992), *Éthiopiques* (1956), *On African Socialism* (1964), *Negritude and Humanism* (1964), *Nocturnes* (1948), and *Anthologie de la nouvelle poésie nègre et malgache de langue française* (1948).

Soyinka, Wole (1934–)

The Nigerian playwright and novelist Wole Soyinka received the Nobel Prize in literature in 1986. Soyinka has significantly contributed to post-colonial African literary productions through his works such as *A Dance of the Forests* (1963), *The Interpreters* (1965), *King's Horseman* (1975), *Myth, Literature and the African World* (1975), and *Aké* (1981). Wole Soyinka has also been a critical voice against military rule in Nigeria.

Thiam, Pierre (1965–)

Pierre Thiam is a renowned chef who has contributed to popularizing West African cuisine in New York. He got interested in cooking while working part-time in a New York City restaurant after he came from Senegal in his twenties to study physics and chemistry in the United States. Pierre Thiam owns restaurants in New York and is also professionally active in Senegal and Nigeria. He has published cookbooks, including *The Fonio Cookbook: An Ancient Grain Rediscovered* (2019), *Yolele! Recipes from the Heart of Senegal* (2008), and *Senegal: Modern Senegalese Recipes from the Source to the Bowl* (2015).

Tovalou-Houénou (born Marc Tovalu Quénum), Prince Kojo (1887–1936)

Born to the royal family of the Kingdom of Dahomey (present-day Benin), Prince Kojo studied in France where he later rose to prominence as a critic of French colonialism, condemning abuses of colonial policies in Africa. He created the Ligue Universelle pour la Defense de la Race Noire in 1924, the same year he also met with Marcus Garvey whom he admired for his leadership of the Universal Negro Improvement Association.

African Heads of State and Government Visits to Harlem (1960s–present)

Washington, DC, New York City, and the neighborhood of Harlem are the three most visited places in the United States by African heads of state and government. African high officials regularly travel to Washington, DC, because it is the federal capital and the seat of the World Bank and the International Monetary Fund. As for New York City, world leaders converge on the Big Apple for the annual UN General Assembly meetings in September. On these visits of African heads of state and government, there are regularly scheduled meetings with countrymen. There are meetings with selected members of the immigrant diasporic community at the hotel where high officials are staying, and sometimes officials travel to areas of the city with a sizable enclave of their nationals. Immigrants are increasingly courted for electoral reasons because many African countries now have laws allowing their nationals living abroad to vote in presidential elections. Also, for domestic political reasons, official international trips with meetings with the immigrant diaspora could contribute to more legitimacy to the ruling party or sitting government. In addition, many African leaders have found in Harlem a perfect international platform and a hospitable ground for their revolutionary or nationalist ideas; this was especially true during the Cold War era. Furthermore, the Harlem International Trade Center project saw African heads of state and government visiting Harlem from the 1980s to the early 1990s.

Here is an inexhaustive list of African heads of state and government who have visited Harlem from the 1960s to the present:

Gowon, Yakubu, President of Nigeria (1966–1975)
Lekhanya, Justin Metsing, Prime Minister of Lesotho (1986–1991)

Mahama, John, President (2012–2017) and Vice President (2009–2012) of Ghana

Momoh, Joseph, President of Sierra Leone (1985–1992)

Motlanthe, Kgalema, President (2008–2009) and Deputy President (2009–2014) of South Africa

Mugabe, Robert, President (1987–2017) and Prime Minister (1980–1987) of Zimbabwe

Museveni, Yoweri, President of Uganda (1986–)

Mnangagwa, Emmerson, President of Zimbabwe (2017–)

Mwinyi, Ali Hassan, President of Tanzania (1985–1995)

Nguesso, Danis Sassou, President of the Republic of the Congo (1997–) and (1979–1992)

Pires, Pedro, President (1991–2011) and Prime Minister (1975–1991) of Cape Verde

Rawlings, Jerry, president of Ghana (1981–2001)

Sall, Macky, President of Senegal (2012–)

Sankara, Thomas, President of Burkina Faso (1983–1987)

Traoré, Moussa, President of Mali (1968–1991)

NOTES

Preface

1. Michelle Young, "The Lost Lewisohn Stadium at City College of New York," March 30, 2021, https://untappedcities.com/2021/03/30/lewisohn-stadium-city-college-ny/.

Introduction: Africa in Harlem

1. *The Economist* published two thematic issues on Africa, one titled "Africa: The Hopeless Continent," *The Economist,* May 13, 2000, and the other titled "Hopeful Continent: Africa Rising," *The Economist,* December 3, 2011.

2. Souleymane Bachir Diagne, "Notre présence africaine dans le monde" [Our African presence in the world], talk at École Polytechnique de Thiès, Senegal, 2017.

3. The African Development Bank Group released "The Middle of the Pyramid: Dynamics of the Middle Class in Africa" report on April 20, 2011. https://www.afdb.org/fileadmin/uploads/afdb/Documents/Publications/The%20Middle%20of%20the%20Pyramid_The%20Middle%20of%20the%20Pyramid.pdf. Accessed December 29, 2021.

4. Donald Carter, Preface to *New African Diasporas*, ed. Khalid Koser (London: Routledge, 2003), xvii.

5. Monica Anderson and Gustavo López, "Key Facts about Black Immigrants in the US," Pew Research Center, January 24, 2018. http://www.pewresearch.org/fact-tank/2018/01/24/key-facts-about-black-immigrants-in-the-u-s/. Accessed July 13, 2018.

6. Jie Zong and Jeanne Batalova, "Sub-Saharan African Immigrants in the United States," Migration Policy Institute, 2017, https://www.migrationpolicy.org/article/sub-saharan-african-immigrants-united-states. Accessed July 10, 2018.

7. Monica Anderson, "African Immigrant Population in US Steadily Climbs," Pew Research Center, February 2017. http://www.pewresearch.org/fact-tank/2017/02/14/african-immigrant-population-in-u-s-steadily-climbs/. Accessed July 10, 2018.

8. Sam Roberts, "More Africans Enter US Than in Days of Slavery," *New York Times*, February 1, 2005; https://www.nytimes.com/2005/02/21/nyregion/more-africans-enter-us-than-in-days-of-slavery.html. Accessed November 17, 2018.

9. Tressie McMillan Cottom, *Thick and Other Essays* (New York: New Press, 2019), 134.

10. Tyler Stovall, *Paris Noir: African Americans in the City of Light* (Scotts Valley, CA: CreateSpace Publishing, 2012); William A. Shack, *Harlem in Montmartre: A Paris Jazz Story between the Great Wars* (Berkeley: University of California Press, 2001); Denean T. Sharpley-Whiting, *Bricktop's Paris: African American Women in Paris between the Two World Wars* (Albany: State University of New York Press, 2015); Michel Fabre, *From Harlem to Paris: Black American Writers in France, 1840–1980* (Champaign: University of Illinois Press, 1991); Bennetta Jules-Rosette, *Black Paris: The African Writers' Landscape* (Urbana: University of Illinois Press, 2000.

11. Nathan Riley Carpenter and Benjamin N. Lawrence, *Africans in Exile: Mobility, Law, and Identity* (Bloomington: Indiana University Press 2018).

12. Katie Kilkenny, "Trevor Noah Fires Back at French Ambassador Who Criticized World Cup Joke," July 18, 2018, https://www.hollywoodreporter.com/tv/tv-news/trevor-noah-fires-back-at-french-ambassador-gerard-araud-world-cup-joke-1128275/.

13. Black Atlantic should be understood here and throughout the book as extending beyond the mostly anglophone diasporic spaces to which the term has oftentimes been contained.

14. The edited volume by the Congolese philosopher and author Valentin Y. Mudimbe offers insights into the critical interventions of the journal; see Mudimbe, ed., *The Surreptitious Speech: Présence Africaine and the Politics of Otherness, 1947–1987* (Chicago: University of Chicago Press, 1992).

15. Carter, Preface to *New African Diasporas*, xii.

16. Paul Stoller, "Marketing Afrocentricity: West African Trade Networks in North America," in Koser, *New African Diasporas*, 72.

17. Khalid Koser, "New African Diasporas: An Introduction," in Koser, ed., *New African Diasporas*, 2.

18. Ibid., 9.

19. Nancy Foner, *New Immigrants in New York*, rev. ed. (New York: Columbia University Press, 2001), 2.

20. Michel Foucault, *Archaeology of Knowledge and the Discourse on Language* (New York: Pantheon Books, 1982).

21. Homi K. Bhabha, "Introduction: On Disciplines and Destinations," in *Territories and Trajectories: Cultures in Circulation,* ed. Diana Sorenson (Durham, NC: Duke University Press, 2018), 2.

1. The History of Black Manhattan:
From Enslaved Africans to African Immigrants

1. Marcy S. Sacks documents this in *Before Harlem: The Black Experience in New York City before World War I* (Philadelphia: University of Pennsylvania Press, 2006).

2. Vivek Bald, *Bengali Harlem and the Lost Histories of South Asian America* (Cambridge, MA: Harvard University Press, 2013), and Irma Watkins-Owens, *Blood Relations: Caribbean Immigrants and Harlem Community, 1900–1930* (Bloomington: Indiana University Press, 1996).

3. Eric W. Sanderson, *Mannahatta: A Natural History of New York City* (New York: Abrams, 2013).

4. A more comprehensive treatment of these slave trades, connecting the trans-Saharan slave trade and the transatlantic one, is provided by New York University history professor Michael A. Gomez in *African Dominion: A New History of Empire in Early and Medieval West Africa* (Princeton, NJ: Princeton University Press, 2017). Here I am not arguing for a unified history of Africa and the diaspora but only underlining how transnational issues such as slavery require a more comprehensive narrative.

5. Anne C. Bailey, "They Sold Human Beings Here," *New York Times Magazine*, February 12, 2020, https://www.nytimes.com/interactive/2020/02/12/magazine/1619-project-slave-auction -sites.html.

6. Andrea E. Frohne, *The African Burial Ground in New York City: Memory, Spirituality, and Space* (Syracuse, NY: Syracuse University Press, 2015), 4.

7. James Barron, "Rezoning a Block in Harlem, Respecting an African Burial Ground," *New York Times*, September 27, 2017, https://www.nytimes.com/2017/09/26/nyregion/rezoning -a-block-in-harlem-respecting-an-african-burial-ground.html. Accessed January 9, 2019.

8. Shane White, *Stories of Freedom in Black New York* (Cambridge, MA: Harvard University Press, 2007), 73–74.

9. Sacks, *Before Harlem*, 188.

10. Sacks, *Before Harlem*, 6.

11. For more on the subject, Paul Laurence Dunbar's novel *The Sport of the Gods* (New York: Dodd, Mead, 1902) provides a fictional account of the experiences of Southern migrants in New York City. Additional sources on this subject are Nicholas Lemann, *The Promised Land: The Great Black Migration and How It Changed America* (New York: Knopf, 1991), Isabel Wilkerson, *The Warmth of Other Suns: The Epic Story of America's Great Migration* (New York: Random House, 2011), and Sabina Arora, ed., *The Great Migration and the Harlem Renaissance* (New York: Britannica Educational Publishing and Rosen Educational Services, 2015).

12. Sacks, *Before Harlem*, 9.

13. Kevin McGruder, *Philip Payton: The Father of Black Harlem*, (New York: Columbia University Press, 2021), and *Race and Real Estate: Conflict and Cooperation in Harlem, 1890– 1920* (New York: Columbia University Press, 2015).

14. The four-episode series is a fictional dramatization of the life of Madam C. J. Walker which is based on A'Lelia Bundles's book, *On Her Own Ground: The Life and Times of Madam C. J. Walker* (New York: Scribner, 2001).

15. Raphaël Confiant, *Madam St. Clair, Queen of Harlem* (New Orleans: Diálogos, 2020), 88.

16. Liberia, in West Africa, was founded in 1822 by freed slaves from the United States and declared its independence from the American Colonization Society in 1847.

17. The latest example is the musical *Fela!* (2008) based on the story of the late Nigerian Afrobeat singer Fela Kuti (1938–1997).

18. Earlier, in 1960, Langston Hughes had edited his anthology *An African Treasury: Articles, Essays, Stories, Poems by Black Africans* (New York: Crown Publishers, 1960). Hughes's edited books of 1960 and 1963 greatly contributed to introducing and promoting African writers to the West.

19. The body of the Black woman is particularly celebrated for its natural beauty and as a symbolic representation of Africa in the poem titled "Black Woman" from the collection *Chants d'Ombre* (Paris: Éditions du Seuil, 1945) by Léopold Sédar Senghor.

20. The other books in Dadié's trilogy are *Un nègre à Paris* [An African in Paris] (Paris: Présence africaine, 1959), and *La ville où nul ne meurt* [The city where no one dies] (Paris: Présence africaine, 1968), which is set in Rome.

21. Bernard Binlin Dadié, *One Way* (Urbana: University of Illinois Press, 1994), 81.

2. Black Radical Politics and African Awakening in the Cold War and Beyond

1. Peter Kihss, "Harlem Hails Ghanaian Leader as Returning Hero," *New York Times*, July 28, 1958, https://www.nytimes.com/1958/07/28/archives/harlem-hails-ghanaian-leader-as-returning-hero-10000-acclaim-leader.html. Accessed December 26, 2019.

2. Kevin Gaines, *American Africans in Ghana: Black Expatriates and the Civil Rights Era* (Chapel Hill: University of North Carolina Press, 2006), 10.

3. Tom Shachtman, "Men with a Mission," *Hoover Digest*, no. 1 (2011), https://www.hoover.org/research/men-mission. Accessed June 19, 2019.

4. Gérald Arnaud, "African Dream in Harlem," *Africultures* 44 (2002): 13–17, quote on 16.

5. David Murphy, "The Performance of Pan-Africanism: Staging the African Renaissance at the First World Festival of Negro Arts," 30, and Dominique Malaquais and Cédric Vincent, "PANAFEST: A Festival Complex Revisited," 197–98, both in *The First World Festival of Negro Arts, Dakar 1966: Contexts and Legacies,* ed. David Murphy (Liverpool: Liverpool University Press, 2016).

6. Murphy, "The Performance of Pan-Africanism," 2.

7. Maya Angelou, *The Heart of a Woman* (1981; New York: Random House, 2009), 118.

8. In that area, specifically on 121 West 125th Street, the seventeen-story mixed-use headquarters of the National Urban League broke ground in March 2021 with a targeted completion in late 2023.

9. Further information is available at the Schomburg Center for Research in Black Culture by accessing the collection "Chronicle of visits of third world nation heads of state to the Harlem community."

10. Given the unsustainable debt burden for poor countries, the Heavily Indebted Poor Countries Initiative for debt relief was implemented by the World Bank and the International Monetary Fund in the 2000s, of which many beneficiary countries were in Africa.

11. Ernest Harsch wrote this account in response to my request that he describe how he experienced this historical event, both in his direct personal witness and in the context of the larger ideological tensions during the Cold War.

12. On a related matter, the novel by Lauren Wilkinson, *American Spy* (New York: Penguin Random House, 2019), is worth reading. It is written as a letter from the narrator Marie Mitchell to her young twin sons. Marie Mitchell, a Black female FBI agent, is recruited by the CIA to undermine the Marxist revolutionary leader Thomas Sankara as part of an effort by the US administration to overthrow his regime. Based on the real historical figure of Sankara, the novel builds connections between Africa and the Black diaspora in a Cold War spy thriller.

13. Acts of the Constituent Assembly of the Institute of the Black Peoples (IBP), Ouagadougou, Burkina Faso, April 7–10, 1990, page 9.

14. The Riverside Church generously gave me access to its archives on its South Africa Task Force detailing the church's active participation in the anti-apartheid movement. From my initial contact by e-mail, to phone calls and site visits to consult the archives, the process could not have been smoother.

15. Boycotted US companies doing business in apartheid South Africa included Pepsi, Mobil Oil, Shell, General Motors, Colgate-Palmolive, Bristol-Myers, and Sterling Drug. There were also protests led by grassroots and community organizations against banks doing business with apartheid South Africa, such as Citibank and Chase. In general, back then and today, corporate America only addressed racism and structural inequities meaningfully when it faces strong public pressure.

16. Shared Interest bulletin 2, no. 2 (1996).

17. Some of the organizations that led anti-apartheid campaigns were the Pan-African Liberation Committee (Brookline Village, Massachusetts), the Philadelphia Southern Africa Solidarity Committee, the American Friends Service Committee (Philadelphia, PA), the Washington Office on Africa (Washington, DC), and the Twin Cities Committee for the Liberation of Southern Africa (Minneapolis, MN).

18. Much of this chapter was drawn from findings made during on-site research at the Riverside Church and the Schomburg Center for Research in Black Culture, which have allowed the author of this book access to archives on the Harlem Third World Trade Institute and the South Africa Task Force Initiative.

19. I myself had an encounter with the police the night I arrived in August 2008 on the campus of the University of Louisiana at Lafayette for the start of my doctoral studies. After a long tiring drive from Iowa, I pulled over in front of the Office of International Affairs late at night, planning to stay in my rental car until morning to check into graduate-student housing. As an F-1 visa student, the Office of International Affairs was my reference point on campus. Paying for a hotel room for the night would have been onerous on my meager savings, which barely covered my moving expenses. Feeling the need to stretch my legs after the long drive, I paced back and forth next to the car. Within few minutes two police cars showed up unexpectedly, and I was asked to spread my legs and put my hands on the car. Blinded by flashlights, I was thoroughly searched down to my intimate parts. Only after this complete body search and search of the rental car did the police officers tell me that they were responding to a call concerning suspicious activity.

3. Push and Pull Factors in African Immigration to Harlem

1. Irma Watkins-Owens, *Blood Relations: Caribbean Immigrants and the Harlem Community, 1900–1930* (Bloomington: Indiana University Press, 1996), 1, 165.

2. Vivek Bald, *Bengali Harlem and the Lost Histories of South Asian America* (Cambridge, MA: Harvard University Press, 2013), 6. The early South Asian presence in the Lower East Side and Harlem during the 1910s through 1930s was built around community leaders such as Ibrahim Choudry, Habib Ullah, and other Bengali ex-seamen (161).

3. Zain Abdullah, *Black Mecca: The African Muslims of Harlem* (New York: Oxford University Press, 2010), 11.

4. Sam Roberts, "Influx of African Immigrants Shifting National and New York Demographics," *New York Times*, September 1, 2014.

5. John Mahama Dramani, *My First Coup d'Etat, and Other True Stories from the Lost Decades of Africa* (New York: Bloomsbury, 2012), 2–3.

6. The larger question that remains to be answered in time is whether these decades must be considered lost decades, or if the chaos and struggle have been enough of a learning experience for African leaders to lay a solid foundation for the economic prosperity and political

stability of future generations. The answers to come will be indicative of new patterns of Africans immigrating within and outside the continent. People under twenty-five years old, as of 2021, account for 60 percent of the total African population, and of this group 60 percent are unemployed. Asiamah, Gildfred, Ousmane Djiby Sambou, and Sadhiska Bhoojedhur. "Are African Governments Doing Enough to Help Young People? Here's What Afrobarometer Surveys Reveal," *Washington Post*, January 15, 2021, https://www.washingtonpost.com /politics/2021/01/15/are-african-governments-doing-enough-help-young-people-heres-what -afrobarometer-surveys-reveal/.

7. Chikouna Cissé and Alassane Diabaté, "Quand Abidjan était la plaque tournante de l'immigration clandestine africaine vers l'Europe (1960–1975)," *Afrika Zamani* 27 (2019): 67.

8. Manthia Diawara, *We Won't Budge: An African Exile in the World* (New York: Basic Civitas, 2003), viii.

9. Pascal Blanchard, ed., *La France Noire: Présences et migrations des Afriques, des Amériques et de l'Océan Indien en Afrique* (Paris: La Découverte, 2012), 182.

10. Diawara, *We Won't Budge*, 59.

11. Examples of such violence include the brutal beating of a street vendor named Souleymane Porgo, from Burkina Faso, who fell victim to a gang assault by three African Americans in the Bronx in 2017, and spent several months in a coma. Another example is that of unarmed twenty-three-year-old Amadou Diallo, an immigrant from Guinea, shot forty-one times in his Bronx apartment building by four white New York City police officers on February 4, 1999. He was shot dead as he reached for his wallet to show his identification, which the police officers assumed was a gun. The police had mistaken him for a rape suspect they were looking for. The officers involved in Diallo's death were all later acquitted on second-degree murder charges. Here there is a parallel with the killing by the police of an unarmed West African immigrant from Burkina Faso, Ousmane Zongo, on May 22, 2003. The thirty-five-year-old Burkinabe lived in Harlem and worked repairing African art and furniture in the Chelsea Mini-Storage warehouse on West 27th Street. Zongo was shot and killed by a police officer in a raid on a CD-counterfeiting operation at the warehouse. Zongo was not involved in CD-counterfeiting. A settlement of $3,000,000 to be paid to the Zongo family was reached in 2006 with the city of New York (Michael Brick and Nicholas Confessore, "Suit Is Settled in 2003 Killing of Immigrant," *New York Times*, July 21, 2006. https://www.nytimes.com/2006/07/21 /nyregion/21zongo.html?searchResultPosition=10).

12. The impact of the devaluation at the macro and micro levels was compounded by ramifications of the bankruptcy earlier in the 1980s of the Denver-based Silverado Savings and Loan (SNL) bank. SNL had stakes in banks in Africa, and since these banks were not protected under the Federal Deposit Insurance Corporation (FDIC), savings by Africans were wiped out with no possible way of recovering any portion of it. This led to further pauperism of the most vulnerable social classes.

13. David Styan, "La Nouvelle Vague? Recent Francophone African Settlement in London," in *New African Diasporas*, ed. Khalid Koser (London: Routledge, 2003), 17–18.

14. This topic is addressed by Michel Fabre in *From Harlem to Paris: Black American Writers in France, 1840–1980* (Champaign: University of Illinois Press, 1991), and Tyler Stovall in *Paris Noir: African Americans in the City of Light* (Scotts Valley, CA: CreateSpace, 2012).

15. In his introduction to *La France Noire*, the writer and scholar Alain Mabanckou notes the invisible history of migration to France from sub-Saharan Africa, North Africa, and Indochina (*La France Noire*, ed. Blanchard, 14).

16. According to Alain Mabanckou and Dominic Thomas, the list includes names such as

Jacques Derrida, Gilles Deleuze, Roland Barthes, Emmanuel Levinas, Michel Foucault, and Jean Baudrillard; see Alain Mabanckou and Dominic Thomas, "Pourquoi a-t-on si peur des études postcoloniales en France?" *L'Express*, January 16, 2020.

17. The "Bienvenue en France" / Choose France" program is meant to make France an attractive destination to foreign students.

18. Bald, *Bengali Harlem*, 5.

19. Marilyn Halter and Violet Showers Johnson, *African and American: West Africans in Post–Civil Rights America* (New York: New York University Press, 2014), 16.

20. Naija music stars include P-Square, Wizkid, Davido, Flavor, and Yemi Alade.

21. For a more detailed account of the impact of COVID-19 on African immigrants in Harlem, see Boukary Sawadogo's article "Pandemic in the City: How African Immigrants in New York City's Manhattan Borough Coped with the COVID-19 Pandemic," *Africa is a Country*, https://africasacountry.com/2020/06/pandemic-in-the-city. June 18, 2020.

22. Ousmane Oumar Kane, *The Homeland Is the Arena: Religion, Transnationalism, and the Integration of Senegalese Immigrants in America* (New York: Oxford University Press, 2011), 59, 69.

23. See Bald, *Bengali Harlem*; Zadi Zokou, dir., *Black N Black* (Zadi Zokou Productions, 2019).

24. To contextualize it historically, the current location of Schomburg Center at the intersection of 135th Street and Lenox Avenue (aka Malcolm X Boulevard) was known as the Speakers' Corner where Black speakers addressed crowds and passersby in the 1920s. In contrast to contemporary times of communication on social media and access to mainstream media, the voices of Black people could hardly be heard in mainstream media at the time. Thus, the soapbox served an essential function as a mass communication instrument—and incidentally as a space of public-speaking training and a public forum.

25. Today's human and musical encounters in Harlem between Africans and African Americans may be regarded as part of a larger historical pattern: In the late 1920s in the Southern port city of Marseille, France, the novelist Claude McKay met and befriended Black dockworkers from French West Africa as he was writing *Banjo: A Story without a Plot* (San Diego, CA: Harcourt Brace Jovanovich and Harvest Books, 1929), a novel in which he describes jazz as a profound linkage between Africa and the diaspora.

4. Social Networks, Community Building, and Gentrification

1. "Data release: Remittances to Low- and Middle-Income Countries on Track to Reach $551 Billion in 2019 and $597 Billion by 2021," https://blogs.worldbank.org/peoplemove/data-release-remittances-low-and-middle-income-countries-track-reach-551-billion-2019. Accessed July 21, 2021.

2. Franceinfo Afrique, "La diaspora africaine est devenue la principale source de financement du continent," https://www.francetvinfo.fr/monde/afrique/economie-africaine/la-diaspora-africaine-est-devenue-la-principale-source-de-financement-du-continent_3747375.html. Accessed March 17, 2021.

3. Nadia Nurhussein, "The Hand of Mysticism: Ethiopianist Writing in Pauline Hopkins's *Of One Blood* and the Colored American Magazine," *Callaloo* 33, no. 1 (2010): 279.

4. Nathaniel Samuel Murrell, William David Spencer, and Adrian Anthony McFarlane, eds., *Chanting Down Babylon: The Rastafari Reader* (Philadelphia: Temple University Press, 1998), 44.

5. *I Remember Harlem*, directed by William Miles, a mini-series released in 1981, includes "Part 1: The Early Years: 1600–1930," "Part 2: The Depression Years: 1930–1940," "Part 3: Toward Freedom: 1940–1965," and "Part 4: Toward a New Day: 1965–1980." The documentary film *Adwa* (1999), directed by Haile Gerima, also addresses the subject matter, specifically the defeat of the Italians at the battle of Adwa and its significance for Africans and the diaspora in a larger pan-African framework.

6. James W. Ford and Harry Gannes, *War in Africa: Italian Fascism Prepares to Enslave Ethiopia* (New York: Workers' Library Publishers, 1935).

7. Andrea E. Frohne, *The African Burial Ground in New York City: Memory, Spirituality, and Space* (Syracuse, NY: Syracuse University Press, 2015).

8. A collection of the Black Religion Project is available at the Schomburg Center for Research in Black Culture which is located Harlem, New York City.

9. Craig Steven Wilder, *In the Company of Black Men: The African Influence on African American Culture in New York City* (New York: New York University Press, 2001), 36.

10. Leslie Alexander, *African or American? Black Identity and Political Activism in New York City, 1784–1861* (Urbana: University of Illinois Press, 2012), 164.

11. O. Marième Daff, "Little Senegal: L'Afrique débarque à Harlem." *Africultures* 44, no. 1 (2002): 19.

12. Data published by Pew Research Center, "Naturalized Citizens Make Up Record One-in-Ten US Eligible Voters in 2020," February 26, 2020.

13. Jobs such as delivery services, dishwashers, food-service workers, cabdrivers, and similar. Middle-class and upper-middle class Africans are mostly diplomats stationed temporarily in New York and a relatively small number of people working in the financial sector.

14. In eminent domain, a government entity pressures private-property owners to sell their property so it can be converted into public use, such as, for example, a new road or mixed-use development. African Americans also have dealt with redlining, a form of discrimination in which services or loans are denied to residents of certain areas based on ethnicity or income. African immigrants stand to learn from the experience of African Americans in battling such exclusionary practices.

5. Relations in Harlem between Africans and African Americans

1. Zain Abdullah, *Black Mecca: The African Muslims of Harlem* (New York: Oxford University Press, 2013), 63, 66, 78.

2. The documentary film *Black N Black* (2019) by Ivorian filmmaker Zadi Zokou, filmed in the United States, Ghana, and Côte d'Ivoire, provides great insights into the relations between African Americans and Africans.

3. For a helpful article addressing the ADOS movement, see the *New York Times*, November 8, 2019, https://www.nytimes.com/2019/11/08/us/slavery-Black-immigrants-ados .html. Accessed November 9, 2019.

4. Tressie McMillan Cottom, *Thick and Other Essays* (New York: New Press, 2019), 143.

5. Ngũgĩ wa Thiong'o, *Re-membering Africa* (Nairobi: East African Educational Publishers, 2009).

6. The Nigerian accent was popular among students in my African cinema courses at City College of New York. For more on "accented cinema" and its different forms, a good resource is Hamid Naficy, *An Accented Cinema: Exilic and Diasporic Filmmaking* (Princeton, NJ: Princeton University Press, 2001).

7. Vivek Bald, *Bengali Harlem and the Lost History of South Asian America* (Cambridge, MA: Harvard University Press, 2013), 50.

6. Depictions of Africa in Cinema, the Arts, and Literature

1. Henry Louis Gates Jr., "Harlem on Our Minds," *Critical Inquiry* 24, no. 1 (1997): 5.

2. Olivier Barlet, "Une Amérique coupée en tranches: Entretien avec Rachid Bouchareb, réalisateur de *Little Senegal*," *Africultures* 44, no. 1 (2002): 26.

3. The challenges of daily survival and integration facing francophone West African immigrants is also the subject of the French language web-series that I directed, "Les aventures de Laangandé à New York City" [The adventures of Laangandé in New York City]. NYC African Movies. YouTube, 2016–18.

4. Boukary Sawadogo, *West African Screen Media: Comedy, TV Series, and Transnationalization* (East Lansing: Michigan State University Press, 2019), 115.

5. Cornelius Moore, "African Cinema in the American Video Market," *Issue: A Journal of Opinion* 20, no. 2 (1992): 38–41.

6. Boukary Sawadogo, "Presence and Exhibition of African Film in Harlem," *Journal of African Cinemas* 12, nos. 2&3 (2021): 169–70.

7. Ezekiel Mphahlele, *The African Image* (New York: Praeger, 1974), 125.

8. The critical term *Blaxploitation* refers to African American movies made in the 1970s targeting mostly Black audiences; the stereotypical portrayals of Black people created a backlash, thus the name.

9. Rebekah J. Kowal, *Dancing the World Smaller: Staging Globalism in Mid-Century America* (New York: Oxford University Press, 2020), 121–22.

10. James Smalls, "Féral Benga: African Muse of Modernism," *Nka: Journal of Contemporary African Art* 41, no. 1 (2017): 58.

11. Charles Molesworth, ed., *The Works of Alain Locke* (New York: Oxford University Press, 2012), 197, 195.

12. Leonard Harris and Charles Molesworth, *Alain L. Locke: The Biography of a Philosopher* (Chicago: University of Chicago Press, 2008), 224.

13. Incidentally, the Brooklyn Museum African art exhibition of 1923 introduced the African American painter and graphic artist James Wells of the Harlem Renaissance to African art.

14. President Macron made the announcement on November 28, 2017, during a speech to African youth at the University of Ouagadougou, Burkina Faso, in which he sought to reestablish new paradigms for the relations between France and Africa. There are reportedly more than 60,000 such colonial-era African artifacts at Quai Branly Museum–Jacques Chirac in Paris.

15. Some exceptions include, for instance, the Metropolitan Museum of Art, which announced, on June 9, 2021, that it planned to return to Nigeria two brass plaques from its collection of 160 items from Benin City. Sarah Bahr, "Met Museum Announces Return of Two Benin Bronzes to Nigeria," https://www.nytimes.com/2021/06/09/arts/design/met-museum -benin-bronzes-nigeria.html.

7. A Few Notable Africans in Harlem in 2022

1. Sara Rimer, "South African Players Find Second Home on Harlem Stage," *New York Times*, August 30, 1984, page B1.

2. Ta-Nehisi Coates, *We Were Eight Years in Power: An American Tragedy*. (New York:

One World, 2017) was published in France under the title *Huit ans au pouvoir: Une tragédie américaine* (Paris: Présence Africaine, 2018).

3. "Il est interdit de collecter ou de traiter des données à caractère personnel qui font apparaître, directement ou indirectement, les origines raciales ou ethniques, les opinions politiques, philosophiques ou religieuses ou l'appartenance syndicale des personnes, ou qui sont relatives à la santé ou à la vie sexuelle de celles-ci." The English translation is quoted from Commission Nationale de l'Informatique et des Libertés (CNIL), https://www.cnil.fr/sites /default/files/typo/document/Act78-17VA.pdf, 10. Rare exceptions are granted through a complex process through the two government bodies of CNIL and Conseil National de l'Information Statistique. These exceptions are for anonymous race-related data for research purposes by scholars. In contrast, US Census Bureau data and certain official forms (employment and school) provide some data on race.

4. Pap Ndiaye is the author of *La Condition noire: Essai sur une minorité française* [The Black condition: An essay on a French minority] (Paris: Gallimard, 2009), considered a foundational work in Black Studies in France.

5. Such books by Souleymane Bachir Diagne include *Open to Reason: Muslim Philosophers in Conversation with the Western Tradition* (New York: Columbia University Press, 2018), and *Islam and Open Society: Fidelity and Movement in the Philosophy of Muhammad Iqbal* (Dakar: CODESRIA, 2011).

6. Manthia Diawara may not be based in Harlem, but his Africa-related public engagements cut across the Lower Manhattan and Uptown divide, thus contributing to the visibility of the African presence in Harlem and New York City at large.

7. In fall 2016 and spring 2017, I had the honor and privilege of curating and moderating the Return to the Source film series, hosting the filmmakers Menelik Shabazz (*Burning an Illusion*, 1981), Biyi Bandele (*Fifty*, 2015), Katy Léna N'diaye (*Waiting for Men*, 2007), and Kewulay Kamara (*In Search of Finah Misa Kule*, 2016).

8. Rashidah Ismaili AbuBakr, *Autobiography of the Lower East Side: A Novel in Stories* (N.p.: Northampton House Press, 2014), *Rice Keepers* (Trenton, NJ: Africa World Press, 2007), *Missing in Action and Presumed Dead* (Trenton, NJ: Africa World Press, 1992), and *Oniybo and Other Poems, with Wilfred Cartey and Louis Reyes Rivera* (New York: Shamal Books, 1986).

9. "Les voix de la diaspora forment l'avant-garde artistique et intellectuelle de l'Afrique" ("The voices of the diaspora form the artistic and intellectual avant-garde of Africa"), *Le Monde Afrique*, January 6, 2019. https://www.lemonde.fr/afrique/article/2019/01/06/les-voix-de-la -diaspora-forment-l-avant-garde-artistique-et-intellectuelle-de-l-afrique_5405691_3212.html Accessed January 10, 2019.

8. Searching for Africa in the Diaspora

1. Fela's formative encounter with Sandra Iszadore is recounted in Benson Idonije, *Dis Fela Self! The Legend(s) Untold: A Memoir* (Lagos, Nigeria: Festac Books, 2016), and Teju Olaniyan, *Arrest the Music: Fela and His Rebel Art and Politics* (Ibadan, Nigeria: Bookcraft, 2009).

2. Other African films on the history and legacy of slavery include productions such as Senegalese director Mahama Johnson Traoré's *Reou-taax* [The town, 1972], Ethiopian director's Haile Gerima's *Sankofa* (1993), Ivorian director Roger Gnoan M'bala's *Adanggaman* (2000), and Burkinabe director Boubakar Diallo's *Coeur de Lion* [Heart of the lion, 2009].

3. Paul Stoller, *The Power of the Between: An Anthropological Odyssey* (Chicago: University of Chicago Press, 2009), 4. He persuasively argues, for example, how West African merchants at

the Malcolm Shabazz Market in Central Harlem have successfully navigated two cultures and ways of being, those of West Africa and New York City.

4. The Africa2020 Season is a series of events (live performance, discussion forum, cinema, fashion/design, arts, music, etc.) all over France to mark the sixtieth anniversary of former French colonies in Africa gaining their political independence. Because of the COVID-19 pandemic, most of the programming took place in 2021.

5. The government of Ghana declared 2019 the year of return for Africans in the diaspora to visit, settle, or invest in the country. The year 2019 marked the four-hundredth anniversary of the first enslaved Africans being brought to the land that would become the United States of America. African American stars such as the actor and producer Danny Glover, the talk-show host Steve Harvey, and the rapper T.I. visited Ghana in 2019 during highly publicized ceremonies. As a follow-up to the Year of Return, Ghana launched the Beyond the Return campaign in 2020.

6. In the event of renunciation, the individual decides to become citizen of an African country that forbids dual citizenship.

7. Maurice Merleau-Ponty, "From Mauss to Claude Lévi-Strauss," in *Signs*, trans. Richard McCleary (Evanston, IL: Northwestern University Press, 1964), 120.

8. The documentary *Our Place in the Sun* (1988) by Ethiopian filmmaker Salem Mekuria documents in the 1980s the history of the Black community on rapidly gentrifying Martha's Vineyard where slaves and freed slaves had settled in the eighteenth century. The writer Dorothy West of the Harlem Renaissance and other Blacks have continued the Black presence on the island.

9. Scott Ellsworth, *The Ground Breaking: An American City and Its Search for Justice* (New York: Dutton/Penguin Random House, 2021), 14.

10. As discussed in Chapter 6, Henry Louis Gates Jr. observes that we are in the midst of the fourth Black Renaissance, which originated in the 1980s with Black women literary writers; see Gates, "Harlem on Our Minds," *Critical Inquiry* 24, no. 1 (1997): 1–12.

11. Boukary Sawadogo, "Parallel Movement: African and African American Cinema," in *African Film Studies: An Introduction* (New York: Routledge, 2018).

12. The four legal pathways to US citizenship include family reunification, employment-based visa, green card lottery, and refugee and asylum status.

13. Achille Mbembe and Sarah Nuttall, "Writing the World from an African Metropolis," *Public Culture* 16, no. 3 (2004): 347–72.

14. Felwine Sarr, *Afrotopia*, trans. Drew S. Burk and Sarah Jones-Boardman (Minneapolis: University of Minnesota Press, 2020).

15. Ngũgĩ wa Thiong'o, *Something Torn and New: An African Renaissance* (New York: Civitas Books, Perseus Books Group, 2009).

16. Wole Soyinka, *Myth, Literature and the African World* (Cambridge: Cambridge University Press, 1976).

BIBLIOGRAPHY AND FILMOGRAPHY

Abdullah, Zain. *Black Mecca: The African Muslims of Harlem*. New York: Oxford University Press, 2010.

Adekeye, Toyin Ibrahim, dir. *Bigger Than Africa*. Motherland Productions, 2018.

Adichie, Chimamanda Ngozi. *Americanah*. New York: Random House, 2013.

African Development Bank Group. "The Middle of the Pyramid: Dynamics of the Middle Class in Africa." April 20, 2011. https://www.afdb.org/fileadmin/uploads/afdb/Documents /Publications/The%20Middle%20of%20the%20Pyramid_The%20Middle%20of%20the%20 Pyramid.pdf. Accessed December 29, 2021.

Alexander, Leslie. *African or American? Black Identity and Political Activism in New York City, 1784–1861*. Urbana: University of Illinois Press, 2012.

Alexander, Michelle. *The New Jim Crow: Mass Incarceration in the Age of Colorblindness*. New York: New Press, 2012.

Amoruso, Marino, dir. *New York Noir: History of Black New York*. MyMar Entertainment, 2008.

Anderson, Monica. "African Immigrant Population in US Steadily Climbs." Pew Research Center, 2017. http://www.pewresearch.org/fact-tank/2017/02/14/african-immigrant -population-in-u-s-steadily-climbs/. Accessed July 10, 2018.

Anderson, Monica, and Gustavo López. "Key Facts about Black Immigrants in the US." Pew Research Center, 2018. http://www.pewresearch.org/fact-tank/2018/01/24/key-facts-about -black-immigrants-in-the-u-s/. Accessed July 13, 2018.

Angelou, Maya. *The Heart of a Woman*. New York: Random House, 2009.

Arnaud, Gérald. "African Dream in Harlem." *Africultures* 44 (2002): 13–17.

Arora, Sabina. *The Great Migration and the Harlem Renaissance*. New York: Britannica Educational Publishing and Rosen Educational Services, 2015.

Asiamah, Gildfred, Ousmane Djiby Sambou, and Sadhiska Bhoojedhur. "Are African Governments Doing Enough to Help Young People? Here's What Afrobarometer Surveys Reveal." *Washington Post*, January 15, 2021. https://www.washingtonpost.com/politics

/2021/01/15/are-african-governments-doing-enough-help-young-people-heres-what
-afrobarometer-surveys-reveal/

Bailey, C. Anne, "They Sold Human Beings Here." *New York Times Magazine*, February 12, 2020. https://www.nytimes.com/interactive/2020/02/12/magazine/1619-project-slave-auction -sites.html.

Bald, Vivek. *Bengali Harlem and the Lost History of South Asian America*. Cambridge, MA: Harvard University Press, 2013.

Balogun, Ola, dir. *Black Goddess or A Deusa Negra*. Embrafilme and Afrocult Foundation, 1978.

Barlet, Olivier. "Une Amérique coupée en tranches: Entretien avec Rachid Bouchareb, réalisateur de *Little Senegal*." *Africultures* 44 (2002): 23–26.

Barron, James. "Rezoning a Block in Harlem, Respecting an African Burial Ground." *New York Times*, September 27, 2017. https://www.nytimes.com/2017/09/26/nyregion/rezoning-a -block-in-harlem-respecting-an-african-burial-ground.html. Accessed January 9, 2019.

Benguigui, Yamina, dir. *Inch'Allah Dimanche* [Sunday God willing]. Film Movement, 2001.

Bhabha, Homi K. "Introduction: On Disciplines and Destinations." In *Territories and Trajectories: Cultures in Circulation*, edited by Diana Sorenson, 1–31. Durham, NC: Duke University Press, 2018.

Blanchard, Pascal, ed. *La France Noire: Présences et migrations des Afriques, des Amériques et de l'Océan Indien en Afrique*. Paris: La Découverte, 2012.

Bouchareb, Rachid, dir. *Little Senegal*. France 2 cinéma, Canal+, 2001.

Boyd, Herb. *Black Detroit: A People's History of Self-Determination*. New York: Harper Collins Publishers, 2017.

———. *The Harlem Reader: A Celebration of New York's Most Famous Neighborhood, from the Renaissance Years to the 21st Century*. New York: Broadway Books, 2003.

Brick, Michael and Nicholas Confessore, "Suit Is Settled in 2003 Killing of Immigrant." *New York Times*, July 27, 2006. https://www.nytimes.com/2006/07/21/nyregion/21zongo .html?searchResultPosition=10).

Budiman, Abby, Luis Noe-Bustamante, and Mark Hugo Lopez. "Naturalized Citizens Make Up Record One-in-Ten US Eligible Voters in 2020." Pew Research Center, 2020. https://www .pewresearch.org/hispanic/2020/02/26/naturalized-citizens-make-up-record-one-in-ten-u-s -eligible-voters-in-2020/. Accessed April 17, 2020.

Bundles, A'Lelia. *On Her Own Ground: The Life and Times of Madam C. J. Walker*. New York: Scribner, 2001.

Carpenter, Nathan Riley, and Benjamin N. Lawrence. *Africans in Exile: Mobility, Law, and Identity*. Bloomington: Indiana University Press, 2018.

Chomsky, J. Marvin, John Erman, David Greene, and Gilbert Moses, dir. *Roots*. Warner Bros. Entertainment, 1977.

Carter, Donald. Preface to *New African Diasporas*. London: Routledge, 2003.

Cissé, Chikouna, and Alassane Diabaté. "Quand Abidjan était la plaque tournante de l'immigration clandestine africaine vers l'Europe (1960–1975)." *Afrika Zamani* 27 (2019): 61–78.

Coates, Ta-Nehisi. *Huit ans au pouvoir: Une tragédie américaine*. Paris: Présence Africaine, 2018.

———. *We Were Eight Years in Power: An American Tragedy*. New York: One World, 2017.

Confiant, Raphaël. *Madam St. Clair, Queen of Harlem*. New Orleans: Diálogos, 2020.

Dadié, Bernard Binlin. *Hommes de tous les continents*. Paris & Abidjan: Présence Africaine / CEDA, 1967.

———. *La ville où nul ne meurt* [The city where no one dies]. Paris: Présence africaine, 1968.

———. *One Way*. Translated by Jo Patterson. Urbana: University of Illinois Press, 1994.

———. *Un nègre à Paris* [An African in Paris]. Paris: Présence africaine, 1959.

Daff, O. Marième. "Little Senegal: L'Afrique débarque à Harlem." *Africultures* 44 (2002): 18–21.

Dash, Julie, dir. *Daughters of the Dust*. Kino International, 1991.

Davis, Miles, and Quincy Troupe. *Miles: The Autobiography*. New York: Simon and Schuster, 1989.

Dia, B. Alioune. "African Immigrants' Views of Gentrification in Central Harlem." MS thesis in Urban Planning, Columbia University, 2012.

Diagne, Souleymane Bachir. *Islam and Open Society: Fidelity and Movement in the Philosophy of Muhammad Iqbal*. Dakar: CODESRIA, 2011.

———. "Notre présence africaine dans le monde" [Our African presence in the world]. Talk at École Polytechnique de Thiès, Senegal, 2017.

———. *Open to Reason: Muslim Philosophers in Conversation with the Western Tradition*. New York: Columbia University Press, 2018.

Diagne, Souleymane Bachir, and Jean-Loup Amselle. *In Search of Africa(s): Universalism and Decolonial Thought*. Medford, MA: Polity Press, 2020.

Diallo, Boubakar, dir. *Coeur de Lion* [Heart of the lion]. Les films du dromadaire, 2009.

Diawara, Manthia. *In Search of Africa*. Cambridge, MA: Harvard University Press, 1998.

———. *We Won't Budge: An African Exile in the World*. New York: Basic Civitas, 2003.

Diop, Djibril Mambéty, dir. *Le franc*. La Mediathèque des trois mondes, 1994.

Dodd, Mark, dir. *The Man Who Stopped the Desert*. Journeyman Pictures, 2012.

Dosunmu, Andrew, dir. *Restless City*. Screen Media Films, 2011.

Dovey, Lindiwe. *Curating Africa in the Age of Film Festivals*. New York: Palgrave Macmillan, 2015.

Dramani, John Mahama. *My First Coup d'Etat, and Other True Stories from the Lost Decades of Africa*. New York: Bloomsbury, 2012.

Dunbar, Paul Laurence. *The Sport of the Gods*. New York: Dodd, Mead, 1902.

DuVernay, Ava, dir. *Selma*. Paramount, 2014.

The Economist. "Hopeful Continent: Africa Rising." December 3, 2011.

———. "Africa: The Hopeless Continent." May 13, 2000.

Ellsworth, Scott. *The Ground Breaking: An American City and Its Search for Justice*. New York: Dutton/Penguin Random House, 2021.

Fabre, Michel. *From Harlem to Paris: Black American Writers in France, 1840–1980*. Urbana: University of Illinois Press, 1991.

Fanon, Frantz. *Black Skin, White Masks*. New York: Pluto Press, 1952.

———. *The Wretched of the Earth*. New York: Grove Press, 1963.

Foner, Nancy. *New Immigrants in New York*. Rev. ed. New York: Columbia University Press, 2001.

Ford, James W., and Harry Gannes. *War in Africa: Italian Fascism Prepares to Enslave Ethiopia*. New York: Workers' Library Publishers, 1935.

Foucault, Michel. *Archaeology of Knowledge and the Discourse on Language*. New York: Pantheon Books, 1982.

Frohne, Andrea E. *The African Burial Ground in New York City: Memory, Spirituality, and Space*. Syracuse, NY: Syracuse University Press, 2015.

Gaines, Kevin. *American Africans in Ghana: Black Expatriates in the Civil Rights Era*. Chapel Hill: University of North Carolina Press, 2006.

Gast, Leon, dir. *When We Were Kings*. Universal Pictures Home Entertainment, 2002.

Gates, Henry Louis Jr., dir. *Black in Latin America*. PBS series, 2011.

———. "Harlem on Our Minds." *Critical Inquiry* 24, no. 1 (1997): 1–12.

Gerima, Haile, dir. *Sankofa*. Mypheduh Films, 1993.

Glissant, Édouard. *Poetics of Relation*. Translated by Betsy Wing. Ann Arbor: University of Michigan Press, 1997.

Gnoan M'bala, Roger, dir. *Adanggaman*. New Yorker Video, 2000.

Gomez, Michael A. *African Dominion: A New History of Empire in Early and Medieval West Africa*. Princeton, NJ: Princeton University Press, 2017.

Guillaume, Paul, and Thomas Munro. *Primitive Negro Sculpture*. London: Jonathan Cape, 1926.

Gyasi, Yaa. *Homegoing*. New York: Alfred A. Knopf, 2016.

Hall, Gwendolyn Midlo. *Africans in Colonial Louisiana: The Development of Afro-Creole Culture in the Eighteenth Century*. Baton Rouge: Louisiana State University Press, 1995.

———. *Slavery and African Ethnicities in the Americas: Restoring the Links*. Chapel Hill: University of North Carolina Press, 2005.

Halter, Marilyn, and Violet Showers Johnson. *African and American: West Africans in Post–Civil Rights America*. New York: New York University Press, 2014.

Harris, Leonard, and Charles Molesworth. *Alain L. Locke: The Biography of a Philosopher*. Chicago: University of Chicago Press, 2008.

Harsch, Ernest. *Thomas Sankara: An African Revolutionary*. Athens: Ohio University Press, 2014.

Hirou, Amandine. "Les obsédés de la race noyautent le CNRS." *L'Express*, December 24, 2019. https://www.lexpress.fr/actualite/societe/les-obsedes-de-la-race-noyautent-le-cnrs_2111788.html

Hopkins, Pauline. *Of One Blood: Or, the Hidden Self*. Boston: Colored American Magazine, 1904.

Hudlin, Reginald, ed. *The Black Godfather*. Netflix, 2019.

Hughes, Langston, ed. *An African Treasury: Articles, Essays, Stories, Poems, by Black Africans*. New York: Crown Publishers, 1960.

———, ed. *Poems from Black Africa*. Bloomington: Indiana University Press, 1963.

Hurston, Zora Neale. *Barracoon: The Story of the Last "Black Cargo."* New York: HarperCollins, 2018.

Idonije, Benson. *Dis Fela Self! The Legend(s) Untold*. Lagos, Nigeria: Festac Books, 2016.

Ismaili, Rashidah. *Autobiography of the Lower East Side: A Novel in Stories*. Northampton House Press, 2014.

———. *Missing in Action and Presumed Dead*. Trenton, NJ: Africa World Press, 1992.

———. *Rice Keepers*. Trenton, NJ: Africa World Press, 2007.

Ismaili, Rashidah, Wilfred Cartey, and Louis Reyes Rivera. *Oniyobo and Other Poems*. New York: Shamal Books, 1986.

Jones, T. Bill, dir. *Fela!* New York: Broadway musical, 2008.

Jules-Rosette, Bennetta. *Black Paris: The African Writers' Landscape*. Urbana: University of Illinois Press, 2000.

Kane, Ousmane Oumar. *Homeland Is the Arena: Religion, Transnationalism, and the Integration of Senegalese Immigrants in America*. New York: Oxford University Press, 2011.

Kihss, Peter. "Harlem Hails Ghanaian Leader as Returning Hero." *New York Times*, July 28, 1958.

Kilkenny, Katie. "Trevor Noah Fires Back at French Ambassador Who Criticized World Cup Joke." *Hollywood Reporter*, July 18, 2018. https://www.hollywoodreporter.com/tv/tv-news/trevor-noah-fires-back-at-french-ambassador-gerard-araud-world-cup-joke-1128275/.

Koser, Khalid, ed. *New African Diasporas*. London: Routledge, 2003.

Kowal, Rebekah J. *Dancing the World Smaller: Staging Globalism in Mid-Century America*. New York: Oxford University Press, 2020.

Lee, Iara, dir. *Burkinabè Rising: The Art of Resistance in Burkina Faso*. Caipirinha Productions, 2018.

Lemann, Nicholas. *The Promised Land: The Great Black Migration and How It Changed America*. New York: Knopf, 1991.

Lemmons, Kasi, dir. *Harriet*. Universal Pictures, 2019

Locke, Alain, ed. *The New Negro: An Interpretation*. New York: Albert and Charles Boni, 1925.

Mabanckou, Alain. *Les cicognes sont immortelles* [Storks are immortal]. Paris: Éditions du Seuil, 2018.

Mabanckou, Alain, and Dominic Thomas. "Pourquoi a-t-on si peur des études postcoloniales en France?" *L'Express* (online), January 16, 2020. https://www-lexpress-fr.cdn.ampproject.org/c/s/www.lexpress.fr/actualite/pourquoi-a-t-on-si-peur-des-etudes-postcoloniales-en-france_2115044.amp.html. Accessed January 18, 2020.

Magee, Carol. *Africa in the American Imagination: Popular Culture, Racialized Identities, and African Visual Culture*. Jackson: University Press of Mississippi, 2013.

Malaquais, Dominique, and Cédric Vincent. "PANAFEST: A Festival Complex Revisited." In *The First World Festival of Negro Arts, Dakar 1966: Contexts and Legacies*, edited by David Murphy, 194–202. Liverpool: Liverpool University Press, 2016.

Massood, J. Paula. *Making a Promised Land: Harlem in Twentieth-Century Photography and Film*. New Brunswick, NJ: Rutgers University Press, 2012.

Mbembe, Achille. "Les voix de la diaspora forment l'avant-garde artistique et intellectuelle de l'Afrique." *Le Monde Afrique*, January 6, 2019. https://www.lemonde.fr/afrique/article/2019/01/06/les-voix-de-la-diaspora-forment-l-avant-garde-artistique-et-intellectuelle-de-l-afrique_5405691_3212.html. Accessed January 10, 2019.

Mbembe, Achille and Sarah Nuttall. "Writing the World from an African Metropolis," *Public Culture* 16, no. 3 (2004): 347–72.

Mbue, Imbolo. *Behold the Dreamers*. New York: Random House, 2016.

McGruder, Kevin. *Philip Payton: The Father of Black Harlem*. New York: Columbia University Press, 2021.

———. *Race and Real Estate: Conflict and Cooperation in Harlem, 1890–1920*. New York: Columbia University Press, 2015.

McKay Claude. *Banjo: A Story without a Plot*. San Diego, CA: Harcourt Brace Jovanovich and Harvest Books, 1929.

McMillan Cottom, Tressie. *Thick and Other Essays*. New York: New Press, 2019.

Mekuria, Salem, dir. *Our Place in the Sun*. WGBH, 1988.

Merleau-Ponty, Maurice. *Signs*. Translated by Richard McCleary. Evanston, IL: Northwestern University Press, 1964.

Miles, William, dir. *I Remember Harlem*. I Remember Harlem Inc. & WNET/Thirteen, 1981.

Mokhtefi, Elaine. *Algiers, Third World Capital: Freedom Fighters, Revolutionaries, Black Panthers*. New York: Verso, 2018.

Molesworth, Charles, ed. *The Works of Alain Locke*. New York: Oxford University Press, 2012.

Moore, Cornelius. "African Cinema in the American Video Market." *Issue: A Journal of Opinion* 20, no. 2 (1992): 38–41.

Mphahlele, Ezekiel. *The African Image*. New York: Praeger, 1974.

Mudimbe, Valentin Yves. *The Invention of Africa*. Bloomington: Indiana University Press, 1988.

———, ed. *The Surreptitious Speech: Présence Africaine and the Politics of Otherness, 1947–1987*. Chicago: University of Chicago Press, 1992.

Muhammad, Gibran Khalil. *The Condemnation of Blackness: Race, Crime, and the Making of Modern America*. Cambridge, MA: Harvard University Press, 2011.

Murphy, David. "The Performance of Pan-Africanism: Staging the African Renaissance at the First World Festival of Negro Arts." In *The First World Festival of Negro Arts, Dakar 1966: Contexts and Legacies*, edited by David Murphy, 1–42. Liverpool: Liverpool University Press, 2016.

Murrell, Nathaniel Samuel, William David Spencer, and Adrian Anthony McFarlane, eds. *Chanting Down Babylon: The Rastafari Reader*. Philadelphia: Temple University Press, 1998.

Murrey, Amber. *A Certain Amount of Madness: The Life, Politics and Legacies of Thomas Sankara*. London: Pluto, 2018.

Naficy, Hamid. *An Accented Cinema: Exilic and Diasporic Filmmaking*. Princeton, NJ: Princeton University Press, 2001.

Ndala, Blaise. *J'irai danser sur la tombe de Senghor*. Ottawa, Canada: Les Éditions de l'Interligne, 2014.

Ndiaye, Pap. *La Condition Noire*. Paris: Gallimard, 2009.

Nelson, Stanley, dir. *The Black Panthers: Vanguard of the Revolution*. PBS, 2015.

New American Economy. "Power of the Purse: How Sub-Saharan Africans Contribute to the US Economy." New American Economy, internet, 2018.

Ngũgĩ wa Thiong'o. *Re-membering Africa*. Nairobi: East African Educational Publishers, 2009.

———. *Something Torn and New: An African Renaissance*. New York: Civitas Books, Perseus, 2009.

Nurhussein, Nadia. 2010. "The Hand of Mysticism: Ethiopianist Writing in Pauline Hopkins's *Of One Blood* and the Colored American Magazine." *Callaloo* 33, no. 1 (2010): 278–89.

Okorafor, Nnedi. *Akata Witch*. New York: Penguin Random House, 2018.

Olaniyan, Teju. *Arrest the Music: Fela and His Rebel Art and Politics*. Ibadan, Nigeria: Bookcraft, 2009.

Osofsky, Gilbert. *Harlem: The Making of a Ghetto, 1890–1930*. New York: Harper & Row, 1996.

Peele, Jordan, dir. *Get Out*. Universal Pictures, 2017.

Ricci, Daniela. *African Diasporic Cinema: Aesthetics of Reconstruction*. East Lansing: Michigan State University Press, 2020.

Rimer, Sara. 1984. "South African Players Find Second Home on Harlem Stage." *New York Times*, August 30, 1984.

Roberts, Sam. "Influx of African Immigrants Shifting National and New York Demographics." *New York Times*, September 1, 2014. https://www.nytimes.com/2014/09/02/nyregion/influx-of-african-immigrants-shifting-national-and-new-york-demographics.html?_r=0. Accessed February 16, 2020.

———."More Africans Enter US Than in Days of Slavery." *New York Times*, February 1, 2005. https://www.nytimes.com/2005/02/21/nyregion/more-africans-enter-us-than-in-days-of-slavery.html. Accessed November 17, 2018.

Sacks, Marcy S. *Before Harlem: The Black Experience in New York City before World War I.* Philadelphia: University of Pennsylvania Press, 2006.

Sanderson, Eric W. *Mannahatta: A Natural History of New York City.* New York: Abrams, 2013.

Sarr, Felwine. *Afrotopia.* Translated by Drew S. Burk and Sarah Jones-Boardman. Minneapolis: University of Minnesota Press, 2020.

Sarr, Felwine, and Bénédicte Savoy. *Restituer le patrimoine africain.* Paris: Philippe Rey and Seuil, 2018.

Sawadogo, Boukary. *African Film Studies: An Introduction.* New York: Routledge, 2018.

———, dir. "Les aventures de Laangandé à New York City" [The adventures of Laangandé in New York City]. *NYC African Movies.* YouTube, 2016–18. https://www.youtube.com/channel/UCn3EDWl9-VXhRXHwsupp3KA. Accessed April 11, 2020.

———"Pandemic in the City: How African Immigrants in New York City's Manhattan Borough Coped with the COVID-19 Pandemic," *Africa is a Country*, https://africasacountry.com/2020/06/pandemic-in-the-city. June 18, 2020.

———. "Presence and Exhibition of African Film in Harlem." *Journal of African Cinemas* 12, nos. 2&3 (2021): 169–70.

———. *West African Screen Media: Comedy, TV Series, and Transnationalization.* East Lansing: Michigan State University Press, 2019.

Sembène, Ousmane, dir. *Camp de Thiaroye* [Camp Thiaroye]. New Yorker Video, 1988.

Senghor, Sédar Léopold. "Ce que l'homme noir apporte." In *L'homme de couleur.* Paris: Plon, 1939.

———. *Chants d'ombre.* Paris: Éditions du Seuil, 1945.

———. "Femme noire" [Black woman]. In *Chants d'ombre.* Paris: Éditions du Seuil, 1945.

———. "To New York." In *Poems from Black Africa*, edited by Langston Hughes. Bloomington: Indiana University Press, 1963.

Shachtman, Tom. "Men with a Mission." *Hoover Digest*, no. 1 (2011). https://www.hoover.org/research/men-mission. Accessed June 19, 2019.

Shack, William A. *Harlem in Montmartre: A Paris Jazz Story between the Great Wars.* Berkeley: University of California Press, 2001.

Sharpley-Whiting, Denean T. *Bricktop's Paris: African American Women in Paris between the Two World Wars.* Albany: State University of New York Press, 2015.

Sherrard-Johnson, Cherene, ed. *A Companion to the Harlem Renaissance.* Malden, MA: Wiley Blackwell, 2015.

Sherwood, Marika. *Kwame Nkrumah: The Years Abroad, 1935–1947.* Legon: Freedom Publications, 1996.

Smalls, James. "Féral Benga: African Muse of Modernism." *Nka: Journal of Contemporary African Art* 41, no. 1 (2017): 44–59.

Solomon, Frances-Anne. *HERO: Inspired by the Extraordinary Life and Times of Mr. Ulric Cross.* HeroFilm and Caribbean Tales Worldwide Distribution, 2018.

Soyinka, Wole. *A Dance of the Forests.* Oxford: Oxford University Press, 1963.

———. *Myth, Literature and the African World.* Cambridge: Cambridge University Press, 1976.

Stockman, Farah. "We're Self-Interested: The Growing Identity Debate in Black America." *New York Times*, November 8, 2019. https://www.nytimes.com/2019/11/08/us/slavery-black-immigrants-ados.html. Accessed November 9, 2019.

Stoller, Paul. "Marketing Afrocentricity: West African Trade Networks in North America." In *New African Diasporas*, edited by Khalid Koser. London: Routledge, 2003.

———. *Money Has No Smell: The Africanization of New York City*. Chicago: University of Chicago Press, 2002.

———. *The Power of the Between: An Anthropological Odyssey*. Chicago: University of Chicago Press, 2009.

Stovall, Tyler. *Paris Noir: African Americans in the City of Light*. Scotts Valley, CA: CreateSpace, 2012.

Styan, David. 2003. "La Nouvelle Vague? Recent Francophone African Settlement in London." In *New African Diasporas*, edited by Khalid Koser, 17–36. London: Routledge, 2003.

Traoré, Mahama Johnson, dir. *Reou-taax* [The town]. 1972.

True, Lynn, dir. *Lumo*. True Walker Productions, 2007.

Tsika, Noah. *Nollywood Stars: Media and Migration in West Africa and the Diaspora*. Bloomington: Indiana University Press, 2015.

Watkins-Owens, Irma. *Blood Relations: Caribbean Immigrants and the Harlem Community, 1900–1930*. Bloomington: Indiana University Press, 1996.

White, Shane. *Stories of Freedom in Black New York*. Cambridge, MA: Harvard University Press, 2007.

Wilder, Craig Steven. *In the Company of Black Men: The African Influence on African American Culture in New York City*. New York: New York University Press, 2001.

Wilkerson, Isabel. *The Warmth of Other Suns: The Epic Story of America's Great Migration*. New York: Random House, 2011.

Wilkinson, Lauren. *American Spy*. New York: Penguin Random House, 2019.

Young, Michelle. "The Lost Lewisohn Stadium at City College of New York." March 30, 2021. https://untappedcities.com/2021/03/30/lewisohn-stadium-city-college-ny/.

Zokou, Zadi, dir. *Black N Black*. Zadi Zokou Productions, 2019.

Zong, Jie, and Jeanne Batalova. "Sub-Saharan African Immigrants in the United States." Migration Policy Institute, 2017.

INDEX

Boukary Sawadogo is an Associate Professor of Cinema Studies and Black Studies at City College–City University of New York. He is the author of *West African Screen: Comedy, TV Series, and Transnationalization*; *African Film Studies: An Introduction*; and *Les cinémas francophones ouest-africains, 1990–2005*.

EMPIRE STATE EDITIONS

SELECT TITLES FROM EMPIRE STATE EDITIONS

For a complete list, visit www.fordhampress.com/empire-state-editions.